Queen Anne Pamphlets

QUEEN ANNE PAMPHLETS

An Annotated Bibliographical Catalogue of Pamphlet Publications
spanning the reign of Queen Anne,
held in the Eighteenth-Century British Pamphlet Collection,
Douglas Library, Queen's University: 1701-1714

by *William F.E. Morley*

Special Collections   Douglas Library   Queen's University   Kingston, Ontario   1987

Copyright 1987 Douglas Library
Queen's University
Kingston, Ontario
ISBN 0-88911-471-4

Designed by Peter Dorn, RCA, FGDC
Printed in Canada on acid-free paper

This volume was published with
the assistance of a fund contributed by
colleagues and friends of William F.E. Morley
on the occasion of his retirement from
Special Collections in September 1985

What, shall whole Reams of Breathless Pamphlets die
And no one Living sing their Elegy?

Elegy on the Death of Pamphlets

(Reprinted: *Poems on Affairs of State*,
ed. F.H. Ellis (London, 1975) VII, 572-3)

CONTENTS

LIST OF ILLUSTRATIONS

PREFACE

Those of us who do intellectual history tend to collect our stock-in-trade
in the form of those books, pamphlets and other printed materials that
promise a store of relevant sources for ready consultation.   One cannot
just expect a library that dates from the nineteenth century to 'have' a
large number of eighteenth-century works, and the task of building a
collection can be a daunting one.   It is only when a bibliographer such
as Bill Morley puts his hand to sorting out the catch that we really know
what we have caught.

I can already attest to the value of this study in terms of its success
in identifying the works which relate to the items here described, though
not themselves initially part of the collection.   It is to Bill Morley's
cogent account of the 'Faults' controversy that I owe an awareness of the
existence of two pamphlets that are vital for purposes of making sense of
several others that were long a part of the collection.   Soon after Bill's
study brought the complexities of this controversy to my attention, I was
able to obtain two of the items needed to fill out the story.   There can
be no better demonstration of the fact - familiar to all buyers of antiquarian
books - that a collector who has been alerted to the importance of some item
is well on the way to acquiring a copy.

The pamphlet literature of the reign of Queen Anne has been well served
by expert bibliographers.   One thinks of Morgan's all-but-exhaustive study,
Moore's checklist of Defoe materials and the various works on the
Sacheverell affair.   The Queen's collection of Queen-Anne imprints is
modest when measured by the universe of possible acquisitions, but it is a
significant one in terms of most other North-American libraries.   We are
indeed lucky that this growing collection found its bibliographer in Bill
Morley, who lent his knowledge, skill, and love of books to this cause, even
though his professional interests lay in other fields.   I can now imagine
the possibility that Bill may be coaxed into bringing some order into our
materials for the reign of George I, an era without its definitive
bibliography.   One may at least hope and I do.

Jock Gunn
November 1985

INTRODUCTION

INTRODUCTION

The period embraced by the publications in this Catalogue, 1701-1714, was marked by two predominant elements of discord in England. The first of these was the War of the Spanish Succession, in which England was involved against France, and English passions were further aggravated (and divided) by the presence in France of the Pretender. The other source of distress was religio-political, and it was evident in the rising conflict over issues which, in this period, gave shape and distinction to the two great parties of the future , born late in the previous century under the names of Whig and Tory[1]. The relationship between these two factions was, of course, heavily permeated with the changing attitudes towards church and state; but it was also deeply affected by the war itself, which provided a dominant theme for the whole period. In such a time of ferment, it was difficult indeed to maintain a non-partisan position, and independent Members of Parliament were "a dying breed in 1702"[2], when Queen Anne's reign began. The influence of the centrist

---

1. "The denominations _Whig_ and _Tory_ were as much religious as political"; politically, Whig meant the acceptance of the legality of King William. Cf. Nigel F. Dennis, _Jonathan Swift_ (New York, 1964), p. 19.
2. _Downie_, p. 83 & 118. (Note: The abbreviations and abridgements used in the footnotes are expanded in the Sources Cited list, following this Introduction.)

groups was, it is true, powerful at times. One such group was the Old Whigs, led by Robert Harley under King William III; another was the Country Members their natural descendents (as opposed to Members of the Court party), who were more likely to be Tories[3]. Yet, despite their influence, they seem not to have had any steadying effect on animosities: Harley (later, Earl of Oxford), a keen advocate of moderation, was "branded as an apostate" by the Whigs, and under Queen Anne, he was "called a turncoat by the Tories"[4]. Even the issue of toleration, so essential a part of liberty, was charged with dissension; the Toleration Act (1689), allowing Protestant dissenters their own preachers and places of worship, was soon regarded as a threat by the High Church. One of the most provocative pamphlets in the early years of Queen Anne, Drake's The Memorial of the Church of England (1705), a frustrated outcry against the loss of the Occasional Conformity Bill, was a forceful attack on the Godolphin administration's policy of moderation; this, and the several responses and counter-responses, are represented in this Catalogue. Five years afterwards, a pamphlet called The Moderator (1710) was still trying to reconcile the Revolution (1688) with the ancient doctrine of non-resistance to royal authority. In 1714, Defoe sketched the sad history of moderation, as it was attempted by his patron Harley, in The Secret History of the White Staff.

Increasing polarization between Whig and Tory, rather than between the old Court and Country parties (though the alignments were mixed at first), marked the progress of William and Mary's reign, and continued throughout the reign of Queen Anne. By 1713, the anonymous author of The Character of

3. Holmes, British Politics, p. 120 & 406; Kenyon, Revolution Principles, p. 202, also notes the "damaging concepts" of freedom and toleration among the Old or Country Whigs. Defoe explains this division of the Whigs into Old and Modern (the Old now inclining to be Tories) in his The Secret History of the October Club (part I), 1711. It is listed in this Catalogue.
4. Downie, p. 83.

a Modern Tory goes on in his title (as this Catalogue shows) to describe a Tory as "the most unnatural and destructive monster (both in religion and politicks) that hath yet appear'd in any community in the world". His language had become but the coin of the day, for just the year before Joseph Trapp, in The Character and Principles of the Present Sett of Whigs, had referred to the common, upstart, money-grubbing Whigs as those who "renounce ... our Saviour" (p. 23), and make chaos by placing all power with the people.

Such bitterness had been some time in brewing. The Triennial Act (1694), requiring Parliament to meet at least once every three years and not to last for a longer period, was an element in promoting party faction[5], as was the formation of the Bank of England (1694), which soon became the Tory bête noire as the symbol of the dark alliance between city money and the Whigs. This convenient association seemed to the Tories to favour war (first that of the League of Augsburg, 1688-97, then that of the Spanish Succession, 1702-13), and the latter war was itself probably the single most divisive factor during Anne's reign. It was presaged by the anonymous The Dangers of Europe, from the Growing Power of France, 1702, written just before King William's death in March. War sentiment allied the Whigs with the Dutch and German Protestants, strengthening their hatred of France and the Pretender, while reinforcing the importance of the Revolution principles for a constitutional monarchy (the right of resistance, rule by consent, the established church, and the Protestant succession). The party of war and patriotism[6]

---

5. Defoe recognized that, for all its benefits, the Act requiring an election every three years kept alive party strife (Review, 5:142, quoted in Downie, p. 1).
6. In the euphemistic cue-word of the day, 'patriot' usually meant Whig, as did 'true lover of Queen and country', and similar epithets, while the expression 'country gentleman' referred to a Tory. Letters to and from Gentlemen, in town or country, are commonplace in the pamphlet titles of the period, as are letters from patriots.

(two activities so often found in combination) could not fail to notice how its success flagged in times of peace or when talk of peace was afoot - as from 1696 to 1702, and after 1710[7].

On the other hand, for the Tories war enriched the mercantile Whigs at the expense of the country squires, and just as the Toleration Act was a blow to the established church, so the Revolution (1688) emphasized the awful disruption of the time-honoured doctrines of divine right and hereditary succession. Sermons marking the death of the 'royal martyr' (30th January, 1649) flourished each 30th of January during the first half of Anne's reign, as they had done intermittently since 1660, when Charles II had proclaimed it a day of fast and humiliation; and they continued throughout the eighteenth century. In this Catalogue, Sherlock and Eyre's sermons of 1708, and those of Smalridge and South in 1709, are examples. Dr. Richard West, a learned divine, drew attention to the divisive effects of these anniversary sermons in A Sermon Preached before the Honourable House of Commons (1710), but the pseudonymous Eugenius Philalethes (see Appendix C) disputed Dr. West's arguments in his Some Modest Animadversions (1710). Yet the archaic nature of these doctrines, in the Whig view, these tenets which denied by implication the very settlement under which Britons now lived and breathed so freely, brought dreadful intimations of eventual defeat not only to Jacobites and nonjurors (of whom Charles Leslie was spokesman; his works are very well represented in this Catalogue), but also to the High-Flyers and de jure Tories[8]. The Abjuration Oath and the Act of Settlement (1701)

---

7. Kenyon, p. 3; and, for the Revolution principles: passim.
8. Kenyon, p.200-202, where it is also pointed out, in fairness, that the Revolution was an embarrassment to the Whigs too, who had to devise the pretence of James II's abdication. Defoe, in his Secret History (cf. footnote 3), gives a brief but misleading history of the expression 'nonjuror' (one who refused the oaths of allegiance to William and Mary on grounds of non-resistance): at the 1688 Revolution, nonjurors were opposed to William and called Jacobites; later, under Queen Anne, they were known as High-Flyers; finally, they were called Tackers, because they were for tacking the Occasional Conformity Bill to the Supply Bill, to ensure its passage through the House of Lords. So said Defoe, but it should be stated that 'nonjuror' and 'Jacobite' were never synonymous terms.

were bitter blows to the Tories, for these instruments not only required recognition of the legitimate succession of William III as he approached the end of his life, but denied it to the exiled Stuarts. The Case of the Abjuration Oath (1702) highlights the Tory dilemma by presenting the Whig point of view.

The Act of Security in Scotland (1703) relieved the Scots from any binding acceptance of the English Protestant succession; but it also provided them with ample opportunity to debate the pros and cons of union with the English, in print as well as in the Edinburgh Parliament. Andrew Fletcher of Saltoun (now Salton, East Lothian), an ardent nationalist, pleaded in 1703 for home rule after Anne's death[9], and an anonymous tract, A Letter to a Member of Parliament, 1705, appeals for caution. In 1706, Fletcher speaks again, opposing with passion the "surrender" of a "united Parliament", a view warmly supported by Lord Belhaven in the same year (these pamphlets all appear in this Catalogue); but the Act of Union was passed nevertheless, by both legislatures, in the following year. Henceforth Anne was Queen of Great Britain and Ireland, instead of England, Scotland, and Ireland.

As a reaction to the entrenchment of the Revolution principles, and the virtual exclusion of High-Church Tories from the top posts under William and Mary (as the Whigs had been under James II), there was a marked increase in the number of sermons preaching non-resistance, and even divine right. The churchmen were protected in some measure by the presence of a Stuart on the throne, and emboldened by their increasing alarm at

---

9. One of the memorable pleasures in reading the background to the pamphlets in this irresistably interesting collection, was the unexpected encounter in one of the writings of this (for me) obscure author, An Account of a Conversation (Edinburgh, 1704), with the source of the famous epigram, so often misquoted: "if a man were permitted to make all the ballads he need not care who should make the laws of a nation".

the absence of any surviving heirs from Anne; but these sentiments delivered from the pulpit were in open rebellion against the spirit of the
Revolution, and in particular against the Act of Settlement by which the
throne passed to the House of Hanover. Here was another fruitful source
of controversy, argued in such pamphlets as: Limitations, 1701, A Letter
to a Member of Parliament (Scotland), 1705, A Letter Written to a Gentleman, 1708; nonjuror Charles Leslie's views in The Constitution, 1709,
were opposed by those in Reasons Against, 1710, by Bishop Benjamin Hoadly,
staunch defender of the Whig doctrine of resistance; there followed All at
Stake, 1712, An Alarm, 1713, and Asgill's two works of 1710 and 1714. The
culmination, however, was reached in the two sermons of Dr. Henry Sacheverell, published in 1709: The Communication of Sin, and The Perils of False
Brethren. The trial and impeachment (1710), and the Tory riots which resulted, taught the Whigs the danger of pressing home the Revolution principles, and cost them their Ministry. The story is told in the largest
accretion of pamphlets to gather about any other issue of the period: there
are 1160 titles, editions, and issues in the Madan(Speck) bibliography of
Sacheverell, over 1100 of which appeared after The Communication of Sin,
October 1709, which marked the beginning of the controversy. A good representation of several dozen Sacheverell and related titles appears in the
Catalogue, including the two already mentioned, and a few which Madan(Speck)
seem to have missed. The main arguments, with some new issues added,
formed the 'Faults' controversy also of 1710 and begun by Bishop Hoadly;
I have dealt with this series of pamphlets separately in Appendix A. The
year 1710, in fact, is the most prolific year of imprints for the period
here covered (at least in the Catalogue, if not at large - see Appendix B.),
and the Sacheverell and 'Faults' controversies were certainly major con-
tributors to this profusion of intellectual activity and factional strife.

The Tory victory, late in 1710, gave that party the long-sought opportunity to set about bringing an end to Britain's part in the war. Their efforts were marked by a crescendo of pamphlets for and against peace negotiations. The Old and New Ministry (1711) was an early one, and in the same year Bishop Francis Hare reviewed the peace efforts in a series of letters published under the title The Negociations for A Treaty of Peace. In 1712 appeared Reflections Upon the Present Posture, A Letter from a Tory Freeholder, A New Project, and others. The time had come for the new Ministry to plead its case, and it chose Jonathan Swift to present the official Tory argument for peace, and this he did in his famous The Conduct of the Allies (1712). Although written under pressure to meet a political demand, its literary technique is of the highest standard. The pamphlet blizzard did not abate though, and continued to the end of our period in such works as Observations, Neck or Nothing, by John Dunton, Dunkirk or Dover, by John Toland, and George Ridpath's Some Thoughts Concerning the Peace, all of 1713; and in 1714 (after the Peace of Utrecht), The Peace-Maker, Charles Povey's An Inquiry into the Miscarriages, The Fears of the Nation Quieted, and John Toland's The Grand Mystery Laid Open, to name only a few. Feeling ran to a fever pitch; but the Whigs closed ranks and achieved in the face of this stress a unity of purpose not approached again by a British political party, one historian has observed[10], till the late nineteenth century, and perhaps not till the twentieth century. The death of Anne, who privately favoured Tory and High-Church principles, marked the end of Tory supremacy; but the termination of the war (1713), and the solidarity of the Whigs, made possible the peaceful accession of the first English Monarch in the long line of the House of Hanover, George I.

---

10. Holmes, British Politics, p. 246.

Many other issues were rampant during this first fourteen years of
the eighteenth century, such as that of occasional conformity, the contest
between the Lords and the Commons, the re-organization of the militia,
Jacobitism, the popular scheme for the widespread establishment of charity
schools, the public accounts and various charges of embezzlement, the moral
position of the Duke of Marlborough, the balance of power in Europe, and
the Dutch barrier. All of these, and many other concerns of the day, are
dealt with by the titles in this Catalogue. One last category of pamphlet
I will mention: those concerned with elections. The Triennial Act of
1694 had spurred factional discussion and, because of the short period between elections, hardly allowed public debate to cool. As early in our
period as 1702, Directions to the Electors of the Ensuing Parliament attempts to circumscribe for electors those congenial qualities to look for in
a candidate for MP, and those which, when discerned in an aspirant, mark
him in advance as a poor representative. Other treatises appeared as each
Ministry's three-year term of office drew to a close; such, for example,
were Defoe's A Speech Without Doors, 1710 (addressing, in the terminology
of the day, the electorate: those outside the doors of Parliament), and
A Letter to the Gentlemen and Freeholders, in 1713. The death of Queen
Anne in 1714, and the plans for the next general election (held in February,
1715), sparked a new set of election pamphlets in 1714, each soliciting
the vote of the electorate by unanswerable logic or gentle persuasion in
favour of the author's particular point of view. Some examples described
in this Catalogue are: A Tender and Hearty Address to all the Freeholders,
A Speech to the People, and Bishop Francis Atterbury's English Advice, to
the Freeholders.

The foregoing literary expressions of the political, military, and
religious excitements of the reign of Queen Anne were reflected in the

activities of the lowly printer and bookseller. Without his energy and enterprise these early years of the Augustan Age could never have flourished - for it was not only the first age of party, but also a period important for its literature, notably in the works of Defoe and Swift. In fact, for these writers and for the writing of the early eighteenth century in general, prose and party were inextricably mixed, so that "it is virtually impossible to divorce literary and political considerations. The finest works of literature of the age were often produced with political intentions", for there was a "complex inter-relationship of literature and politics"[11]. It was the spectacular rise of Grub Street, and the cult of pamphlet readers it encouraged, that opened the way for the ascending popularity of a higher form of literature, after the effects of the Septennial Act (1716) allowed the factional tumult to subside. For the printers and booksellers, it was a time of unprecedented opportunity for expansion; but this could never have been seized without the ending of press censorship. It is to the expiration of the Licensing Act in 1695 (introduced by Charles II in 1662) that the growth of the political press is directly attributed[12]. Printing shops sprang up, at the close of the century, in Bristol, Exeter, Chester, York, Norwich, and other cities, with new presses being established every year during our period[13]. Probably the most important of the early beneficiaries of this freedom from censorship (the laws of libel and treason remained as a safeguard[14]), was the newspaper; the Daily Courant (1702) and Defoe's Review (1704) are early examples in our period, and Ichabod Dawks' Dawks's Newsletter, printed in

---

11. Downie, p. 15.
12. Holmes, Divided Society, p. 66.
13. Plomer, p. [vii].
14. Downie, p. [ix]; the active propaganda machine of Harley was also a deterrent to sedition: the vigorous search for the author of Drake's The Memorial of the Church of England (1705), and the threats and rewards offered, form a notable instance.

a cursive type, is earlier still (London, 1696). "By 1709 almost a score

of newspapers were appearing in London alone, and most of them were politi-

cally committed"[15]. Pamphlets were about 40 years older than newspapers

in England however, beginning in 1622 with weekly Corantos, or pamphlets

of foreign news[16]. Success did not come to the pamphlet trade for almost

a hundred years though, and even the stimulus created when the Licensing

Act was allowed to lapse in 1695, was partially offset by the introduction

of a paper duty by William III in 1696, on imported and domestic paper.

In 1709, a copyright Act was passed, giving the author or his delegate the

sole right to print or reprint a work for a term of twenty-one or twenty-

eight years. In 1711, also under Queen Anne, duties on paper were com-

bined with a stamp duty on pamphlets (and newspapers), of up to 16s. a

ream imported and 1s.6d. domestic. Finally, a new set of duties was

placed on pamphlets (and newspapers) in an Act of 1712. These duties

raised an outcry from English printers and bookseller/publishers, and they

15. Holmes, Divided Society, p. 67. John Dyer's newsletter was of the same period, but it was handwritten.
16. Part of the story is told in The Cambridge History of English Literature, edited by A.W. Ward and A.R. Waller, vol. 9 (Cambridge, 1962), p.1-5. The story is further developed in OED: 'coranto' is the Spanish word for 'running', which derives from the French 'courante', for current (in use till about 1650), a lively dance or its music. Clearly, the English Daily Courant is also derivative. Both the pamphlet and the news sheet developed from the corantos, but it is interesting to note that the word 'pamphleteer' has often a contemptuous usage. Published just at the end of our period was a work by Myles Davies, with the title in Greek (transliterated): Eikon mikro-biblike, then in Latin and English: sive Icon libellorum, or A critical history of pamphlets: tracing the rise growth and different views of all sorts of small tracts or writings ... Part I (London, 1715) – cf. BM and NUC. Another interesting work, also unavailable for consultation, is Abel Boyer's The Political State of Great Britain, Being an Impartial Account of the Most Material Occurrences, Ecclesiastical, Civil, and Military ... (38 vols., London, 1711-29); this was a monthly newspaper, and it is said to include abstracts of the most important pamphlets from both political parties, issued during each month (see DNB, 'Boyer', and the title of Boyer's Political State, 1711, q.v. in the Catalogue). No copies are recorded in the Canadian Union Catalogue in the National Library, Ottawa, and those copies at Queen's University do not contain any pamphlet abstracts; neither is it the impression of Dr. J.A.W. Gunn, who has seen the collection, that the remainder of the items is remarkable for its pamphlet abstracts.

pressed the perfectly valid argument that a great advantage was given to
Dutch and Irish printers in the English market. By this time, though, the
pamphlet war was at its height (see Appendix B.), so the duties could act
only as a minimal discouragement; and even the copyright legislation did
little to stop piracy. Printers were kept busy running off their libellous tracts and, in between, dodging government agents bent on seeking
them out for punishment. One has an impression of faces on Tower Hill
glowing red in the light of condemned pamphlets being burned in disgrace
by the public hangman. Small wonder that the quality of the printer's
workmanship was usually low, and that their names and those of the authors,
were so frequently omitted from their title-pages[17] - to the everlasting
bewilderment and delight of the bibliographer. But print they did, and
so did the booksellers sell, in ever-increasing numbers. Some of the
figures of edition-sizes and total sales of a single title that have come
down to us, are startling even by today's standards. Swift's The Conduct
of the Allies (1711) sold eleven thousand copies in six editions in two
months (see the annotation in the Catalogue entry)[18]. Even more astonish-
ing are the printing and sales reports of William Benson's A Letter to Sir
J[acob] B[anks] (1711), of which it is said that the eleven or more editions totalled about 100,000 copies[19]; and even earlier, Dr. Henry Sacheverell's The Perils of False Brethren (1709), the second of his two controversial sermons (all these titles appear in this Catalogue), of which one
edition alone sold between 35,000 and 40,000 copies[20]. An authoritative
estimate places the total number of copies of Perils sold in the British
Isles at 100,000, with the sale of Dutch, German, and French translations

17. For much of this information I am indebted to Plomer, p. vii-ix.
18. Journal to Stella, 28 Jan. 1712 (N.S.). H. Davis, editor of Swift's
Works, in "Political Tracts" vol. 6, p. ix, says that the first edition
sold out in two days, and the second in five hours!
19. DNB, 'Benson'.
20. Downie, p. 114.

over and above this. The same source[21] shows the appearance of four
genuine editions and at least six piracies, all within about twelve months,
1709-10. Earlier still and most spectacularly is Lord Belhaven's Speech
in Parliament, 1706, mentioned earlier as one of the Scottish protests
against union with the English Parliament, of which Morgan,BBH:vol.1, p.
421, alleges "some hundreds of thousands of it were reported to have been
sold in the two kingdoms"; this seems to be an anachronistic achievement
for the presses of the day, though, unless many different presses were
involved. Not till 1750 were these printing and sales-records broken,
and then only by a narrow margin over the specific figure of 100,000:
Bishop Thomas Sherlock's Letter from the Lord Bishop of London to the
Clergy and People of London on the Occasion of the Late Earthquakes (London,
1750) attained a circulation of 105,000 copies; but it was a religious
treatise of sensational character, and many copies were distributed without
charge, for evangelical promotion[22]. The pamphlets of the age of Queen
Anne, dealt with in this Catalogue of some 160 titles, did indeed provide
a baroque flourish to the century-long glories of Stuart tracts.

                    *   *   *

The Eighteenth-century British Political Pamphlet Collection at
Queen's University covers from the Civil War to the Reform Bill of 1832,
but is intensive for the eighteenth century. This Catalogue is based on
an examination of the actual pamphlets in that part of the collection which

---

21.   Madan(Speck):60.
22.   Ian Watt, The Rise of the Novel (Berkeley, Cal., 1960), p. 36.

covers imprints for the years 1701-1714. For a more general description,
readers are referred to the separate "A Note on the Collection", below.
All mention in the Catalogue entries of editions and titles not presently in this part of the collection, are drawn from bibliographies, catalogues[23], and other works of reference, and not from any personal inspection
of such works themselves. The time and expense involved in visiting
libraries for access to these rare pamphlets (no doubt widely scattered)
made that approach prohibitive. It is hoped that the dangers inherent in
any bibliographical acknowledgement of titles and editions not actually
seen, will be averted by my clear statement of sources in every case. For
the same reason, it has not been possible to compare editions, issues, or
copies, excepting where they were in the collection; but where variations
are noted in the bibliographies consulted, these are cited for their possible utility (though without verification), and compared with the work in
hand.

Policy of Exclusion. Where size is concerned, some items in the present
collection stand as tall as folios; but for thickness, a work not exceed-
ing one centimetre, excluding covers, may be safely regarded, though not
defined, as a pamphlet. (The number of pages was not used because of
variations in paper thickness.) This is a working rule only, not often
invoked; but scanning later items in the collection, I find perhaps half-
a-dozen that measure somewhat more than a centimetre. One is 1.5 cm.

---

23. I understand a catalogue to be a bibliography (enumerative, descriptive or analytical) of a specific collection; it is therefore cir-
cumscribed by the items in that collection, whereas no such limitation
applies to a general bibliography of a subject. Examples are catalogues
of private or other libraries, and dealers' catalogues of sections of
their stock.

thick, yet describes itself in its Advertisement as a pamphlet. (This is Sir Brooke Boothby's Observations on the Appeal from the New to the Old Whigs, London, 1792.) Clearly it must be regarded as a tract, though a plump one. Ultimately, one must call upon a sense of the period. In the eighteenth century, a pamphlet was recognized by the nature of its content and purpose as much as by its format. A volume of 2 or 3 cm., unless of large and open type, is not likely to have been regarded as a tract; the sustained reading involved could only have hindered its intention to provoke immediate controversy on a current topic.

Arrangement. The plan of the Catalogue is chronological, by the year of publication (or the estimated year), the items then being arranged alphabetically by author (or else by title) under each year.

Bibliographical Description

1. General. The Cataloguing Principles set forth by R.C. Alston and M.J. Jannetta, in Bibliography, Machine Readable Cataloguing and the ESTC (London, British Library, 1978, esp. p.5-20) have been noted, and generally observed; but this is not a machine-readable catalogue, so I have departed from the ESTC Principles when the requirements of rare-book description demanded it. For example, it has not been necessary to use indicators or fields; ellipses have been used to indicate the omission of quotations from title-page transcriptions; my aim has not been to transcribe only as much of the title as would ensure correct filing sequence or differentiate from other titles, but rather to indicate comprehensively what the author had to say about his subject; and the spelling of the title-page is retained; but while capital letters are rendered into lower-case excepting for the first word of a title, and proper nouns and proper adjectives are indeed capitalized, I have also followed the informative Library of Congress practice of capitalizing the first words of the titles of other

works quoted in the title being transcribed. Also, outside of the title and imprint, direct quotations (in the notes, for example) follow the capitalization of the original. Title and imprint punctuation follow that of the title-page (in the Catalogue, though not in the lists of sources), and in the collation a roman sequence is expressed in roman whether or not it leads directly into an arabic sequence. These latter are two illustrations of the need to depart from the Anglo-American Cataloguing Rules, 2d Edition (AACR II), to meet the needs of eighteenth-century book description, until the special rules for rare-book cataloguing (the International Standard Bibliographic Description (Antiquarian), or ISBD(A), rules) have been fully established. In the meantime, I have been guided by the informal draft report issued by a Working Group of IFLA (International Federation of Library Associations and Institutions) in London, 1980. In any event the problem has not been a vexatious one, and NUC entries have been most helpful because its rare-book cataloguing has in the past usually been more elaborate than that for other books[24].

I have not observed the AACR II prescription of separating certain elements of the title-page and imprint by means of an oblique slash, for this is quite alien to rare-book transcription; and neither have I supplied letters omitted from words on a title-page (usually to avoid the charge of libel) in their proper place, but have inserted them after the words in brackets, so as not to obliterate the signs of omission which may themselves help to distinquish variants. The AACR II imprint abbreviations 's.l.' and 's.n.', though, have been used, as well as an additional one, 's.d.'.

2. _Author or Main Entry_. Generally, I have followed the form of entry adopted for a work by NUC, and in such cases the source of my entry is not

---

24. NUC practice is to catalogue new accessions by AACR II rules; but the intake of eighteenth-century works being relatively low, the new forms of entry and cataloguing for such works are slow to appear in NUC.

given. Where I have not followed the NUC entry, it is because I have pre-ferred what has seemed to be better evidence; the source of this evidence is always given (usually the _Dictionary of National Biography_).

Where there are indications which run counter to the NUC form of entry but which yet are inconclusive, I have followed NUC and provided the con-trary sources. The great number of anonymous pamphlets issued during the period of this Catalogue has presented a special challenge[25], and one with which I would dearly love to have become more fully engaged had circum-stances allowed (see Appendix C for a consideration of the authorship of just one pamphlet, from internal evidence). However, I have been alert to authorship clues, and have examined further in cases of conflicting author attributions.

3. _Transcription of Title_. The present work is not a short-title catalogue, where titles are given in sufficient fullness only to distin-guish each work from the others; it is instead an annotated catalogue with its entries conforming with descriptive rather than enumerative biblio-graphy. The objective is to identify each work physically, and to convey at least an impression of each pamphlet's character and message. To this end, titles are given in subject fullness rather than simply in a distin-guishing fullness.

No attempt is made to produce a type-facsimile of a title-page, because

---

25. The literary artifices used by the authors writing about public aff-airs, such as concealing their own names and disguising those of their subjects, was a cumbersome but necessary protection; however, Sir Charles H. Firth has suggested a compensating advantage in being allusive and in-direct (_The Political Significance of 'Gullivers Travels'_, London, 1919, p.ix), for while it protected the author, it also stimulated the curiosity of the reader. Perhaps this is why even manifestly innocent pamphlets are sometimes published anonymously!

of the limitations of the typewriter[26], and also because anyone needing such typographical detail would find it more reliable to examine the original pamphlet. If you need to know the time of day you don't consult a calendar! However, where it is useful for bibliographical purposes, photocopies of some title-pages have been inserted, and also copies of some other pages of historical interest, to enliven the text.

I have tried to identify the biblical sources (in the King James Version) of sermons which take scriptural passages as their text, and also to reveal places, events, and particularly persons[27], who are only alluded to in the title. Half titles and running titles are noted, though the former only when actually present in the copy in hand. A record of the running title will help users to identify a copy of the work which lacks its title-page - bibliographically the most important, yet most vulnerable, leaf in a pamphlet.

The long 's' is always rendered in its modern 'short' form, but title-page spellings are preserved, as are all aberrations, in verbatim transcription, excepting for words in non-roman alphabets (such as those in Greek), which are transliterated but always with an indication, to distinguish from matter already transliterated in the title-page.

4. The Imprint. The imprint statement, which includes the place of printing, the name of the printer and/or bookseller, and the year of public release, is given as it appears on the title-page, with the same punctuation (in disregard of the AACR II imprint punctuation rules) but not the same

---

26. Professor W.A. Speck, in the introduction (p.vi) to his edition of Madan - cited in the Catalogue as Madan(Speck) - notes the unsatisfactory compromise of indicating italics and capitals, as Madan had done, yet ignoring black letter.
27. Addison, in his essay on the "Potency of Mystery and Innuendo" (Spectator, no. 567) refers to writers who omit the vowels of great men's names "and fall must unmercifully upon all the consonants", and adds that Tom Brown (1663-1704), "of facetious memory", was the first to bring this practice into fashion (cf.DNB, 'Thos. Brown').

capitalization - that is, in conformity with the title transcription - so
far as the three main elements are concerned: place, person(s), year; and
always in this order, changes to that end being made silently. These
imprint details may sometimes assist users in establishing, or at least
suspecting, significant bibliographical variations. The price of the
pamphlet, which is usually placed following the imprint, at times differs
from that given in (for example) Morgan, BBH, suggesting a cheaper reprint
perhaps. The information on printers' and booksellers' addresses occasionally supplements or improves upon that found in Plomer's Dictionary,
and I have regularly used that splendid source to identify printer's and
bookseller's names more precisely in recording imprints. If any of these
three elements is lacking from the title-page I have endeavoured, because
of their importance, to discover them from other sources. If found, they
are given in square brackets, the elements separated by commas only, and
with or without question marks in accordance with the strength of the evidence. When it seemed useful, the source of such information has been recorded in the notes. Imprint dates in roman figures are always rendered
into arabic numerals, as being less liable to transcription and typing
error and more convenient to the average user today. Attention is drawn
to Old Style (O.S.) and New Style (N.S.) dates when the specific day or
month of publication affects the year as given in the imprint - or elsewhere[28]. The N.S. year is the one used in the chronological arrangement
of entries. However, the advance required to correct O.S. dates to N.S.
(10 days by 1752) has been ignored; thus 31st December O.S. is regarded
as December N.S., not as, say, 8th January N.S., the next year.

---

28. An explanation of calendar usage in Britain under Queen Anne is given
in the list of Abbreviations following this Introduction, under 'N.S.' and
'O.S.'.

As a general example, the following title-page imprint:

> Printed for T. Hodson, over Against
> Gray's Inn Gate in Holborn, And The
> Bible and Three Crowns, Cheapside,
> in London, Near Mercer's Chapel, Book-
> sellers. First Day of March, MDCCIX.
> Price 6d.

would be rendered as:

> London, printed for T[homas] Hodson,
> over against Gray's Inn Gate in Holborn,
> and The Bible and Three Crowns, Cheapside
> near Mercer's Chapel, booksellers. First
> day of March, 1709 [1710 N.S.]. Price 6d.

5. <u>Collation</u>. This being a catalogue of a particular collection, my objective has not been to describe an ideal copy, but to record details of the specific copy in hand. However, in a spirit of compromise, obvious deficiencies have been noted, as have variations from copies described in cited bibliographical sources.

Every pamphlet has been collated by pages, and the pagination expressed according to the old Library of Congress rules, which required every printed page to be accounted for, including medial blank ones, but not terminal blank pages even though cognate. When beginning leaves are printed on one side only, they are described as 'p.l.' - preliminary leaves. Signatures, or gatherings, have not usually been examined excepting so far as is necessary to determine formats; but where necessary for bibliographical purposes the make-up of gatherings <u>has</u> been investigated, and the collation recorded by standard signature marks. Formats are expressed in the abridged symbols, for example: 4°, 8°, for quarto, octavo; but when the leaves of the gathering do not agree with the signature marks, as when half-sheets or other partial sheets have been used, then this is indicated parenthetically, thus (for instance): 8°(in 4s). The height of the <u>bound</u> pamphlet is given, to the nearest whole centimetre; unbound pamphlet heights are indicated by 'unbd.' in parentheses directly following the centimetre size.

A word about cancels. Ninety-five per cent of the Queen's collection is in an attractive twentieth-century acid-free binding, with marbled boards of various designs and colours. The binding programme was considered essential because of the fragility of unbound items, and it continues; but this binding naturally resists any attempt to examine the make-up of the pamphlets: its sheet-fold and leaf structure. Some bibliographical advantage has been sacrificed for security, for cancel leaves and similar irregularities cannot usually be identified by direct examination. An eye has been kept open for stubs and non-matching catchwords however, and cancels searched for when recorded in bibliographies; the results are reported in the notes.

Bibliographical Notes

The bibliographical notes, which follow the description, concern a wide variety of subjects, but in general may be brought under two headings: those concerning the whole edition or issue, and those relating only to the specific copy in hand. A note on the errata, if any, is always given first, to alert readers to the possibility of error in the text. The rest of the first-category notes follow in the same order as the title-page elements (author, title, imprint), and conclude with notes on related titles: A reply to, Answered by, Further to, and so forth. Notes in the second category, those concerning the specific copy, begin with descriptions of imperfections, and end with notes on provenance, if any (the kinds of association, given in abridged form, are listed below with the Abbreviations). All bindings are of the twentieth century, unless otherwise indicated.

A more complete list of notes, and the order in which they are given, appears as Appendix D, after the Catalogue.

Bibliographical Citations

A separate list expanding the abbreviations used for bibliographies appears under 'Sources Cited', below, but it is hoped that in most cases the work cited will be recognized by users from the abbreviation. 'No bibliographical citation found' means that none has been found amongst the bibliographies consulted: those named in the list just mentioned. When a library symbol is given in parentheses after the NUC citation, this indicates that only a single copy of the title is located in the National Union Catalog of the United States: the one in the library represented by the symbol given. When NUC, the citation given first, is not given at all, then of course there is no copy of that title recorded in NUC; when NUC appears after 'Cf.', then only another edition or issue is recorded in NUC. Other abridged and parenthetic information supplied after a bibliographical citation usually refers to editions, issues, or variants mentioned in that source which differ from the work in hand.

Annotations

The annotations which conclude the entries are not intended to be summaries or condensations of the entire text of each pamphlet, and even less are they critical reviews; instead, they aim to present selected important points which seem to convey the thread of the arguments, and the religio-political stance of the writer. By quotation and paraphrase, I hope to have transmitted a little of the original style, vocabulary, and particular ingenuity of the writers and their period, and perhaps too something of the fervour and weight of concern which motivated so many of the authors. In the heat of these fierce controversies, I may not always have succeeded in my attempt to be impartial. Some pamphlets, such as those by Leslie, are models of lucidity; and a few writers, such as Swift and St.-John, are quite conscious of literary style. Defoe, as well as

Swift, produced masterpieces of satire, though the satire of the period,
added to the deliberate obscurity to evade charges of libel, is not always
easy to penetrate.   Many of the pamphlets are rambling and repetitive,
and certainly writing in haste to meet the sudden needs of a new situation
is not conducive to planning and logical development.   Neither is it helpful to the understanding of readers a quarter-millennium later: many arguments are indeed difficult to follow.

One cannot fail to notice that many arguments are repeated in pamphlet after pamphlet, just as there are several (sometimes, indeed, numerous)
works tackling the same issue at each turn of the cycle of successive
issues.   In these cases, I have tried to bring out new answers to old
questions, and new questions addressed to old issues.   However, on the
grounds that a user needing to consult a single title only will not be en-
lightened by being told that the author "follows the usual arguments", I
have felt justified in allowing some repetition, albeit with variations,
of familiar arguments and viewpoints.   Some writers present their case with
such remarkable clarity, or with such force and logic, that it has seemed
worthwhile to dwell upon their texts in extended annotations, and to refer
to these annotations from other works on similar issues.

Abbreviations for bibliographies (not italicized) or works of reference (in italics) follow those given in the Sources Cited, below; other
works are cited in full within the annotation.   All scriptural quotations
are taken from the Authorized (King James) Version of the Bible.   Users
should note that other editions, variant titles, and even other copies of
a given work are best sought in the Index, because there the additional
titles in Appendix E (of works acquired after the main Catalogue was compiled) are interfiled with those of the main Catalogue of the collection.

I would like to take this opportunity to express publicly my grateful appreciation to Dr John M. Stedmond (who supervised my compilation of this work in its original format as a Queen's Master of Arts thesis) and Dr W.C. Ferguson, both of the Department of English, and Dr J.A.W. Gunn, Department of Political Studies, for their never-failing efforts to guide me and to improve this work, by their expert counsel in their respective fields of eighteenth-century literature, bibliography, and politics.   I must also thank my daughter Vivian Morley-Simurda for her painstaking work in compiling the original index, Ms Beth B. Watters for her invaluable help with extending the index and with proof reading, and Ms Maureen Tasker and Ms Eileen Kemp for typing the manuscript.   Finally, my sincere gratitude to Mr Peter Dorn for attempting to design a silk purse from a sow's ear, and to Ms Barbara Teatero for guiding the typescript through the press.

                                        William F.E. Morley

                                        Kingston, Ontario, October 1986

Sources Cited

Besides those listed here, a few other sources (those cited only
once, e.g., that under Laconics) appear within the text, with full information. General works of reference, such as Encyclopaedia Britannica and
The Oxford Companion to English Literature, consulted for orientation in
a field, are excluded. It is hoped that the abbreviations used are not
so contracted that they will be unrecognizable to most users, even in
their cited form. Abbreviations for works which are not bibliographical
are italicized (underlined), to distinguish texts from bibliographies,
catalogues, and similar compilations. It should be noted that the abbreviations appearing at the left in this list are used precisely in this
form in the bibliographical citations paragraph, which terminates each
entry; within the text, these forms may be further abridged. For example,
"Morgan,BBH:N:615" or "NUC(Pre-1956)600:43" will be cited in the text
as simply "Morgan" or "NUC", unless the item cited in the text differs
from that in the citations paragraph. The form of the specific citation is usually obvious (referring to volume number then page, column,
or item number, separated by a colon); where there may be a misinterpretation, the form used is explained at the end of each entry here.

Arber

  Arber, Edward. <u>The term catalogues, 1668-1709 A.D.; with a number for</u> <u>Easter Term, 1711 A.D.</u> ... London: 1903-6. 3 vols.

BM(to 1955)

  British Museum. Department of Printed Books. <u>General catalogue of</u> <u>printed books. Photolithographic edition, to 1955.</u> London: 1965-66. 263 vols.

BN

  Bibliothèque nationale. Départment des Imprimés. <u>Catalogue générale</u> <u>des livres imprimés</u> ... <u>Auteurs.</u> Paris: 1897 to date (for publications to 1960).

BPL(Defoe)

  Boston. Public Library. <u>A catalog of the Defoe Collection.</u> Boston: 1966. (Cited by page no. only.)

<u>Briquet</u>

  Briquet, Charles M. <u>Les filigranes; dictionnaire historiques des</u> <u>marques du papier</u> ... Leipzig: K.W. Hiersemann, 1923. 4 v. (paged continuously).

CBEL

  Watson, George. <u>The new Cambridge bibliography of English literature,</u> <u>edited by George Watson.</u> Cambridge: 1969-77. 5 vols. (v.1: 1974).

Carabelli

  Carabelli, Giancarlo. <u>Tolandiana; materiali bibliografici per lo studio</u> <u>dell' opera e della fortuna di John Toland (1670-1722).</u> Firenze: 1975. (If not a main entry, cited with 'n' after page no., <u>e.g.</u>, Carabelli:115n.)

Cordeaux & Merry

  Cordeaux, E.H., and D.H. Merry. <u>A bibliography of printed works relating</u> <u>to the University of Oxford.</u> Oxford: 1968.

DNB

Dictionary of national biography. ... Edited by Sir Leslie Stephen and Sir Sidney Lee. From the earliest time to 1900. London: 1967-8. 21 vols. & Suppl. (Cited by vol. and page no. for a specific passage, or by name of person for a general biography.)

Downie

Downie, James A. Robert Harley and the press: propaganda and public opinion in the age of Swift and Defoe. Cambridge: 1979.

Espasa

Enciclopedia universal ilustrada, Europeo-Americana ... Barcelona [etc]: [1907?]-1930. 70 vols. & Apéndice & Suplemento.

Halkett & Laing

Halkett, Samuel, and John Laing. Dictionary of anonymous and pseud-onymous English Literature. New and enl. ed. by Dr. James Kennedy [etc.] ... Edinburgh: 1926-34. 7 vols. (incl. Suppls.; subsequent vols. deal with later persons).

Hazen(Walpole)

Hazen, Allen T. A catalogue of Horace Walpole's library. New Haven, Conn., 1969. 3 vols.

JCB

Brown, John C. Bibliotheca Americana; a catalogue of books relating to North and South America in the library of John Carter Brown of Providence, R.I. With notes by John Russell Bartlett. Providence, R.I.: 1865-71. Part 3: 1701-1800, vol. 1: 1701-1771.

Knuttel

Knuttel, W.P.C. Catalogus van de pamfletten-verzameling berustende in de Koninklijke bibliotheek. s'Gravenhage [The Hague]: 1889-1916. 8 vols. (v. 8 is a Suppl.) in 10, and Register, 1920. Covers 1486-1853; vol. 3: 1689-1713; vol. 4:1714-1775.

Kress

   Harvard University. Kress Library of Business and Economics. Catalogue
   ... Boston: 1940-1967. 5 vols. (incl. 2 Suppls.). Covers 1473-1848;
   vol. 1: 1473-1776.

LC

   Library of Congress. Library of Congress catalog; a cumulative list of
   works represented by Library of Congress printed cards. Books: authors.
   1947-1955. Washington, D.C.: 1947-55. 47 vols. & Suppls. (superseded
   by NUC, q.v.) 'LC' may also be used for the Library of Congress itself.

London Library.

   Wright, C.T. Hagberg, and C.J. Parnell. Catalogue of the London Library,
   St. James's Square, London. London: 1913-14. 2 vols., and Suppl., 1913-
   20. London: 1920.

Madan(Speck)

   Madan, F.F. A critical bibliography of Dr. Henry Sacheverell. Edited
   by W.A. Speck. Lawrence Kan.: 1978.

Moore(2d ed.)

   Moore, John R. A checklist of the writings of Daniel Defoe. 2d ed.
   [Hamden, Conn.]: 1971.

Morgan,BBH

   Morgan, William T. A bibliography of British History, 1700-1715. Bloom-
   ington, Ind.: 1934-42. 5 vols. (Each chapter begins with a review of
   the year's pamphlets.)

NUC(Pre-1956)

   The national union catalog, pre-1956 imprints; a cumulative author list
   representing Library of Congress printed cards and titles reported by
   other American libraries. London [etc.]: 1968-80. 685 vols. & Suppls.
   to date.

Plomer

    Plomer, Henry R. A dictionary of the printers and booksellers who were at work in England, Scotland and Ireland from 1668-1725. Oxford: 1922.

Rothschild

    Rothschild, Nathaniel M.V., baron. The Rothschild Library; a catalogue of the collection of eighteenth-century printed books and manuscripts ... Cambridge: 1954. 2 vols.

Stonehill

    Stonehill, Charles A., and Andrew Block. Anonyma and Pseudonyma. 2d ed. Pound Ridge, N.Y.: 1969. 2 vols.

Straus(Curll)

    Straus, Ralph. The unspeakable Curll; being some account of Edmund Curll, bookseller; to which is added a full list of his books. London: 1927. "A handlist (1706-1746)": p. 201-314.

Teerink-Scouten

    Teerink, H. A bibliography of the writings of Jonathan Swift. 2d ed., rev. and corr. by Dr. H. Teerink. Edited by Arthur H. Scouten. Philadelphia: 1963.

Term catalogues, see Arber

Thomason

    Thomason, George. Catalogue of the pamphlets, books, newspapers, and manuscripts relating to the Civil War ... 1640-1661. London: 1908. 2 vols.

WingSTC

    Wing, Donald. Short-title catalogue of books printed in England, Scotland, Ireland, Wales, and British America, and of English books printed in other countries, 1641-1700. New York: 1945-48. 3 vols. (2d ed., vol. 1 only, 1972)

Wright(Defoe)

Wright, Thomas. The Life of Daniel Defoe ... London: 1931. "List of

Defoe's principal works": p. 412-23. (A 'p.' refers to pages in the

text; 'no.' refers to the number in the bibliography.)

Other Sources Consulted

Anglo-American cataloguing rules. 2d ed. ... Chicago: American Library

Association; Ottawa: Canadian Library Association, 1978. (Familiarily

known as: AACR II.)

Bowers, Fredson

Principles of bibliographical description. New York: 1962.

Ehrenpreis, Irvin

Swift: the man, his works, and his age. Vol. 2. London: 1967. (Volume

2 covers the period 1699 to August 1714.)

English historical documents. General editor: David C. Douglas. [London]:

1953-75. (Volume 8, 1953, edited by Andrew Browning, covers the period

1660-1714. Bibliography: p. 39-45.)

Holmes, Geoffrey

The trial of Doctor Sacheverell. London: 1973.

_____

British politics in the age of Anne. London: 1967.

_____, and W.A. Speck.

The divided society: party conflict in England, 1694-1716. London: 1967

(Title taken from correction slip tipped onto t.-p., and varying from

the t.-p. title).

Kenyon, John P.

Revolution principles; the politics of party, 1689-1720. Cambridge: 1977. (The Ford lectures, 1975-6; Cambridge studies in the history and theory of politics.)

Luttrell, Narcissus

A brief historical relation of state affairs from September 1678 to April 1714. Oxford: 1857. 6 vols.

McKerrow, Ronald B.

An introduction to bibliography for literary students. Oxford: 1965.

The political state of Great Britain ... Vol. 1-60, Jan. 1710/11-Dec. 1740. (Abel Boyer, editor, 1711-29, 38 vols. Includes in its early years abstracts of important pamphlets relating to affairs of state, but none seen in issues available.)

Smith, Robert A.

Eighteenth-century English politics: patrons and place-hunters. New York: [1972] Bibliography: p. 187-203.

[Somers tracts]

A collection of scarce and valuable tracts ... chiefly such as relate to the history and constitution of these kingdoms ... The 2d ed., rev., augm., and arr., by Walter Scott ... London: 1809-15. 13 vols. (Volumes 5, 6, 12, and 13 especially relevant.)

Steinberg, Sigfrid H., editor

A new dictionary of British history. London: 1963.

Swift, Jonathan

The Examiner, and other pieces written in 1710-11. Edited by Herbert Davis. Oxford: 1966. (This is the edition cited in the Catalogue. The title of the Journal is Examiner, not The examiner.)

Swift, Jonathan

Journal to Stella. Edited by Harold Williams. Oxford: 1974. 2 vols.
(This is the edition used, whenever the Journal is cited.)

_____

Political tracts, 1711-1713. VI. Edited by Herbert Davis. Oxford:
1973. (Includes The conduct of the Allies, text and comment.)

_____

Political tracts, 1713-1719. VIII. Edited by Herbert Davis and
Irvin Ehrenpreis. Oxford: 1973. Several other volumes also were examined, in this set of Swift's works published by Basil Blackwell.

Toland, John

A collection of several pieces of Mr. John Toland ... with some memoirs
of his life and writings. London: 1726. 2 vols. (The 'Life', by
Pierre Desmaizeaux: v.1, p. iii-xcii.)

Abbreviations

Commonly-accepted abbreviations, such as sic, e.g., are not included here.

arr. - arranged

augm. - augmented

autogr. - autograph(ed)
   (provenance)

Bible - Books of the Bible are
   cited in brief form (Rom.,
   but Acts) followed by chapter and verse separated by a

colon.

bk. pl. - bookplate (provenance)

cf. - confer, consult

corr. - corrected

ed. - edition

enl. - enlarged

fol. - folio

incl. - includes, including

inscr. - inscribed (provenance)

introd. - introduction

l. - leaf, leaves (when followed by
a number)

ms(s). - manuscript(s)

n. - note

N.S. - New Style; refers to the
Gregorian calendar, used in
Britain from 3d Sept. 1752,
O.S. (which required an immediate correction of 11 days
advance), but often unofficially earlier. Before that
date the new year began officially on 25th March. See
also: O.S.

no(s). - number(s)
(Note: Roman numerals are
usually changed into the more
easily recognized arabic
numerals.)

O.S. - Old Style; refers to the
Julian calendar used in Britain
officially till 3d Sept. 1752,
O.S., when the Civil, Ecclesiastical, and Legal years began
25th March, though the Historical
year had begun unofficially on
1st Jan. since 1582. See also: N.S.

p. - page, pages

p.l. - preliminary leaf,
leaves

pref. - preface

pt(s) - part(s)

pub. - publisher, published

q.v. - the special usage here,
after a title, is to indicate that the title is in
the collection, and thus
has its own separate entry
in this catalogue.

r. - recto: right hand page of
a book, normally bearing an
odd page number, or the
front of a broadside or
broadsheet. Used as a
superior letter, with signature marks.

rev. - revised

s.d. - sine dato: no publication date, though I usually
give an estimated year.

s.l. - sine loco: without place
(of publication), though
I have tried to indicate
the most likely place; AACR II.

s.n. - sine nomine: without
name (of publisher); AACR II

sig(s). - signature(s),
signature mark(s)

suppl(s). - supplement(s)

t.-p. - title-page

transl. - translated,
translation

unbd. - unbound (in collation)

v. or vol(s). - volume(s).
When used as a superior letter
with signature marks, this
indicates 'verso': the left-
hand page of a book,
normally bearing an
even page number; or
the back of a broad-
side or broadsheet.

4° - quarto

8° - octavo

8°(in 4s) - 4 leaves to
signature (probably
half-sheets)

A NOTE ON THE COLLECTION

The University has owned British political pamphlets from the first decade of its existence; the earliest accession number presently known is 5228, and it was published in 1641.   The first recorded gifts were from Dr Duncan McArthur (1885-1943), made in 1934 when he left Queen's Department of History.   The present separate collection had its earliest beginnings in a box of printed items donated in 1965 by Dr A.R.M. Lower, then retired from Queen's but widely known for his important contributions to the study of Canadian history.   The box included twenty-five unbound and disbound British pamphlets, mostly eighteenth-century and political - the nucleus of an interesting special collection.   At this juncture, Dr John A.W. Gunn returned to Queen's Department of Political Studies from two years at Oxford, where he had read seventeenth-century political pamphlets at the Bodleian Library.   The author of books on both the seventeenth and eighteenth centuries, his fortuitous arrival was most opportune: he began to develop the Library's holdings in British political pamphlets, devoting long hours to the Collection over many years, and up to the present time.   Dr Gunn has made, and still makes, every effort to acquire

the really important items of the period: in the seventeenth century,
from the Civil War to the Standing Army Controversy, and through to the
latter end of the eighteenth century, when the struggle for reform in
the 1780's and 1790's, because interrupted by the French Revolution, in
fact continued until the Reform Bill of 1832 was passed.   The collection
reflects this continuity.   Interest is focussed on the eighteenth
century, and we have recorded our holdings with the great ESTC project;
but the Collection represents the whole period of importance of the
British political pamphlet, from 1642 to 1832.

THE CATALOGUE

AN ESSAY for regulating and making more useful the militia of this kingdom. To which is added a scheme for the distributing musters and exercise. The second edition corrected. London, printed for A[nn]. Baldwin near the Oxford Arms in Warwick-Lane, 1701. 1 p.l., 12 [i.e., 10] p. 4° 21 cm.

The recto of p.1 is numbered 4, thus omitting two page numbers.

Leaves foxed up to p. 8; lower margin closely trimmed with loss of text, p. 9-10.

Re-organized by Acts of 1662-3, the militiamen were still not effectively trained. The author demonstrates that "a well regulated Militia" could be as effective as a standing army, and at a lesser cost; but at present the militia lacks discipline and experience (p.3). He sets about showing how this could be remedied, and only by enforcing existing laws, 12 brief extracts from which are presented in evidence. Each extract is followed by a commentary, illustrating the beneficial results to be expected if the law were fully applied, or if the law were made more fully effective. Instances support his arguments. A proposed county budget, and a scheme for an annual calendar of "Musters and Exercise" for each county, brings the work to a conclusion (p.10-12). This

is a last ember in the fiery controversy of 1697-99 on the 'standing
army'.

  No bibliographical citations found. **Cf**. Morgan,BBH:D146 (variant but
close title, same imprint, ii, 10 p.); NUC(Pre-1956)722:117 (variant
title, 1715 ed., 12 p.).

  ANOTHER copy.

The recto of p. 1 is numbered 4, thus omitting two page numbers.

Upper margin closely trimmed, some page numbers wanting.

(See copy 1, above, for other notes).

GT. BRIT. Parliament, 1701. House of Commons.

A state of the proceedings in the House of Commons, with relation to
the impeached lords: and what happened thereupon between the two Houses.
London, printed for Edward Jones, and Timothy Goodwin. 1701. 61 p.,
1 l. fol. 31 cm.

  Order to print, dated 24 June, 1701: p. [2].

  Another edition: London, 1701, but 100 p. (cf. Morgan, BBH:D411).

  Edward Russell, Earl of Orford, First Lord of the Admiralty; John Somers,
Baron Somers, Lord Chancellor; and Charles Montague, Baron Halifax, Auditor
of the Exchequer, were impeached by the Commons (p.15-16) for advising King
William III to endorse both Partition Treaties (1698 and 1700) between
England, France, and the Netherlands, "concerning the Partition of the
Spanish Dominions" (p.14), and William Bentinck, Earl of Portland, as Pleni-
potentiary in Paris, was impeached for negotiating and concluding the
Treaties, without the knowledge of the Commons (p. 12 and 16). Orford
and Somers were acquitted, while Portland and Halifax were dismissed for
want of prosecution (cf.DNB, 'Bentinck' and 'Montagu').

  NUC(Pre-1956)466:395,556:38, & 214:552; Morgan,BBH:D411.

LACONICS: or, New maxims of state and conversation. Relating to the
affairs and manners of the Present times. In three parts. ... London,
printed for Thomas Hodgson over against Grays-Inn-Gate in Holborn. 1701.
1 p.l., [6], 120 p. 8° 18 cm.

Authorship is attributed to Thomas Brown (1663-1704) by Dr. J.A.W. Gunn
in "Mandeville and Wither: individualism and the workings of providence",
in Mandeville studies: new explorations ..., edited by Irwin Primer (The
Hague, M. Nijhoff, 1975), where the work is described as anonymous (p.107)
but cited as by "[Thomas Brown et al.]" (p.107n31). "... The Third Part
was done by a different Hand from that of the Two First" (cf. Preface,
p. [6]); the "et al." may refer to the author of this 3d Part.

First edition. Second edition "with additions": London, 1702. For a
similar title, by John Timbs (1801-1875), cf. BM,128:321 and 239:246.

In 3 Parts, starting on p. 1, 35, and 81 respectively.

Bound in near-contemporary calf, blind-stamped monograms on covers, re-
backed.

Provenance: 1. bookplate (and cover monograms?) of William Stirling:
inside front cover. 2. bookplate of A.N.A. (?) Keir: inside back cover.

The Preface (p.[1], 1st count) indicates that this collection of "Apoph-
thegms, and Maxims" is the first in English, other than translations of
La Bruyère (in turn influenced by Theophrastus), and others. The 3 Parts
are rich in comments on love and women ("Lovers always complain of their
Hearts, but nevertheless their Distemper lies in their Heads", p. 37;
"Women are neither those Angels nor those Devils we describe 'em", p. 43),
but Parts 1 and 2 treat profusely of kings, princes, and affairs of state
("Both King and People ought to dissemble small Dissatisfactions", p. 4;
"A Prince had better Govern amiss than impotently", p. 12; "The People are
agitated by Parties and Factions, as Seas are by contrary Winds", p. 32).

The aphorisms of Part 3, though, tend to be longer, and to concern literary

and social life ("Gaming find's [sic] a Man a Cully, and leaves him a Knave",

p. 85; "Some Books like the City of London fare the better for being

Burnt", p. 119).

NUC(Pre-1956)310:544 (1st & 2d eds.); BM(to 1955)128:321 (1st & 2d);

Morgan,BBH:D251a (1st & 2d).

A LETTER, directed to the Honourable Robert Harley, Esq; Speaker to the

Honourable House of Commons, relating to the great abuses of the nation.

[s.l.; London, s.d.; 1701] 4 p. 4° 20 cm.(unbd.)

Signed (p. 4): England's Well-wisher. London, May the 3d. 1701.

Caption title; text begins: Sir, Having such a Worthy Person in the Chair

...

First (and only?) edition.

Complains of corruption among customs officers, Justices of the Peace,

and Deputy Lieutenants, with examples (the under-reporting of the quantities

of beer brewed, for tax purposes; the illegal doubling of duty on merchan-

dise for private gain - and if a complaint is reported, the revenue officers

may damage your goods at the wharf; etc.). Some corrective measures are

proposed. For fear of reprisals from those whose secrets he has revealed,

says the writer, he must remain anonymous or else "thereby hazard my life".

NUC(Pre-1956)328:650; Morgan,BBH:D271; Kress:S2231.

LIMITATIONS for the next foreign successor, or new Saxon race. Debated

in a conference betwixt two gentlemen. Sent in a letter to a Member of

Parliament. ... London, printed in the year 1701. 1 p.l., 5-34 p. 4°

21 cm.

Signed (p. 34): Your Humble Servant. March 3d 1700/1 [i.e. 1701 N.S.].

Second edition; the 1st ed., 23 p., 8°, was also pub. London, 1701.

Reprinted in State tracts, 1707, 3:381-93.

Bibliographical footnotes.

This tract purports to review a lengthy dialogue between the writer, a
Whig, and a Tory (cf. p. 33), in order to present a perspective on the
succession issues being widely debated towards the end of William IIIs
reign (he died just 12 months later). The Protestant line is now fixed
(in the Revolution principles) but the person not named, says the writer,
and "the Late King [James II] having abdicated, or rather being depos'd",
the succession falls on the line of the Princess of Orange (Queen Mary II,
d.1694). The debate then considers that this line is Lutheran, while "the
Electress Dowager of Hanover" (Sophia, granddaughter of James I), the first
in line, is a Calvinist, and we have had trouble enough with religious
differences already, so there must be no religious innovation (p. 5-8).
Other possible foreign contenders are discussed (cf. the title; Anne, Queen
Mary's sister and an Anglican, is not mentioned), and the security for the
constitution needed from a "Foreign Successor", the terms of which are then
enumerated (p. 11-13). But these would lead to a commonwealth, says the
writer, and no successor would agree to such conditions. King William did,
is the response, and King John with the Magna Charta. Further conditions
are debated, against the historical background, and whether the Elector
of Hanover and the Elector of Saxony would accept such terms (p.14-30), and
if so, whether the Dutch might not join with Scotland to restore the balance of power (p. 25). In the end the debaters agree that "The pretended
Prince of Wales" (the Old Pretender) has no claim, that this matter of
the terms and religion of the successor must be examined narrowly, but that
in any event government is safe in the hands of Parliament.

NUC(Pre-1956)333:464 (1st & 2d eds.); Morgan,BBH:D274 (1st & 2d).

[MACKWORTH, Sir Humphrey], 1657-1727.

A vindication of the rights of the Commons of England. By a Member of
the Honourable the House of Commons. ... London: printed, and are to be
sold by J. Nutt, near Stationers-Hall. 1701. 1 p.l., [10], 40 p. fol.
30 cm.

Authorship: Epistle dedicatory and other dedications, written by the
author, signed (p. [3], [4], and [5], 1st count): Humphrey Mackworth.

First edition; 2d has same date and collation; reprinted in Somers
tracts, 1814, 11:276, and in 1750 ed., vol. 4, which gives authorship to
Robert Harley (evidently in error, since Harley is a dedicatee).

Upper margin closely trimmed.

History and description of the respective constitutional rights, powers,
and prerogatives of the king, Lords, and Commons, illustrated by actual
practices and procedures. Morgan notes: valuable material on the history
of the Constitution.

NUC(Pre-1956)352:479 (& 2d ed., 1701). Cf. London Library,2:169 (2d ed.);
Morgan,BBH:D282 (2d ed.).

A VIEW of the posture of affairs in Europe, both in Church and state.
Viz. I. The antient pretensions of the two families of Austria and Bourbon
to the Spanish monarchy, historically stated. II. The balance of the power
of Europe, settled by Charles V. and how it came to be broken. III. A
view of the courts of Europe, and their present disposition and state,
relating to peace and war. IV. Of the state of the Church of Rome, and
the decay of the Protestant interest in Europe. Written by a Gentleman,
by way of letter. ... London: printed for James Knapton, at the Crown
in S. Paul's Churchyard. 1701. 4 p.l., 84, [4] p. 8° 17 cm.(unbd.)

Errata: verso of 4th p.l.

Authorship: Dedication, to Lord John "Sommers" (2d l.) signed: A.C.
Arthur Capel, Earl of Essex (1631-83), to whom a work by Somers was once
ascribed (DNB, 'Somers'), is excluded as author because some events here
described are posthumous, e.g. Duke of Anjou became King of Spain (p. 26)
in 1700.

Pages 49-56 are misnumbered 41-48.

Preface (says the tract relates to religion and justice, the pillars of
every state, but sullied in many; in England though, both are "happily
settled by a most benign Constitution". The aim of publication here is
"to undeceive some, and divert others"): 3d & 4th p.l. List of "Books
printed for, and sold by James Knapton ..." (mainly on commerce, travel
and science): 4 p. at end.

Each of the 4 parts of the t.-p. is a separate letter. I. The French
King has the power to annex Spain at any time, but his ancient claim was
only to a part, though the House of Bourbon claims all, making France and
Spain as one. Charles of Anjou also holds a claim to Spain through Naples,
while Austria's claim is through Charles V (p. 1-9). II. Emperor Charles
V had divided his Empire (1556) between Philip II (Spain, Netherlands,
etc.) and Ferdinand I (Austria, Hungary, etc.), the new Emperor; but this
balance was at last broken when Philip IVs daughter married Louis XIV of
France, and while the Civil War raged in England, "France over-powered the
Spaniards" and Austrian power declined, upsetting the "Caroline Balance"
(p. 11-27). III. This part is an account of the various powers in Europe,
their governments, strength of arms, geography, and political alignments
(p. 29-69). IV. Review of the Christian Church (Roman, Greek, Protestant)
from the Roman to the Holy Roman Empires and the Reformation; but the
Council of Trent and the rise of science, scepticism, and trade, have led
to the decay of Protestantism, while the influence of missionaries at court

and in education, have increased the power of Rome.

   NUC(Pre-1956)637:110; Morgan,BBH:D466.

[WAGSTAFFE, Thomas], 1645-1712.

   Rights and liberties of Englishmen asserted. With a collection of statutes and records of Parliament against foreigners. Shewing, that by the
Constitution of England, no outlandish man, whether naturaliz'd or not, is
capable of any office in England or Ireland. That no man ought to be made
a bishop, but he that is English born. That no outlandish man ought to work
or trade, but under the governance of English men. That no outlandish
broker ought to be imployed here. With other useful observations. Humbly
offered to the consideration of the Honourable House of Commons. London,
printed for A[nn]. Baldwin in Warwicklane. 1701. 26, [2] p. 4° 20 cm.

   Signed in **letterpress** (p. 26): D--f G--d, but crossed out in this copy
and 'James Graves' written under in ink. On last page, in manuscript:
'R-h---d N-----c-ffe' (Richard Northcliffe?).

   List of "Books sold by A. Baldwin in Warwick-lane" (including books
against a standing army): 2 p. at end.

   Although ordained in the English church, Dr. Wagstaffe was a nonjuror
(he was secretly consecrated Bishop of Ipswich in 1694 - DNB); but by prac-
tising as a physician, he avoided the poverty of most of the nonjuring
clergy. The uncertainties of the succession at this time gave Parliament
the opportunity to increase its powers, and Wagstaffe here presents historical instances from Rome and Richard II forward, of troubles which ensued
whenever resident foreigners (especially Frenchmen) were active in the
councils and commerce of England, and they were not under parliamentary
control - matters dealt with in the Act of Settlement (1701). The present
poverty of our tradesmen "proceeds from the vast Crowd of Outlandish men"

in the kingdom (p. 15). Our wars are prolonged and misdirected when the generals are "foreign Foxes to keep English Geese" (p. 18), and these generals should be replaced by English ones before the next war (of Spanish Succession). Charity begins at home; if foreigners want English laws, freedoms, and religion, they should "go to the English foreign Plantations" to enjoy them (p. 21-2). English sources, and precedents in antiquity, are also plentifully cited for state restrictions on foreigners; and what was true then is seasonable still under William III: we must "expel Outlandishmen from all Places Civil and Military in England and Ireland" (p. 26).

NUC(Pre-1956)644:665; Morgan,BBH:D472; Kress:2328.

THE WHIGS thirty two queries, and as many of the Tories in answer to them. With a speech made at the general Quarter-Sessions held for the county of G----r [i.e. Gloucester]. As also another learned speech made at the town hall of R-d-g [i.e. Reading]. To which is added, a copy of a late printed paper, pretended to be a vindication of the Earl of Rochester. London: printed and sold by the booksellers of London and Westminster. 1701. Price six pence. 38 p. 8° 20 cm.

The queries (p. 3-15) concern loyalty to King William, factious matters relating to Jacobitism, the Church, relations with France, and animadversions upon individuals (Mackworth, Davenant, etc.), in a style close to malicious gossip. The speeches (p. 16-22) are typical of an M.P. reporting to his constituents about his arduous efforts on their behalf. "The True Patriot Vindicated, Or, A Justification of his Excellency the Earl of Rochester, Lord Lieutenant of Ireland" (p. 22-38) defends the Earl "From several False and Scandalous Reports" relating to the concerns in the earlier queries, as well as to the Earl's alleged levying of customs duties without warrant, his actions in the High Commission Court, and the

charges against him of misuse of funds and peculation while he served
as First Lord of the Treasury.

   NUC(Pre-1956)659:353; Morgan, BBH:D487(28 p.); BM(1955)256:397.

THE CASE of the Abjuration Oath endeavoured to be cleared, to the satisfaction of those who are required to take it. London, printed for J[ohn]. Nutt, near Stationer's Hall, 1702. 1 p.l., 20 p. 4° 20 cm.(unbd.)

From refs. to the Queen, this was pub. after 8th March 1702, when Anne ascended to the throne.

The Abjuration Oath, renouncing the Stuart claim to the throne, was imposed by Parliament in 1701. This discusses in catechistic form the 4 main points of the Oath: 1. the Queen has the rightful claim to the throne; 2. "the Pretended Prince of Wales" (James Edward, the Old Pretender) has not; 3. all allegiance to this Pretender is renouced; and 4. this abjuration is made "heartily and willingly" (p. 2). The meaning of a rightful claim is explored, and the evidence found in favour of a de facto crowned king over any de jure heir by blood, when it is for the public good: only one prince at a time can have the right (p. 11), therefore if Her Majesty "has an undoubted Right" then "The P[retended]. P[rince]. can have none at all" (p. 13). The publication of this argument (a Whig view, supporting the revolution principles) it is hoped will further national unity and loyalty (p. 19-20).

NUC(Pre-1956)97:620; Morgan,BBH:E103; BM(to 1955)34:944.

THE DANGERS of Europe, from the growing power of France. With some
free thoughts on remedies. And particularly on the cure of our divisions
at home: in order to a successful war abroad against the French King and
his allies. ... By the author of, The Duke of Anjou's succession considered. London: printed, and sold by A[nn]. Baldwin, in Warwick-Lane. 1702.
1 p.l., [2], 68 p. 4° 21 cm.

Errata: p. 68.

Caption title (p. 1, sig. B1): A view of the dangerous state of Europe,
&c. This does not accord with catchword 'TH' on preceding page, sig. A2.
The only copy in NUC, that at Duke University, has catchword 'THE',
in reset type, but it too has no text between A2^v and B1^r, and the identical text of the 'Errata' (p. 68) has also been reset. The type batter of
the title-page, A2^v, B1^r, and p. 68 (photocopy seen), is all identical in
both copies.

The Duke of Anjou's succession considered was pub. in London, 1701, as
was The Duke of Anjou's succession further considered (cf.NUC(Pre-1956)
151:55).

Page 66-8 set in smaller type, pagination, and catchwords continuous.

Lower margin closely trimmed, p. 61-3, with partial loss of footnote,
p. 61.

Domestic disagreements (e.g. p. 18-22), especially over succession, have
encouraged Louis XIV to support the (Old) Pretender, master the Spanish
Netherlands, advance his grandson the Duke of Anjou to succession in Spain,
enlarge his armed forces, and generally to threaten England and "his
majesty" (e.g. Pref.; thus this was written before William IIIs death, Mar.
1702, N.S.). British unity is urged, and war with France (e.g. p. 44,
48-9); the War of the Spanish Succession was declared May, 1702.

NUC(Pre-1956)132:351 (NcD; & 2d ed., 1702); Morgan,BBH:E133; Kress:2346.

DIRECTIONS to the electors of the ensuing Parliament, which is to meet on Tuesday the 30th of December ... [s.l.; London?] Printed in the year, 1702. 1 p.l., 22 p. 4°(in 2s) 20 cm.(unbd.)

Sets forth precepts for use in electing Members of Parliament, adducing past mischiefs of legislators in support of judicious electoral choice, without fear or favour. For example, those you elect should be of "Competent Years and sound Understandings, well read ...", for they must comprehend "the True Interest of England, in relation to our Affairs at Home and Abroad"; and while in England a man is of age at 21, in most other places he must be 25, and the writer does not think that anyone should be considered for Parliament "before that Age at least" (p. 9-13). He must support the "Legal Prerogative" of the Crown, without extension or diminution, for past calamities were "inflicted upon us by Parliaments" (such as the tyranny which followed Charles I); so we must seek a "Balance between the two Extreams of an Absolute Monarchy, and a Popular Anarchy" (p. 2-3). Our present King (William III, d. 8 Mar. of the year of pub., 1702 N.S.) "is supported by the best of Titles, _viz_. The General consent and Election of the People" (p. 7). Above all, "forbear Chusing such Men as are inseparably link'd to a Party of Faction" (p. 18). "All our Hopes" rest "in the Choice of a Good Parliament" (p. 21), so we must "Chuse Men truly Fearing God, Loyal to their King, Lovers of their Country, Sound in their Understandings, Just in their Dealings ..." (p. 22) - in short, though Whiggish, an unusually impartial election pamphlet.

NUC(Pre-1956)144:356.

SOME remarks on the Bill for taking, examining and stating the publick accounts of the Kingdom: and on the proceedings thereon in both Houses, the last session. London: printed in the year, 1702. 28 p. 4° 19 cm.(unbd.)

Second edition; 1st ed.: 1701. Reprinted in State tracts, 1707, 3:302-12 (cf. Morgan).

Further to: The several proceedings and resolutions of the House of Commons in relation to the Bill for taking, examining, and stating the publick accounts of the Kingdom, together with a copy of the Bill. London, 1701 (cf. Morgan,BBH:D386).

Imperfect: hole in p. 25-8, inner margin, with loss of parts of 3 words, p. 27.

The Bill concerned the appointment of Commissioners for the public accounts, and while the 1701 pamphlet showed "the Lords to be in the Wrong", this shows why the author "is not of the same Opinion" (cf. p. 3-4).

NUC(Pre-1956)556:7; Kress: 2371. Cf. Morgan,BBH:D404 (1701 ed.).

THE TRYAL, sentence, and condemnation of Fidelity, as it was lately acted on the publick stage. With a dialogue between Corruption and Fidelity: wherein is discovered the vitious and corrupt practices of those who publickly exclaim against the members, and proceedings of true English parliaments. ... London, printed, and sold by the booksellers of London and Westminster. 1702. 1 p.l., [2], 28 p. 4°(in 2s) 20 cm.

Dedication (p. [1]-[2], 1st count), "To the Honourable, the Commons of England, in Parliament assembled", signed: Fidelity.

Upper margin closely trimmed.

The 'character' Fidelity, a loyal supporter of King William, is indicted because "he made it his Business to discover Frauds, Abuses and Mismanagements committed in the Government, and made Proposals to redress the same, and Save the public Treasure" (p. 15). The jurymen in a mock trial, all of whom, along with many of the witnesses, bear names personifying human vices, find the prisoner guilty as indicted, and the judge's sentence is to change Fidelity's name to "Faction, alias Jacobite, Lewisdenian [supporter of Louis XIV], Rogue, Rebel, and Mad-man" (p. 17). "A Dialogue between Corruption and Fidelity", and 21 Queries, follow, all in the same satirical vein.

NUC(Pre-1956)603:201 (ICN); Morgan,BBH:E505a; London Library,2:1130.

1703

[CROSFEILD, Robert], fl. 1693-1704.

  The government unhing'd: or, An account of many great encroachments made
upon the liberties and propertie of the people of England. Shewing the
notorious breach of trust of some publick ministers and officers. Humbly
offered to the consideration of the Honourable House of Commons. ...
London, printed for the author, at the Cock-Pit House in Clerkenwell-[Close;
and sold by the booksellers, 1703.] 23 p. 4° 19 cm.

  Signed (p. 23): Robert Crosfeild. Cock-Pit House, Clarkenwel-Close, Nov.
15th, 1702. Referring to the imprint, this address seems to establish
Crosfeild as author. That he was a publisher too is confirmed by references to his publications on p. 4 and 5, though he is unknown to Plomer.

  Imperfect: lower margin closely trimmed with loss of 1 or 2 lines of text
on each page, and of part of title-page imprint, completed (in brackets,
above) from copy in Newberry Library, Chicago, and supplied in facsimile,
tipped in at the end.

  Provenance: bookplate of James, Earl of Bute: verso of t.-p.

  The "Lords of the Admiralty, &c." are charged with the "encroachments"
(p. 3), and the attempt here is to bring them, and other corrupt ministers,
"to open shame" (p. 4). The evidence of John Woodgate is adduced, over his

Laudatur et Alget
Juven. Sat. 1.

Portrait of Daniel Defoe from the frontispiece
of <u>Jure Divino</u>, 1706, described as by Taverner
and Vandergucht. The motto <u>Laudatur et Alget</u>
(He is praised, yet not cherished) is from
Juvenal's <u>Satires</u>.

name, on p. 18-19.

NUC(Pre-1956)128:56 (ICN); Morgan,BBH:F433.

[_____].

The government unhing'd: or, An account of many great encroachments
made upon the liberties and propertie of the people of England. ...
London, printed for the author, at the Cock-Pit House in Clerkenwell-
Close; and sold by the booksellers, 1703. 23 p. 4° 30 x 22 cm.

Signed (p. 23): Robert Crosfeild. Cock-Pit House, Clarkenwel-Close,
Nov. 15th. 1702. Referring to the imprint, this address seems to establish
Crosfeild as the author.

This is a facsimile of the original in the Newberry Library, Chicago,
bound as 2 original pages on one side of each leaf. For other notes, see
entry above for an imperfect original.

NUC(Pre-1956)128:56(ICN); Morgan,BBH:F433.

[DEFOE, Daniel], 1661?-1731.

A new test of the Church of England's loyalty: or, Whiggish loyalty and
Church loyalty compar'd. [Edinburgh?] Re-printed in the year 1703. 1
p.l., 23 p. 4° 20 cm.

Authorship established in Moore (2d ed.):44, though Morgan,BBH:E508,
apparently citing Halkett & Laing 4:180, gives authorship to John Tutchin
(1661?-1707). Defoe's birth date: LC and DNB; actual year still uncertain.

First pub. [London?], Jun. 1702, 34 p. (cf. BM, Moore, Wright, Morgan);
other printings are given in Moore, including this one (in National Library
of Scotland), and a 1704 and 1705 in Morgan. NUC & BM give [Edinburgh]
for a 1703, 23-p. edition. A London, 1715, edition appeared: BM, 50:115,
under the title: A defence of Mr. Withers's History of the resistance: or,
A new test of the Church of England's loyalty, referring to John Withers,

A history of the resistance, as practis'd by the Church of England (London, 1710, q.v.), which presented a case similar to Defoe's (cf.NUC(Pre-1956)669:694).

Imperfect: small tear top of p. 23, with loss of about 4 words; upper margins closely trimmed.

Provenance: official stamp of "Devon & Exeter Institution" (verso of t.-p.).

Morgan notes: "Defoe urges the Church of England to cease looking towards St. Germain", where the exiled Stuarts reside, in France.

In close historical argument, Defoe complains that dissenters have suffered more and longer ill-usage (under the Established Church) than have adherents to the Church of England, themselves schismatics once, and that the latter acted with similar loyal dissent when threatened (e.g. under Mary Queen of Scots), as have "The Protestant Brethren the Dissenters, or Whigs" under the Established Church. "The Laws are the Test both of the Royal Authority, and of the Subjects Obedience" (p. 22).

NUC(Pre-1956)136:574; BM(to 1955)50:115; Morgan,BBH:F116 (wrongly given as 1st ed.); Wright(Defoe), no. 30; BPL(Defoe):96; Moore(2d ed.):44n.

[FLETCHER, Andrew],1655-1716.

Speeches, by a Member of the Parliament, which began at Edinburgh the 6th of May 1703. Edinburgh; printed in the year 1703. 95 p. 8° 17 cm.

Morgan,BBH:F147, has also 66-p. and 78-p. editions of 1703.

Fletcher, leading advocate of the nationalists in the important 1703 Scottish Parliament, pleaded for the restoration of all rights and liberties of Scotland as before the Union with the Crown of England (1603), for home rule after Queen Anne's death (Act of Security), and for raising a national militia. These events were important in their influence on Anne, as leading towards the legislative union of Scotland and England in 1707

(Treaty of Union).

NUC(Pre-1956)175:166 (95 p., called "second edition"); Kress:2385 (95 p.).

1704

[BURNET, Gilbert, bp. of Salisbury], 1643-1715.

The Bishop of Salisbury's speech in the House of Lords, upon the Bill against Occasional Conformity. [London: printed for Ri[chard]. Chiswell, at the Rose and Crown in St. Paul's Church-Yard. 1704. Price two-pence.

Authorship: NUC, and DNB, 'Burnet'.

Caption title; imprint taken from colophon.

Closely bound at inner margin, with slight loss of text on 1st and last pages.

Review of occasional conformity practices from Elizabeth's reign, with reasoned arguments against the Bill and for occasional conformity.

NUC(Pre-1956)85:621; Morgan,BBH:G94.

[HAVERSHAM, John Thompson, 1st baron], 1641-1710.

The speech of a noble peer upon the reading of the Bill for preventing Occasional Conformity. [London, printed in the year, 1704.] 4 p. 4° 20 cm.

Caption title; imprint taken from colophon.

Morgan gives the printer (or publisher?) as "J. Simon".

Addressed to the House of Lords, and argues against the passage of the

Bill. The Test Act (1673, 1678) is "one of the best Bills [i.e. Acts]
that ever was made for the Security of the Protestant Religion", and it
should not be evaded by occasional conformity; but the expensive Spanish
Succession War has not gone well for Britain, and we cannot afford to lose
good leaders by such a Bill at this time. (The Bill was passed in the
Commons 14 Dec., 1704 - cf. BM(to 1955)63:909 - but rejected in the Lords.)

NUC(Pre-1956)235:322; BM(to 1955)238:116; Morgan,BBH:G226.

[LESLIE, Charles] 1650-1722.

Cassandra. (But I hope not) Telling what will come of it. Num. I.
In answer to The occasional letter. Num. I. Wherein the New-Associations,
&c. are considered. London: printed and sold by the booksellers of London
and Westminster, 1704. 2 p.l., 76 p. 4° 20 cm.

Errata: verso of t.-p.

Authorship: NUC, BM & DNB ('Leslie').

Number I advertised in Defoe's Review, 18 April, 1704, as "now in press",
and 20 June as "just published"; 18 July, Cassandra No. II announced;
Leslie's The rehearsal, 15 March, 1706, advertised Nos. I and II (cf.Morgan,
BBH:V31 & *V31).

A reply to: The occasional letter. Number I. Concerning ... The new
association ... With a postscript, relating to Sir Humphrey Mackworth's
book, intituled, Peace at home: or his defence of the Occasional Bill
[i.e. Mackworth's Peace at home: or, A vindication of ... the Bill for
preventing danger from Occasional Conformity ... London, 1703 (cf. Arber,
3:372; NUC(Pre-1956)352:478).] London, 1704 (cf. NUC(Pre-1956)426:189).
Morgan,BBH:V31, assigns all The occasional letter. Number I to Mackworth's
authorship.

Bound with his: Cassandra. (But I hope not) Numb. II. ... London, 1704
(q.v., 'Leslie').

Having waited in vain since February (cf.Arber,3:389) for a second Occasional letter to explain its arguments (cf. Advertisement, verso of t.-p.),
Leslie, a nonjuror, here presents the counter arguments for non-resistance
to change in Church and state, against the anonymous author of The occasional letter no. I, who had criticized the Church of England doctrine of
passive obedience.

NUC(Pre-1956)328:212; BM(to 1955)135:690; Morgan,BBH:V31 & [*]V31.

[_____].

Cassandra. (But I hope not) Telling what will come of it. Numb. II.
In answer to The occasional letter. Numb I. Wherein the New-Associations,
&c. are considered. London: Printed and sold by the booksellers of London
and Westminster, 1704. 1 p.l., 98 p. 4° 20 cm.

Errata: p. [2].

Page numbers 58-9, 62-3, misnumbered 50-51, 54-5, respectively.

The second part of a reply to: The occasional letter. Number I. London,
1704. (For other notes, see Leslie's Cassandra ... Num. I.)

Bound with his: Cassandra. ... Num. I. London, 1704 (q.v.).

Partial contents: "A declaration by the King's Majesty", Dumfermling,
August 1650 (in black letter): p. 45-52; "The declaration of the Commissioners of the General Assembly of Scotland", signed August, 1650, A. Ker; "A
letter from Lieutenant General David Leslie to the Lord General Cromwell",
August 1650: p. 55-6; "Some observations upon this declaration": p. 57-61.

NUC(Pre-1956)328:212; Morgan,BBH:V31 & [*]V31.

[MACKWORTH, Sir Humphrey], 1657-1727.

A letter from a Member of Parliament to his friend in the country.
Giving a short account of the proceedings of the Tackers, upon the Occ-

asional and Self-denying Bills, the Act of Security in Scotland, and other

occurrences in the last session of Parliament. [London: printed and are

to be sold by the booksellers of London and Westminster, 1704] 8 p. 4°

21 cm.

Authorship and pub. date: NUC & BM; Morgan,BBH:G316, notes that author-

ship is also ascribed to William Pulteney, Earl of Bath.

Caption title; imprint taken from colophon; date from sources above.

Refers to the Tory Bill to prevent Occasional Conformity, the Act of

Security for Scottish home rule after Queen Anne's death, and other Bills,

and "the Right of Tacking, or joining two Bills together" (p. 2). Mackworth

argues in favour of Tacking; in his A brief account of the Tack. London?

1705 (q.v. below), after two rejections of the Bill, 1703-4, Mackworth (if

he is the author) opposes Tacking.

NUC(Pre-1956)352:477; BM(to 1955)149:268.

[NICOLSON, William, abp. of Cashel], 1655-1727.

A true state of the controversy betwixt the present Bishop and Dean of

Carlile, touching the regal supremacy. In a letter from a northern divine,

to a member of the University of Oxford. London: printed in the year 1704.

1 p.l., 20 p. 4° 20 cm.(unbd.)

Authorship: NUC & BM; Morgan,BBH, says W. Nicolson and F. Atterbury,

acknowledging the section contributed by the latter. In the text, the

author is seemingly referred to as a third person, other than Bishop Nicol-

son and Dean designate Atterbury (e.g. p. 12 & 20), but the main arguments

(p. 12-20) opposing Dr. Atterbury's institution as Dean are from a view-

point peculiar to the Bishop. Referring to the letter's destination, both

Bishop and Dean were educated at Oxford. Francis G. James, in his bio-

graphy of Nicolson North Country Bishop (New Haven, 1956, p. 160-61), assumes Nicolson was the author.

First edition. Second edition: ... to which is added a Letter from the south, giving an account of a very strange attempt made by Dr. A[tterbury]. towards antedating the resignation of his predecessor in the Deanery of Carlisle. London, 1705, in 2 parts (cf. BM & Morgan).

Contents include: "Letters Patents" from Queen Anne, Westminster, 13 Nov. 1704, appointing Dr. Francis Atterbury as Dean of Carlisle, signed: Clayton (p. 2-4); a recantation by the Dean at Rose-Castle [Carlisle], 15 Sept. 1704, of whatever "may reasonably seem to impeach Her Majesty's Royal Supremacy", signed: Fran. Atterbury (p. 7-11).

Concerns the institution of Francis Atterbury as Dean of Carlisle, and the opposition of Bishop Nicolson to the form and wording of the "Letters Patents" and to a statement of the Dean seeming to question the royal supremacy.

NUC(Pre-1956)418:566; BM(to 1955)171:879; Morgan,BBH:G480.

1705

A DEFENCE of liberty and property, giving an account of the contest between the L--ds [i.e. Lords] and C---ns [i.e. Commons] of Athens. London,
printed in the year 1705. 1 p.l., 10 p. fol. 32 cm.

First edition; another ed., 1706, has 23 p.

Further to the Parliamentary election of 1700 in Aylesbury, Bucks., and
the case of the Tory, William White vs. the Whig, Matthew Ashby over the
right to vote, which led to a contest between the Upper and Lower House
(discussed by Sir Humphrey Mackworth, in Free parliaments, 1704, and in
his An abstract of a treatise, 1705, q.v.). This presents the arguments
of both the Lords and the Commons, concluding that the Commons hope to
satisfy the Lords without "Sealing their own Ruine", for the sacrifices
in wars abroad are unjustified if liberty is lost at home (p. 10).

NUC(Pre-1956)136:469; Morgan,BBH:H119 (1705 & 1706).

[DRAKE, James], 1667-1707.

The memorial of the Church of England, humbly offer'd to the consideration
of all true lovers of our church and constitution. London: printed in the
year 1705. 56 p. 4° 21 cm.

Authorship: It was Defoe who pointed to Dr. Drake as the author, but what

appears to be the best evidence is found in the Preface to the 1711 ed.
(q.v., below), and this clearly proves Drake to be the author. Downie,
p. 84-8, names many other suspects in the intensive authorship hunt, including William Pittis, but considers Sir Humphrey Mackworth to be a serious contender; Drake is accepted, however, till better evidence arises
(p. 87). DNB ('Thos. Pittis') says William Pittis participated, while
The history of the Mitre and Purse (1714, q.v., below), perhaps itself by
Wm. Pittis, states without reservation (p. 28) that the authors were "Dr.
Drake and Mr. Pooley" (i.e. Henry Poley), at Robert Harley's instigation.
BM accepts this.

First edition? First pub. about 9th July, 1705 (Downie, p. 82 and 209n5;
composed 1704: DNB, 'Drake', and the 1711 ed. Preface, p.v), and printed
in 250 copies by the Roman Catholic David Edwards (p. vi of 1711 ed.,
Downie, p. 11 & 83, and Rothschild:1559; unidentified in Plomer). In this
ed., p. 17, 1.34 begins "shall here" (cf. NUC).

Answered by: 1. John Toland, The memorial of the state of England. London, 1705 (q.v., below; itself answered by: William Stephens, A letter to
the author of The memorial of the state of England. London, 1705, q.v.,
below); 2. Daniel Defoe, The High-Church legion: or, The memorial examin'd;
being, a new test of moderation. London, 1705 (Moore,103; here Defoe tried
to discredit The memorial, on behalf of the Ministry); 3. The memorial of
the Church of England, humbly offer'd ... With remarks upon the whole
paragraph by paragraph. 2d ed. London, 1705 (from NUC,375:319, the cross
reference in NUC,17:573, and BM,65:2928-9, this is the 2d ed. of: An
answer paragraph by paragraph, to The memorial of the Church of England.
London, 1705; both are identical in sentiment to The memorial of the Church,
this 'answer' serving cleverly only to reprint the proscribed original.
A "2d. ed., corrected" was pub. in 1706; cf. NUC & BM); and 4. The case of

the Church of England's memorial fairly stated: or, A modest enquiry into
the grounds of those prejudices ... against it. London, 1705 (by William
Pittis or, says Morgan,H248 and followed by NUC,328:211, by Charles Leslie; this is a vindication of Drake's The memorial. "The 2d. ed.":
London, 1705, with errata, p. 56. According to The history of the Mitre
and Purse, 1714 (q.v., below), a confession of authorship of this tract
was wheedled from a gentlemen, who was then brought to trial: p.29). See
also the notes to the 1711 ed., following.

The circumstances giving rise to the writing of this tract (mainly, the
rejection of the Occasional Conformity Bills) are given in the anonymous
Preface to the posthumous 1711 edition (q.v., below), and the results of
its publication were to precipitate a fierce pamphlet controversy, a vigorous but ineffective search for the writer directed by Robert Harley, and
parliamentary debate on the alleged danger to the church and the implied
insult to Queen Anne, its head. Drake was suspected, cleared, but under a
cloud, while William Pittis was fined and pilloried (DNB, 'Wm. Pittis')
for the libel, and the tract itself was sentenced to be burnt by the common
hangman in September (Abel Boyer, The political state of Great Britain,
Apr. 1711, cited by DNB and Rothschild). It is said that this work was
the cause of Earl Godolphin's turn from a Tory to a Whig commitment (Downie,
p. 11). In this satirical reproach upon moderation Drake, a physician and
author of the weekly Mercurus politicus, expresses the High-Church, Tory
fear of occasional conformity (p. 14, &c.), and of the growth of other
threats from dissenting 'Sectaries' to the doctrine and discipline of the
Established Church (p. 15-20, &c.). He upbraids the Godolphin Ministry for
its policy of moderation (p. 23-36), from his frustration at the failure
of the three Occasional Conformity Bills, 1703-5. This defeat had alarmed
the High-Churchmen, and here the memorialist warns them to preach the dis-

tinction between latitudinarianism, which betokens a lack of interest in
religion and the church, and Christian virtue, which is true moderation
(p. 13, &c.). This cry that the church is in danger reached a crescendo
four years later in the Sacheverell pamphlets (1709), trial, and impeachment, and now in 1705 it had already become a torrid election issue, in the
face of the best efforts of Harley (and, in his service, Defoe, who called
The memorial "A virulent pamphlet" - Review, 12 July, 1705), to cool down
the public fever.

   NUC(Pre-1956)375:319 (1705 & 1711 eds.); BM(to 1955)65:2928 (2 eds., 1705);
Morgan,BBH:G379 (both; & 2d ed., 1705; 78 p., 1706; under: Wm. Pittis);
Carabelli:116n (ed. unspecified); Rothschild:1559 (both; under: Wm. Pittis,
from Halkett & Laing).

[LAWTON, Charlwood], 1660-1721.

   Civil comprehension, &c. in a letter to a friend, from one who wishes
the general good of England, and particularly well to the Establish'd
Church. [London. Sold by the booksellers of London and Westminster. 1705.
Price 2d.] 8 p. 4° 22 cm.

   Signed (p. 8), 15 Oct. 1705: N.N. (to which BM,168:70 adds: [i.e. C. Law-
ton]). Halkett & Laing and Stonehill are in agreement.

   Caption title; imprint taken from colophon.

   Imperfect?: t.-p. wanting? Arber & Morgan give title as: Civil comprehension recommended as an expedient for peace and union; in a letter to a
friend who wishes ... well to the Established Church, no paging, otherwise
the same; from a variant ed. with a t.-p.? NUC (also a caption title) &
BM both have title as: Civil comprehension, &c. in a letter ...

   Reprinted in Somers tracts, 1814, 12:574-80 (also has caption title, as
above).

Further to this is his: A second letter concerning civil comprehension.
London, 1706.

In this tract (in epistolary form), the writer purports to respond to
his friend's command to speak freely, without regard to current factions;
but the writer's arguments proceed with more vehemence than order. "Liberty of conscience" is part of the Christian religion, he says, evidently
meaning Protestantism for "Persecution could never have been introduced ...
[but for] the dark times of Popery" (p. 2). All Protestants favour moderation, and "If Men had Moderation enough to come into a Civil Comprehension,
neither our Church, nor our Civil Rights, nor Toleration could ever be
destroy'd (p. 3-4). Even Presbyterians were against the execution of Charles I, and next to Papists our Church (Anglican) fears them most (p. 3).
The Whigs said only the Exclusion Bill (introduced 1680) and the Bill against occasional conformity (introduced 1702/3/4) could save our rights and
our Church, and they opposed the Triennial Bill (passed 1694). The Church
Party (Tories) were violent during the Revolution to avoid the suspicion
of Jacobitism (p. 5-6). The Popish Plot and the Test Act (1678), and
the Rye House Plot (1683), are not examples of moderation. The Whigs say
the Tories are High-Flyers and Papists, and will destroy civil rights; the
Tories say the Whigs want a commonwealth. Without domestic peace, we can't
refuse a standing army, nor procure a good foreign peace treaty. All
sides must be moderate, and withstand self-interest.

   NUC(Pre-1956)319:636; BM(to 1955)132:97 & 168:70. Cf. Morgan,BBH:H245
(variant title, same imprint); Arber,3:479-8 (variant title and imprint).

A LETTER to a Member of Parliament, concerning the true interest of Scotland, with respect to the Succession. [s.l., Edinburgh? s.d., 1705?]
7 p. 4° 19 cm.(unbd.)

Caption title; place of pub.: not in Arber, but pro-Scottish; pub. date: Morgan & NUC, in brackets but without query; the most likely years are 1703 to 1706.

One in the spate of pamphlets preceding the Act of Union, discussing the successor to Queen Anne, this urges the M.P. "never to name the ... Successor to the Crown of England, till th' Articles of Union were agreed to", but to insist on "Commissioners for an Union" first, to better conditions for Scotland (p. 3-4). "Let us Either be separated altogether ... or let us have an Honourable Union" (p. 7).

NUC(Pre-1956)329:30; Morgan,BBH:H257.

MACKWORTH, Sir Humphrey, 1657-1727.

An abstract of a treatise, intituled, Free parliaments: written by Sir Humphrey Mackworth, in defence of the proceedings of the House of Commons, in the case of Ashby and White. With some additions, in defence of their commitments, and other proceedings on the late writs of habeas corpus, and writ of error. The fourth edition. [London: printed, and are to be sold by John Nutt near Stationers-Hall, 1705.] 4 p. fol. 33 cm.

Caption title; imprint taken from colophon.

An abstract of Mackworth's Free parliaments; or, A vindication of the fundamental right of the Commons of England ... to be sole judges of all those privileges of the electors, and of the elected, which are absolutely necessary to preserve free parliaments ... Being a justification of the ... House of Commons, in the case of Ashby against White. [London], 1704.

William White, a Tory, and Constable of Aylesbury, Bucks., denied Matthew Ashby, a Whig, his vote at the 1700 Parliamentary elections in Aylesbury, but Ashby brought successful suit against White. Queen's Bench ruled (1704) the case as one of Parliamentary privilege and thus outside common law, but the Lords reversed the decision, thus in effect making themselves judges

of Commons' rights. This contest gave rise to many publications: cf.BM

(to 1955)7:809; see also entry for A defence of liberty and property ...

London, 1705, above, and Arber,3:455 & 483 for another work on this case,

by Mackworth.

   NUC(Pre-1956)352:476(& 477); BM(to 1955)149:268; Morgan,BBH:H1.

[_____].

   A brief account of the Tack, in a letter to a friend. [s.l.; London?

printed in the year 1705.] 8 p. 4° 19 cm.

   NUC(4-p. ed.) notes "Attributed by Lowndes to Daniel Defoe", but unfound

in Moore, and all 3 bibliographies cited below list this under Mackworth.

   Caption title; imprint taken from colophon.

   Reprinted in Somers tracts, 1814, 12:466-83 (cf.Morgan).

   After two rejections of the Bill to prevent occasional conformity (1703-

4) by the House of Lords, "the only way to have it Pass'd was to Tack it to

a Money Bill". The author is opposed to Tacking, and to the Occasional Con-

formity Bill, and thinks the Established Church is in less danger now from

dissenters than it used to be from Papists.

   NUC(Pre-1956)352:477; Morgan,BBH:H276; Kress:S2312.

[STEPHENS, William], 1647?-1718, Supposed Author.

   A letter to the author of The memorial of the state of England. London,

printed in the year 1705. 2 p.l., 32 p. 4° 20 cm.

   Authorship: DNB ('Stephens') assigns this to John Toland, to whose work

in fact it replies, but says Stephens was indicted as the writer (and that

Thos. Rawlins was "the reputed author"). Pierre Desmaizeaux, in his "Mem-

oirs" to Toland's A collection of several pieces (London, 1726, p.lx) says

Stephens was the publisher, and Rawlins the author, an attribution entertained by <u>Downie</u> (p. 91-2), where further evidence is adduced. The case

for Rawlins is strong, and accepted by Morgan, but the ms. ascription to

Stephens' authorship on the t.-p. of Cambridge University Library's copy

(Carabelli) and in a letter on the back of the t.-p. of the Bodleian copy

(<u>Halkett & Laing</u>) seems better evidence, and is accepted by NUC and BM.

Half-title: A letter to the author ... England.

First edition, and probably the only one, though an anonymous work with

the same 1st 13 words in the title but ... <u>England, answer'd paragraph by</u>

<u>paragraph</u> (London, 1706, <u>q.v.</u>, below) is sometimes mistaken for a 1706

edition - cf. bibliographical citations, below.

A reply to: John Toland, <u>The memorial of the state of England</u>. London,

1705 (<u>q.v.</u>, below), itself a reply to: James Drake, <u>The memorial of the</u>

<u>Church of England</u>. London, 1705 (<u>q.v.</u>, above).

Answered by: <u>A letter to the author of The memorial of the state of Eng-</u>

<u>land, answer'd paragraph by paragraph</u>. London, 1706, and Daniel Defoe,

<u>Remarks on the Letter to the author of the state-memorial</u>. London, 1706.

A further reply by John Toland, <u>A defence of Her Majesty's administration:</u>

<u>particularly, against the notorious ... calumnies with which ... Marl-</u>

<u>borough, and ... Harley, are ... aspers'd in ... A letter to the author of</u>

<u>The memorial of the state of England</u>, was suppressed "when six or seven

sheets were already printed" (cf. Desmaizeaux, "Memoirs", <u>loc</u>. <u>cit</u>., above).

Upper margins closely trimmed.

A Church of England divine with strong Whig and deist inclinations (<u>DNB</u>),

Stephens (if he be the author) sympathized with Toland's argument for

toleration towards the dissenters: "You have stated the Case of Dissenters

so distinctly ... that I think no good Man can find any just Cause of Ex-

ception", and toleration "is a Claim which all Christians may demand as a

... Right" (p. 1-2); thus, Stephens says, he has no argument with three-fourths of Toland's book, so will devote himself to Toland's blind praise

of the present Ministry, which part of Toland's tract is less candid than

the other three parts (p. 7). The author then elaborates on his resent-

ments against Toland's fawning defence of the Ministry in power, and spares

no pains in assaulting Marlborough and Robert Harley (Godolphin, the other

leader, escapes reproof). Harley, says the author, is "a Man who has de-

serted and betray'd all Parties" (p. 29). Toland had said Harley "hated

extremes in all Parties" ("in every Party he always hated extreams": p. 69

of Toland's Memorial), but it would have been more to the point to say he

is "hated extremely in all Parties"; and as to "his aversion to extremes

... I never heard that he was extremely Honest, or extremely Sincere", so

I agree (p. 30). According to Downie (p. 90-91) this pamphlet subjects

Harley to the strongest public censure hitherto, and it set a long-standing

precedent for the regular Whig judgement of Harley as a man of intellect

and skill, trying to draw all power into his own hands, and to maintain good

relations with both Hanoverians and Jacobites (cf. DNB, 'Harley'). The

author concludes with the mordant observation that there can be no attain-

ment of high places without first "abandoning all Sense of Truth, Honour,

Modesty or Shame" (p. 31).

    NUC(Pre-1956)567:629 (1705; also 1706, 44 p., probably meaning A letter

... answer'd paragraph by paragraph, q.v., below); BM(to 1955)229:658

(1705 only); Carabelli:124 (1705); Morgan,BBH:H369 (under Rawlins, but also

attributed to Stephens; & 1706, probably in error, as NUC).

[TOLAND, John], 1670-1722.

The memorial of the state of England, in vindication of the Queen, the

church, and the administration: design'd to rectify the mutual mistakes of

Protestants, and to unite their affections in defence of our religion and liberty. London: printed and sold by the booksellers of London and West-

minster. 1705. 1 p.l., [2], 104 p. 4° 21 cm.

"Escapes of the Press corrected": p. [2], 1st count.

Authorship: London Library follows Somers tracts in assigning this to the

Earl of Nottingham's pen, but the evidence of DNB, 'Toland', Halkett & Laing,

and particularly of the Pierre Desmaizeaux "Memoirs" to vol. 1 of Toland's

A collection of several pieces (London, 1726, p.lix-lx), is overwhelmingly

for Toland and is accepted in most bibliographies, including NUC & BM;

Carabelli weighs other evidence, and also finds in favour of Toland.

Caption and running title: The memorial of the state of England, &c.

An earlier issue appeared, same imprint and collation, but without the

errata list on p. [2]; cf.NUC. Reprinted (errata corrected) in Somers

tracts, 1814, 12:526-74. Carabelli has also: Dublin, 1705, and Somers

Tracts, 1751, eds.

To the Reader (The present controversy involves many issues, known to

all but understood by few, such as the problems of High and Low-Church,

dissenters, Quakers, toleration, conventicles, sacramental test, occasion-

al communion, Whig and Tory, the new and old Ministry, and union of the

two kingdoms, etc., which are all here set in a fair light, to dispel the

sophistry of The memorial of the Church of England, here quoted from the

2d, 8° ed.): p. [1]-[2], 1st count. The Principal Heads (p. [2], 1st

count): Of the Church; Of the Dissenters; Of the Toleration; Of the Minis-

try.

A reply to: James Drake, The memorial of the Church of England. London,

1705 (q.v., above).

Answered by: William Stephens, A letter to the author of The memorial of

the state of England. London, 1705 (q.v., above; itself answered by A letter

to the author of The memorial of the state of England, answer'd ... London,

1706, q.v., below, and Daniel Defoe, Remarks on the Letter to the author
of the state-memorial. London, 1706).

Toland was educated for the church but became a deist; his Christianity
not mysterious (1696), ordered to be burnt by the common hangman and its
author prosecuted (1697), was "the first act of warfare between deists and
the orthodox which occupied the next generation" (DNB, 'Toland'). He
(with Swift and Defoe) become one of Robert Harley's ablest propaganda writers, and was "employed" by Harley to write the present work (DNB), or wrote
it under Harley's "protection" (a letter from Toland, probably to Harley,
1705, cited in Carabelli). Desmaizeaux (loc. cit., above) says it was published "by the direction of Mr. Harley, Secretary of State". Defoe was
also influenced by Harley to answer James Drake's powerful The memorial to
the Church of England, but Toland's reply is "The definitive Harleyite response to the Memorial", written in just a few days, with the advice only
of William Penn, the Quaker, and distributed by himself (Downie, p. 89-90).
The purpose of the tract is to cool the public temper, inflamed against the
Marlborough-Godolphin-Harley Ministry by Drake who, deeply moved by the
failure of the Occasional Conformity Bills, had exaggerated the growing
dangers to the Church of England under that administration. Toland defends
the official policies in general, and Robert Harley in particular (even
though he is "not once nam'd ... in the Memorial [to the Church of England]",
p. 68), describing those qualities in his patron which give him the best
claim of anyone "to encounter those, who would confound all our Rights",
and to protect us from "barbarous Subjection" (p. 68-9). An outline of
the text is given in the preliminary "To The Reader" (cf. note above). The
ringing close praises High and Low-Churchmen for their moderation and learning, rendering them "the Glory of the Reformation" (p. 104). Able though
this vindication was, it did not silence debate; instead, it provoked

William Stephens into his stinging reply (q.v., above, 1705).

NUC(Pre-1956)596:325 (both issues); BM(to 1955)65:2929,239:721, &c.;

Morgan,BBH:H442; Carabelli:115-6; London Library,2:955(D. Finch, Earl of

Notts.).

1706

BELHAVEN, John Hamilton, 2d. baron, 1656-1708.

The Lord Belhaven's speech in Parliament, the 15th day of November 1706, on the Second Article of the Treaty. [London? 1706] 8 p. 4° 19 cm.(unbd.)

Caption title.

First pub. as a broadside, Edinburgh (cf. DNB, 'John Hamilton' 1st baron); other eds. have "second speech" in the title.

Upper margins closely trimmed, some page numbers lost.

This is the second of Lord Belhaven's two nationalist speeches before the Scottish Parliament in Nov. 1706, the other being given on the 2d. Nov. (cf. Morgan: I39 & London Library, 1:204). "A passionate opponent of the union" (DNB), Belhaven here considers "the Motives, that should engage us to take England's Successor upon their own Terms" (p. 1), referring to the settlement of the succession after Queen Anne, for Scotland. (The succession had been provided for England in the Act of Settlement, 1701, but the Scots Act of Security, 1703, did not oblige them to follow the English Act.) Belhaven argues eloquently against the Articles of the proposed Treaty lying before them, for the parliamentary union of Scotland and England. They offer nothing to Scotland, and have not been well-enough considered by the Members; we should at least hold out for some trade advantages. Where we have the power, we have the security; not so where it is

lodged in others, as it would be if we go "into the English Succession"

(p. 6). Let us be warned, he concludes, by past injuries from the English.

   NUC(Pre-1956)44:462 (2d and 15th Nov. speeches); BM(to 1955)96:905 (both);

Kress:2491. Cf. Morgan,BBH:I38 (omits date from title, otherwise same);

Kress:2487 ("... Beilhaven's second speech ...", [1706?], else same); S1155

& S2333 (2d speech, [Edinburgh?] 1706, broadside).

[CROMARTY, George MacKenzie, 1st earl of], 1630-1714.

   Trialogus. A conference betwixt Mr. Con, Mr. Pro, and Mr. Indifferent,

concerning the Union. To be continued weekly. [s.l.; London?] Printed

in the year 1706. 1 p.l., 8 [i.e. 6] p. 4° 18 cm.(unbd.)

   Authorship: Morgan, & DNB, 'Mackenzie'.

   Page numbers 2-3 omitted in pagination.

   No subsequent weekly numbers have been identified; in this number, only

"Indif." and "Con." speak, though "Indif." clearly advocates the parlia-

mentary Union of Scotland and England, as did the author himself.

   Morgan,BBH:I96.

[FLETCHER, Andrew,] 1655-1716.

   State of the controversy betwixt united and separate parliaments.

Whether these interests which are to be united by the present treaty, and

these interests which by the same treaty are to remain separate and dis-

tinct. Are more properly and safely lodged under the guardianship of an

united Parliament, or under that of separate parliaments. [s.l.; Lon-

don?] Printed in the year 1706. 28 p. 4° 24 cm.

   First few leaves foxed.

   In the controversy, which was settled by the Act of Union (1707) of the

English and Scottish Parliaments, Fletcher was firmly opposed to union because with a "united Parliament, the Scots do make a formal Surrender ...
and are for ever left to the Mercy of the English" (p. 16).

  NUC(Pre-1956)175:166(NNC); BM(to 1955)74:334; Morgan,BBH:I156.

HALIFAX, George Savile, 1st Marquis of, 1633-1695.

  The anatomy of an equivalent, by the Marquis of Halifax, adapted to the
equivalent in the present Articles, 1706. [Edinburgh, 1706] 8 p. 4°
19 cm.(unbd.)

  Caption title.

  Imprint from BM.

  First pub. as: The anatomy of an equivalent. [London? 1688?] (cf. NUC &
BM), further to his A letter to a dissenter, by T.W. [London, 1687], and
reprinted in Fourteen papers, 1689, and State tracts, 1693 (cf.BM(to 1955)
4:1068), but this posthumous text is adapted to contemporary concerns, and
somewhat abridged, by an unknown hand.

  Further to: Daniel Defoe, An inquiry into the disposal of the equivalent. Edinburgh, 1706, and An essay upon the equivalent. In a letter to
a friend ... [s.l.] 1706 (cf. Kress:2501, 2508).

  "If you Scots will Acquiesce in the Articles [of Union with England] Proposed [to "take away the Oaths and Tests", cf. 1688 text, Savile's Works,
Oxford, 1912, p. 104], You shall sometime or other have as good a thing for
them, This put into Fashionable Word, is now called an Equivalent" (p.1).
Part of the literature of the Revolution of 1688, the original text was
"directed against James the Second's famous attempt to buy off the hostil-
ity of the dissenters by including them in his project of toleration"
(Walter Raleigh's Introd. to Savile's Works, op. cit., p. xix-xx).

  NUC(Pre-1956)227:98; BM(to 1955)213:767; Morgan,BBH:B171; Kress:2512.

A LETTER to the author of The memorial of the state of England, answer'd paragraph by paragraph. London: printed in the year 1706. 44 p. 8° 19 cm.

Authorship: Pierre Desmaizeaux, in his "Memoirs" to John Toland's A collection of several pieces (London, 1726, p. lx) says that Toland (whose The memorial, 1705, q.v., above, favours toleration and dissenters) was directed to answer Stephens' A letter (1705, q.v., above). This reply to Stephens, who agreed with Toland's views of dissenters and toleration, presents a firm Church of England perspective however.

This title should not be confused with the title of Stephens' work, the first 13 words of which are identical, but to which this is an answer; nor with The memorial of the Church of England ... With remarks upon the whole paragraph by paragraph (London, 1705), the last words of which are the same. The similarity of several titles in this 'memorial' series, beginning with James Drake, The memorial of the Church of England (1705, q.v., above) has led to confusion in several bibliographies.

A reply to: William Stephens, A letter to the author of The memorial of the state of England. London, 1705.

Further to this is: Daniel Defoe, Remarks on the Letter to the author of the state-memorial. London, 1706 (another reply to Stephens' A letter).

This close analysis of Stephens' attack on the politics of the Ministry (made more effective by Stephens assuming "the Face ... of an old Whigg", instead of which "he has a Cloven Foot", p. 4), returns to stressing the High-Church considerations of the original The memorial of the Church of England, by Jas. Drake, 1705 (q.v., above). The author here purports to show, with casuistry and the method of extensive quotations from Stephens each followed by his own comment, that Stephens (or whoever the author of A letter might be) is insincere or misguided. He does this by making (as examples): toleration of dissenters ridiculous by using extreme arguments

(p. 7); by showing that moderation does not mean tolerance of sin, so churchmen should not be rebuked for condemning sin (p. 9-12); that the constitution is defended by laws and liberty, not a standing army (p. 19-20); and ("coming to the only Drift and Aim of his [Stephens'] Writing", p. 24) by disputing Stephens' claim of mismanagement of the war and its campaigns (sometimes with logistical detail), and particularly by defending Marlborough against the malicious (though often covert or indirect) attempts by Stephens to "Blacken the Fame and Reputation of my Lord Duke" (p. 38). Stephens should have given us better proof of his charges, else he is "a Libeller fitter for the Rod than the Pen" (p. 44).

Carabelli:124n. Cf. NUC(Pre-1956)567:629 (1706, 44 p., under Stephens, with the title given only to "England ...": probably this is the "... answer'd paragraph by paragraph" work).

THE PLEA of publick good not sufficient to justifie the taking up arms against our rightful and lawful sovereigns. In a letter to the Reverend Mr. Hoadly. ... [s.l.; London?] Sold by the booksellers of London and Westminster. 1706. 12 p. 4° 19 cm.

A reply to: Benjamin Hoadly, The measures of submission to the civil magistrate consider'd. In a defense of the doctrine delivered in a sermon preach'd ... Sept. 29, 1705. London, 1706. Includes the sermon, on Romans XIII, 1 (cf. BM(to 1955)104:607, & Morgan,BBH:H211).

Dated (p. 12): March 13. 1705/6, i.e. 1706 N.S.

Provenance: T. Cross (t.-p. autogr.).

You say (says the author, of Hoadly) that the public good, when invaded by the sovereign, demands resistance to the sovereign, and that passive obedience is "a very criminal Omission"; but this 'public' is that body of which the King is head, so the public good must be a mutual good (p. 3).

"Publick Good is the End and Motive of Allegiance" to the sovereign (p. 4),
and is served not by following private fancy "but by what the Laws have
determined". Otherwise, the writer concludes, the public's allegiance "is
to be deemed against the publick Good, when they say it is", the public
becoming the judge for the king <u>and</u> themselves (p. 12).

NUC(Pre-1956)461:475 (InU).

TRAPP, Joseph, 1679-1747.

The mischiefs of changes in government; and the influence of religious
princes to prevent them. A sermon [on <u>Prov</u>. 28:2] preach'd before the
Mayor, and Corporation of Oxford, on Friday March 8. 1705/6. Being the
anniversary of Her Majesty's inauguration. By Joseph Trapp M.A. Fellow
of Wadham College Oxon. Publish'd at the request of the Common Council.
Oxford, printed at the Theater, for John Stephens 1705 [O.S., 1706 N.S.].
And sold by J[ames]. Knapton at the Crown in St. Paul's Ch Yard, London.
1 p.l., 29 p. 4° 21 cm.(unbd.)

The Council's request to print, 11 Mar. 1705 (verso of t.-p.) signed:
Samuel Thurston Clericus Com. Civit. Oxon.

Printed at the Theatre Press, Oxford University where, <u>Plomer</u> (p. 280-
81) notes, the bookseller Stephens had items printed without paying University dues.

The lesson from <u>Proverbs</u> reads: "For the Transgression of a Land many
are the Princes thereof; but by a Man of Understanding and knowledge the
State thereof shall be prolong'd". The sermon, on this special occasion,
makes the point that "it is certainly a most pressing Calamity to any
People ... to have several Competitors or Rival Kings contending together
for the supreme Authority, or to have the civil Constitution often chang'd
and vary'd: or even to have frequent Successions of Princes ..." (p. 2);

so, long may Good Queen Anne reign (p. 29).

NUC(Pre-1956)600:44; BM(to 1955)240:908; Morgan,BBH:I387.

[PUCKLE, James,] 1667?-1724.

England's path to wealth and honour, in a dialogue between an Englishman and a Dutch-man. ... Printed, 1700. London: reprinted, in the year,
1707. 60 p. 12° 14 cm.

Dedication, to Thomas, Duke of Leeds, "Governour of the Royal Fishery of
England", signed (p. [4]): James Puckle.

First pub. under title: England's interest; or, A brief discourse of the
royal fishery. London, 1696, 2d ed. same year; then as A new dialogue between a burgermaster and an English gentleman. London, 1697, and England's
way to wealth ... London, 1699. England's path ... 2d ed. with additions,
London, 1700, preceded the present work, followed by a London, 1718 ed.,
and The advantages of the fishery to Great Britain demonstrated. In a dialogue ... London, 1719. Then came a Swedish transl. by J. Porteus, Eng-
landz Gen-Stijg til Macht och Ahra. Stockholm, 1723, followed by England's
path ... To which is added, articles relating to the Dutch herring-fishery
... London, 1750, and further reprints in the Somers tracts, vol. 4, 1750,
and vol. 11, 1809.

Upper margin closely trimmed; inner margin tightly bound.

"... the great and best Nursery for Seamen is the Fishery" (p. [6]; its

development (by floating stock in a National Fishery, p. 49) is advocated
as the "Path to Wealth" and for the relief of the poor.

   NUC(Pre-1956)474:538(CLU-C); BM(to 1955)196:404; Morgan,BBH:B280;
London Library,2:956. Cf. Kress:2253 (2d ed. with adds., 1700, 40 p.).

AN ACCOUNT of the Charity-Schools lately erected in ... England and
Wales: with the benefactions thereto; and of the methods whereby they
were set up, and are governed. Also a proposal for enlarging their number, and adding some work to the childrens learning ... The seventh
edition, with large additions. London, printed and sold by Joseph Downing, in Bartholomew-Close near West-Smithfield, 1708. 41, [1] p. tables.
4° 23 cm.

First pub. 1704 (? cf. Morgan; Kress:2534 says 1706); see also 1711,
1712 eds.

Includes list of Charity-Schools: p. [10]-36.

List of books printed and sold by J. Downing: 1 p. at end.

Bound with: Robert Moss, The providential division. London, 1708 (q.v.),
and 3 other works, in a vol. lettered on spine: Pamphlets on Charity
Schools.

Provenance: stamp of Mercantile Library, Philadelphia: p. 5, etc.

The purpose of Charity Schools is "the Education of Poor Children in ...
the Christian Religion, as ... taught in the Church of England; and for
Teaching them such other Things as are most suitable to their Condition"
(p. 4). Then appears an account of their erection and management. They

begin with a subscription list and the establishing of rules; these are set forth (p. 4-8), and statistical lists of schools follow. It is interesting to note that Bishop White Kennett's great contribution to this subject, The charity of schools for poor children, was a sermon preached and published in London in 1706, two years after the probable first appearance of the present work. Thousands of charity schools were endowed throughout the eighteenth century, in the four countries of the British Isles, for the free education of poor children (education, that is, guided by the middle and upper classes to establish social discipline among the lower orders against rebellion and infidelity, intending to solve the Church and state problems of irreligion and pauperism by preparing them for life as hewers of wood: see Mary G. Jones, The charity school movement, London, 1964, p. 4-5, 19); but much of the inspiration was truly benevolent, and it is remarkable that the movement began when England was painfully occupied with a long and costly war (op. cit., p. 23n).

NUC(Pre-1956)2:559 (London, 1706-10); Morgan,BBH:G4 (1704-17); Kress: S1188 & S2387.

BEVERIDGE, William bp. of St. Asaph, 1637-1708.

A sermon [on Acts 22:20] preach'd before the lords spiritual and temporal, in Parliament assembled, in the Abby[sic]-Church at Westminster, January the 30th. 1695/6. being the day of the martyrdom of King Charles I. By William, Lord Bishop of St. Asaph. [Acts 22:20 quoted] ... London: printed by H[enry]. Hills [jun.], Black-fryars, near the Water-side, for the benefit of the poor. 1708. 15[i.e. 16] p. 8° 18 cm.(unbd.)

Title within black mourning border.

Apparently the 1st ed. (e.g., Arber); reprinted in his Theological works (Oxford, 1843-8, 12 v.), v. 6, p. [432]-46.

Page 16 numbered 15.

Upper margin closely trimmed.

The text from Acts reads, in part: "And when the blood of thy martyr Stephen was shed, I also was standing by, and consenting unto his death ..." All-Saints' Day, 1st Nov., memorializes Christian martyrs, but King Charles suffered death 30th Jan. (1649) "for the sake of Christ, and his Church", so this day "is set apart for the Anniversary commemoration of it" (p. 3). Dr. Beveridge then preaches on the suffering and cause of St. Stephen and of Charles I. "If King Charles had died in the Communion of the Church of Rome ... He would have been Canonized long ago by the Pope" (p. 10).

NUC(Pre-1956)51:598; BM(to 1955)16:924; Arber,3:489.

EYRE, Robert, 1657?-1722.

A sermon [on Joel 3:19] preach'd before the Honourable House of Commons, at Saint Margaret, Westminster, on Friday, Jan. 30. 1707/8. ... By Robert Eyre, D.D. Prebendary of the Cathedral Church of Winchester. London: printed by H[enry]. Hills [jun.], in Black-fryars, near the Waterside. For the benefit of the poor. [s.d.; 1708?] 16 p. 8° 18 cm.

Title within black mourning border.

Request to print Dr. Eyre's sermon, 31 Jan. 1707 (O.S.), "Yesterday, being the Day appointed for a Solemn Fast and Humiliation, for the Murder of King Charles the First": verso of t.-p.

Upper margin closely trimmed.

The lesson from Joel reads: "Egypt shall be a desolation ... because they have shed innocent blood in their land" (p. 3), and the sermon deals with scriptural examples of violence and punishment, their relevance to the execution of Charles I, repentence, and loyalty to the present monarch, in accord with the Tory doctrine of non-resistance.

NUC(Pre-1956)165:44([n.d.]); BM(to 1955)69:1030(1707, evidently O.S.;
& 3 1708 eds.); Morgan,BBH:J186 (& 3 other eds. of 1708); London Library
(Suppl.1920):243.

A LETTER written to a gentleman in the country about the late northern-
invasion; and the lawfulness of taking the oaths to the present government.
By a minister of the Church of England. London: printed in the year 1708.
16 p. 4° 22 cm.

"The opinion of a Divine ... about the Oath of Abjuration ..." (p. 14-16)
is signed: J.E. ['llesby' added in ink ms. in this copy], and 'By J. Ellesby' in pencil on t.-p. J. Ellesby's authorship of any part of this work
has not been confirmed, but NUC lists a James Ellersby writing in this period.

The main letter (p. 3-14) is unsigned, but dated (p. 14): July, 8. 1708.

The 'late northern-invasion' was in Scotland, but was a threatened one
only for it was by the "Providence of God ... Happily prevented and crusht"
(p. 4). The taking of oaths refers to the Abjuration Oath (cf. caption
title "The Opinion of the Divine", p. 14); one in 1662 required Scots to
renounce the Solemn League and Covenant between English and Scots, 1643,
but the more recent one was passed by Parliament in 1701, and it imposed
an oath abjuring the exiled Stuarts (father and son; James II died in
Sept.). Here, it is taken "that the Oath of Abjuration refers only to the
Act of Settlement", passed March 1701 when Princess Anne's young son (Duke
of Gloucester) died, requiring that if William and Mary, and Anne, had no
heirs, the crown would pass to Sophia, Electress of Hanover (granddaughter
of James I, mother of George I), so that "the Crown is now entail'd in the
Protestant Line" (p. 14). In the present work, the letter-writer, fearing
for the welfare of his correspondent "for not complying with the Govern-

ment", explains with Christian "Tenderness and Charity" that it is only
the Pretender's legal not hereditary right he must renounce, and draws
attention to the danger of encouraging the Pretender's return to Britain
from his exile in France, to which end his friend is "Mutinously inclin'd"
(p. 3). The writer hopes his friend can accept the oath, as described in
the enclosure ("The Opinion of a Divine") without straining his conscience
(p. 4). The invasion was prevented, so law-abiding peace is counselled,
for no good end can justify an evil action (p. 5); anyway, there's no
prospect for the Pretender whose birthright has been excluded, without the
aid of "French Power" and "Popish Interest" which might ruin our church,
state, and liberties. So, we must support Queen and government, and suppress all actions in favour of the Pretender - or risk the punishment of
God (p. 5-8). Your supposed King cannot hope for success, his birth is
darkly uncertain, and he is bred "in a Popish and French Education" (p. 9).
Think carefully, without a "false Notion of Honour", abiding by Christian
rules - that is, "not upon Revolution but Revelation Principles" (p. 10-13).
"The Opinion of a Divine", mentioned above, concerns the sense of the oath
and when it "may be safely taken": the Pretender's right is now excluded,
and his uncertain birth make his claim doubtful; but nothing uncertain may
be the subject of an oath. Thus, the oath refers literally to the Protestant settlement, so is quite safe for the whole Protestant clergy to take
(p. 14-16).

No bibliographical citations discovered.

MOSS, Robert, 1666-1729.

The providential division of men into rich and poor, and the respective
duties thence arising, briefly consider'd in a sermon [on Prov. 22:2]
preach'd in the parish church of St. Sepulchres, May 27. 1708. ... at

the anniversary meeting of the chief promoters of the Charity-Schools;
together with the masters and mistresses of the said schools; and the
children there educated, to the number of three thousand, and upwards.
... London: printed for Richard Sare at Gray's-Inn Gate in Holborn; and
Jacob Tonson at Gray's-Inn Gate next Gray's-Inn Lane. 1708. 1 p.l., 28 p.
4° 23 cm.

Imperfect: p. 7-10 (sig. B4 & C1) wanting; text supplied in facsimile
from another edition.

Bound with: An account of the Charity-Schools. London, 1708 [and 1711,
and 1712], (q.v.) in a vol. lettered on spine: Pamphlets on Charity Schools.

Provenance: bookplate (inside front cover) and stamp (t.-p., etc.) of
Mercantile Library Company, Philadelphia.

The lesson from Proverbs reads: "The rich and poor meet together: the
Lord is the maker of them all"; and while there may be outward differences
amongst people, there is "manifest Equality as to their Nature and Origine".
Moss, who was Chaplain to Queen Anne, then makes 3 points: God has provided sufficient for the happiness of all, has made rich and poor mutually
needful of each other (p. 5), and smiles upon the charitable work which has
brought Christian care and education to 3000 destitute children of the London area (p. 22). He then describes the charitable services performed,
by and for ever-increasing numbers.

"Charity School was an early (usually Anglican) elementary school, established through the activities of the Society for Promoting Christian Knowledge (1698), usually in the first 30 years of the 18th century. There
were some 1,500 of these ..." (Chambers's Encycl., London, 1966, 12:273,
'School'). Yet the eighteenth century saw only 128 new grammar schools
established in England and Wales (see Mary G. Jones, The charity school

movement, London, 1964, p. 18-19). Until Sunday schools appeared towards
the end of the century, these thousands of charity schools were the principal, and for many children of the poor the only, means of education
throughout the British Isles (op. cit., p. 23).

NUC(Pre-1956)397:486 (& 'Print. by H. Hills, [1708?]', & 1708, 16 p.);
BM(to 1955)165:441; Morgan,BBH:K291 (also: [1708], 12°); Kress:S2411
(16 p., else same).

SHERLOCK, Thomas, bp. of London, 1678-1761.

A sermon [on Prov.24:21] preach'd before the Queen at St. James's,
on Munday [sic] January 31. 1703/4 being the anniversary of the martyrdom
of King Charles the First. By Thomas Sherlock, M.A. Rector of Therfield,
Hertfordshire. Published by Her Majesties special command. London:
printed by H[enry]. Hills [jun.], in Black-fryars, near the water side.
For the benefit of the poor. 1708. 16 p. 8° 18 cm.

Text within a black mourning border.

First pub. London, printed for William Rogers, 1704 (cf. NUC).

Upper margin closely trimmed.

The lesson from Proverbs reads: "My son, fear thou the Lord and the King:
and meddle not with them that are given to change"; the sermon considers
"What Obedience to our Governours is enjoyned by the Law of God" and how
consistent with this law are those who practice change (p. 3); it relates
this to King Charles and Queen Anne in accordance with the Tory doctrine
of non-resistance.

NUC(Pre-1956)543:322: BM(to 1955)221:333; Morgan,BBH:G427 (also 1704
ed.).

WAKE, William, abp. of Canterbury, 1657-1737.

A sermon [on Matt. 26:51-2] preach'd before the House of Lords, at the
Abbey-Church in Westminster, on Friday, Jan. 30. 1707/8. ... By the
Right Reverend Father in God, William Lord Bishop of Lincoln. London:
printed by H[enry]. Hills [jun.], in Black fryars, near the waterside.
For the benefit of the poor. [s.d.; 1708?] 16 p. 8° 18 cm.

There is a variant in NUC, and Morgan,BBH:K438: ... on Friday, Jan.
XXX. MDCCVII. ... London, printed by W.B. for Richard Sare, 1708. 4°

Upper margin closely trimmed, affecting some page numbers; inner margin
tightly bound, affecting text.

The Scriptural lesson is: "All they that take the Sword, shall perish
with the Sword", and Abp. Wake refers this to the "Murder of our Royal
Sovereign" (p. 13), marked "on this Day, set apart ... [for] National Humiliation" (p. 16). By a proclamation of 1660, the year of his Restoration,
Charles II established the 30th Jan. each year as a day of fasting and
humiliation, in memory of his royal father, executed on that day, 1649.

NUC(Pre-1956)645:167(NjPT); BM(to 1955)251:682 (1708, 8°).

BLACKALL, Offspring, bp. of Exeter, 1654-1716.

The divine institution of magistracy, and the gracious design of its institution.   A sermon [on Rom. 13:4] preach'd before the Queen, at St. James's, on Tuesday, March 8. 1708 [O.S., or 1709 N.S.].   Being the anniversary of Her Majesty's happy accession to the throne.   By Offspring Lord Bishop of Exon.   Published by Her Majesty's special command.   London: printed by J.R. for W[illiam]. Rogers, at the Sun against St. Dunstan's Church in Fleetstreet.   1709.   24 p.   8°   19 cm.

Running title: A sermon preach'd before the Queen.

Answered by: Benjamin Hoadly, Some considerations humbly offered to the ... Bishop of Exeter.   London, 1709 (q.v.).   This began the long controversy with bp. Hoadly; see also Charles Leslie's defence of bp. Blackall, The best answer ever was made.   London, 1709.

The text from Romans reads: "For he is the minister of God to thee for good", and the sermon (which quotes widely elsewhere from the Bible) seeks to show that Queen Anne (the magistrate) has a "Divine Appointment" and a "Divine Authority" (p. 3), and that this is quite compatible with her obligations to her subjects because her power is for their good (p. 11, etc.); it is thus her subjects' duty to obey her (p. 23).   This sermon "called forth the wrath of the whigs" (DNB, 'Blackall'), as supporting the High-Church doctrine of non-resistance to royal commands.

NUC(Pre-1956)59:533 (& 2 other 1708/9 eds.); BM(to 1955)21:178; Morgan,BBH:L42 (4°); Rothschild:398; Arber,3:634 & 636; London Library (Suppl. 1920):84.

_____.

The Lord Bishop of Exeter's answer to Mr. Hoadly's letter. Prov. xxvii. 6. Faithful are the wounds of a friend, but the kisses of an enemy are deceitful. London: printed by J[ohn]. Leake for W[illiam]. Rogers, at the Sun over-against St. Dunstan's Church in Fleetstreet, 1709. 56 p. 8° 20 cm.

A reply to: Benjamin Hoadly, Some considerations humbly offered. London, 1709 (q.v.). See also the reply to Hoadly by Charles Leslie, The best answer ever was made. London, 1709.

Answered by: Benjamin Hoadly, A humble reply to the ... Bishop of Exeter's answer ... London, 1709.

A page-by-page refutation (precise editions cited are identified, p. 56) of Hoadly's Whig arguments against the Tory doctrine of non-resistance, as expounded earlier by Bp. Blackall in The divine institution of magistracy. London, 1709 (q.v.).

NUC(Pre-1956)59:533 (2 eds. & 2d ed., all 1709); Morgan,BBH:L41 (with 2 other 1709 eds.). Cf. Rothschild:399 (variant imprint); Arber,3:642.

[GANDY, Henry], 1649-1734.

Remarks on Mr. Higden's Utopian constitution; or, An answer to his unanswerable book. By an English-man. With an appendix. ... [Quotation from bp. Gilbert Burnet's sermon on Romans 13:5, p. 17, and from Numbers

30:20.] London; printed, and sold by the booksellers of Westminster and
London.   (Price B[oun]d. 2s. 6d.)   [s.d.; 1709?] 1 p.l., [6], 126, [2],
lxxx p. 8° 19 cm.

"Wrongly attributed to George Hickes, D.D.": Halkett & Laing,5:69.

Pref. signed (p. [6], 1st count): A.B.; the oath (p. lxxx) begins: I
A.B. do swear ... ("A.B." refers, perhaps, to A. & B., the interlocutors.)

Page xlii and lxxvii misnumbered lxii and lxxviii, respectively.

The Appendix contains "some Passages of Law and History, applicable to
the Subject in hand", supporting de jure monarchy.

Morgan has 2d. ed. with this collation, [1711?]; but his 1st ed., un-
collated, is also 1711, which would be after Higden's 1710 reply.

A reply to: William Higden, A view of the English Constitution.   London,
1709. (Cf. also Charles Leslie's The Constitution, laws and government,
of England, vindicated. London, 1709; Higden's response, A defence of the
View of the English Constitution. London,1710; and Leslie's further reply:
"Remarks on Mr. Higden's late Defence", appended to Leslie's The finishing
stroke. London, 1711 (which Morgan,BBH:N347, ascribes to H. Gandy).

List of religio-political works on similar subjects: [2] p. ff. p. 126
(probably misbound; NUC entry has [2] p. at end).

A page-by-page critique quoting many sources, in the form of a dialogue
between "A." and "B.", of Higden's title, from the viewpoint of nonjurors.
Supports the argument for "the King de jure, against a King de facto", the
latter claim being one only of "Possession without any prior Claim, and
without Right" (p. 27-8). Cf. also Leslie's The Constitution, laws and
government (op. cit., supra) for other notes.

NUC(Pre-1956)190:302 ([17--?]; also 3d ed., 1713). Cf. Morgan,BBH:N228
(same collation, but 2d ed., [1711?]).

GIBSON, Edmund, bp. of London, 1669-1748.

Against speaking evil of princes, and those in authority under them: a sermon [on <u>Acts</u> 23:5] preach'd at the assizes held at Croyden in Surrey, March 7th, 1705/6. before the Right Honourable the L[ord]. Chief-Justice Holt, and Mr. Justice Tracey. ... By Edm. Gibson, D.D. Rector of Lambeth, and Chaplain to his Grace the Lord Archbishop of Canterbury. Publish'd at the request of the judges, High-Sheriff, Grand-Jury, and other gentlemen. London: printed and sold by H[enry] Hills [jun.] in Black-fryars, near the Water-side. For the benefit of the poor. 1709. 16 p. 8° 18 cm.

First pub. London, [1706?].

Upper margin closely trimmed.

The lesson from <u>Acts</u> reads: "Thou shalt not speak evil of the ruler of thy people". The sermon describes the circumstances of St. Paul's words, says this seditious spirit has never been more malignant, with less reason, than today (p. 4), and cites scripture against the censure of princes in the spirit of the High-Church doctrine of non-resistance.

Cf. NUC(Pre-1956)198:640([1706?]); London Library,1:940 (1706); Morgan,BBH:I169 (two 1706 eds.).

HOADLY, Benjamin, bp. of Winchester, 1676-1761.

Some considerations humbly offered to the Right Reverend the Lord Bishop of Exeter. Occasioned by his Lordship's sermon preached before Her Majesty, March 8. 1708 [O.S., or 1709 N.S.]. London, printed for J[ohn]. Morphew near Stationers-Hall, 1709. 52 p. 8° 20 cm.

A reply to: Offspring Blackall, <u>The divine institution of magistracy</u> ... London, 1709 (<u>q.v.</u>).

Answered by: Offspring Blackall, <u>The Lord Bishop of Exeter's answer to</u>

Mr. Hoadly's letter. London, 1709 (q.v.), and Charles Leslie, The best
answer ever was made. London, 1709 (q.v., below).

In the contentious matter of the duty of subjects and the authority of
governors (p. 5), which bp. Blackall had argued was the duty to divine
authority (doctrine of non-resistance), Rev. Hoadly points out that the
magistrate's authority is limited to governing for the good of his subjects
(p. 9; from Rom. 13:4) and thus, he argues, the magistrate (or monarch) is
not exempt from questioning and censure by his subjects: absolute non-
resistance shall not impose a doctrine of servitude (cf. p. 51) - thus
expressing the Whig view of the doctrine of non-resistance. The polemics
begun here between Hoadly and Blackall anticipate, on a smaller scale, the
fierce controversy sparked later in 1709 by Sacheverell's two pamphlets
(q.v.).

   NUC(Pre-1956)248:478 (also 47-p. & 16-p. eds., & 2d and 3d eds., all
1709); BM(to 1955)104:608 (plus 3d ed., 1709); Morgan,BBH:L186 (plus 16-p.
& 3d eds., 1709). Cf. Rothschild:1139 (variant imprint).

[LESLIE, Charles], 1650-1722

   The best answer ever was made. And to which no answer ever will be made.
(Not to be behind Mr. Hoadly in assurance) In answer to his bill of complaint exhibited against the Lord Bishop of Exeter, for his Lordship's
sermon preach'd before Her Majesty, March 8. 1708. Address'd in a letter
to the said M. Hoadly himself. By a student of the Temple. ... London:
printed and sold by J[ohn]. Morphew, near Stationers-Hall, 1709. Price
3d. [4], 28 p. 8°(in 4s.) 19 cm.

   Signed, April 18. 1709, Your Unknown and yet Well known Servant: p. 28.

   "Advertisement" (p. 28) for St. Paul, no mover of sedition; or, A brief
vindication of that apostle from the false ... exposition of Mr. Hoadly

(London, 1706), attributed to John Haslewood (b.1647) in Morgan,BBH:I183

& London Library, Suppl. 1913-20, p. 324 (cf. NUC(Pre-1956)515:204, title);

this, and An enquiry into the nature of the liberty of the subject (London,

1706), attributed to Francis Atterbury (in Morgan,BBH:I146, but NUC(Pre-

1956)160:470, under title) were replies to: Benjamin Hoadly, A sermon

preach'd before the Right Honourable the Lord-Mayor ... of London ...

September 29th. 1705 (London, 1705).

Numerous typographical errors throughout.

A reply to Benjamin Hoadly, Some considerations humbly offered to the

... Bishop of Exeter. London, 1709 (q.v.).

Answered by: Hoadly, The foundation of the present government. London,

1710 ("Postscript"), and William Stephens, A modest reply to the unanswer-

able answer to Mr. Hoadly. London, 1709 (q.v.).

This defends bp. Blackall's arguments (in The divine institution of

magistracy, London, 1709, q.v.) supporting the High-Church doctrine of non-

resistance, and attacks Hoadly's response. (The Bishop's Answer brought

Hoadly's further Low-Church criticism: A humble reply to the ... Bishop of

Exeter's answer ... London, 1709.) The preface explains the purpose of

Leslie's "Vapouring Title" as to show Hoadly "in what manner you have treat-

ed the Lord Bishop of Exeter", Blackall, a disrespect Leslie deplores

(p. [3], 1st count). His close argument has page references to Hoadly's

work; a sampling of its flavour follows: people are not the origin of

government for, as bp. Blackall shows, none has power over his or another's

life, so this power can't be transferred to the government. Killing in

self-defence is not authority over another, else this would be Hobbes'

state of nature (p. 8). Ultimate appeal of government can't be to the

people (i.e. everybody), for this would be anarchy; but without appeal,

power is absolute. Thus with the king, whose power ends all controversy,

while appeal to the people perpetuates confusion (p. 14). Wherever is
the last resort, there is absolute power. The origin of civil government,
from Adam's time, is not in the people but the family, whence grew the
nation; and this is not a state of equality, even among the 'Hottentotes'
(cf. 'A battle royal' in Leslie's The finishing stroke, London, 1711, q.v.),
but of nature and self-preservation requiring God-given authority (p. 15-
18). What if spouses, children, and servants said: if you do not cherish
us, we are not bound to obey? No, a magistrate does not lose his commission by the manner of its execution (p. 19-22), for there will always be
some "who Snarl at the Administration" (p. 26). One may appreciate Dr.
Johnson's observation that Leslie was the only reasoning nonjuror, and one
"who was not to be reasoned against" (DNB, 'Leslie').

NUC(Pre-1956)328:210; BM(to 1955)135:688; Morgan,BBH:L222 (& another
1709 ed., price 1s., while this is "Price 3d." on t.-p.). Cf. Rothschild:
1325 (sold by booksellers of London & Westminster).

[_____].

The Constitution, laws and government, of England, vindicated. In a
letter to the Reverend Mr. William Higden. On account of his View of the
English Constitution, with respect to the sovereign authority of the
prince, &c. In vindication of the lawfulness of taking the oaths, &c.
By a Natural Born Subject. ... London printed, and sold by the booksellers
of London and Westminster. 1709. 1 p.l., [6], 124, [3] p. 8° 19 cm.

Errata: p. [6], 1st count.

A reply to: William Higden, A view of the English Constitution. London,
1709. (Cf. also Henry Gandy, Remarks on Mr. Higden's Utopian constitution.
London [1711?].)

Answered by: William Higden, A defence of the View of the English Constitution. London, 1710.

Displays the present and historical case for succession from the nonjuror
viewpoint, arguing that both monarch and constitution (which depends on
the monarch and the 3 estates) are established de jure, not just de facto
(e.g., p. 5-7); "God made Kings and Kings made parliaments" (DNB, 'Leslie').
NUC(Pre-1956)328:213; BM(to 1955)135:690 & 103:689; Morgan,BBH:L224.

[OLDISWORTH, William], 1680-1734.

A vindication of the Right Reverend the Lord Bishop of Exeter, occasioned
by Mr. Benjamin Hoadly's reflections on his Lordship's two sermons of government, preached in St. Dunstan's Church, March 8, 1704 [O.S., 1709 N.S.].
and before Her Majesty, March 8, 1708 [O.S., 1709 N.S.]. ... [Paraphrase
from:] Acts 23. 2, 3, 4. London, printed for A[nn]. Baldwin at the Oxford-
Arms in Warwick-Lane. 1709. 2 p.l., 5-87 p. 8° 20 cm.

Authorship: DNB, 'Oldisworth', assigns this without query, and NUC,
Halkett & Laing, and Stonehill concur.

Half-title: A vindication of the Bishop of Exeter. Price one shilling.

Another edition, 1709, was "printed and sold by booksellers of London and
Westminster", with only 24 p. (cf. NUC); priority of issue not determined.

A reply to: Benjamin Hoadly, Some considerations humbly offered to ...
the Lord Bishop of Exeter. Occasioned by His Lordship's sermon ... March
8. 1708 (anniversary of Queen Anne's accession). London, 1709 (q.v.)
(which itself considers: Bp. Offspring Blackall's The subject's duty: a
sermon [on Prov. 24:21] preached March 8, 1704/5, 1705, and The divine
institution of magistracy ... A sermon [on Rom. 13:4] preach'd ... March
8. 1708, 1709, q.v.). Besides Oldisworth's Vindication, Hoadly's Some
considerations was also answered by: Bp. Blackall's The Lord Bishop of
Exeter's answer to Mr. Hoadly's letter. London, 1709 (q.v.) (in turn,

answered by: Hoadly's <u>An humble reply to the Bishop of Exeter's answer</u>, 1709), and Charles Leslie, <u>The best answer ever was made</u>. London, 1709 (<u>q.v.</u>). The controversy was extensive, and many other titles, and indeed writers, were involved; many of the titles were reprinted, often several times.

Answered by: Benjamin Hoadly, <u>The divine rights of the British nation and constitution vindicated</u> ... London, 1710. Hoadly was also supported by the wits of <u>The Tatler</u> (cf. <u>DNB</u>, 'Blackall').

Oldisworth enters this prolific controversy by claiming that he knows Bp. Blackall only by reputation, and writing as an admirer wishes only to defend his two excellent sermons, but without forgetting his obligations to Mr. Hoadly (cf. p. 6; then a Low-Church rector) and to truth - for Mr. Hoadly's love of truth causes him to detect an opposite tendency throughout Bp. Blackall's sermons (instances are cited by page number, and in satiric manner; p. 8-11). The Bishop opposes occasional conformity to the Anglican Church, and believes in non-resistance and passive obedience, while Hoadly (later a bishop under George I) upholds the Whig doctrine of resistance and the Revolution principles. The "Supream Governor" is, Bp. Blackwell had argued, in the words of St. Paul, a servant to God, so cannot be a "Peoples Servant"; accountable only to God, says Oldisworth, "no Power on Earth, can question ... him". This is the old allegory that compares the world to a household (or family, cf. Chas. Leslie, <u>The finishing stroke</u>, 1711, <u>q.v.</u> below), with master and degrees of servants (p. 33). As to Hoadly, what he states on p. 49 (of <u>Some considerations</u>) observes Oldisworth, may be applied to his whole book: "All Separation is not Schism; All Resistance is not Rebellion [says Hoadly]; To which I add: All Supreamacy is not Tyranny; All Non-Resistance is not Slavery" (p. 25). This pamphlet is a page-by-page refutation of Hoadly's arguments, with frequent reference

'The Church in Danger', 1706: impression of an inn
sign put up at Stoke by Naland, Suffolk. The amused
and delighted spectators are dissenting pastors.
(Picture and caption from
The Trial of Doctor Sacheverell, 1973,
Courtesy of the author,
Professor G. Holmes.)

to the scriptures, showing that the true right of the magistrate (sovereign) is hereditary and supreme, and that the doctrine of non-resistance
cannot destroy liberty. Although the points at issue are the power of
the monarch as impinging on the power of Parliament, and the place of the
established church in this equation, the issues are, as so often, clouded
by a spirit of contention which become tedious. Oldisworth, described in
DNB as a "hack-writer", ends with an apology for trespassing upon the
Bishop - "For all this is supposing his Lordship to be in the wrong, and
a Thought like that ought never to be forgiven me" (p. 87).

NUC(Pre-1956)429:305 (& 24 p. ed., 1709); BM(to 1955)104:609 (both eds.;
Oldisworth queried); Morgan,BBH:L308; Arber,3:638.

CRIDPATH, George], d.1726.

The peril of being zealously affected, but not well: or, Reflections on
Dr. Sacheverel's [sic] sermon, preach'd before the Right Honourable the
Lord Mayor. ... of London, at the Cathedral Church of St. Paul, on the
fifth of November, 1709. ... London, printed for J. Baker at the Black
Boy in Pater-Noster-Row. 1709. 24 p. 8° 19 cm.(unbd.)

Also attributed to "D.W." and Matthew Tindal (cf. Madan).

A reply to: Henry Sacheverell, The perils of false brethren. London,
1709 (q.v.), one of the 2 sermons for which Sacheverell was impeached in
1710.

Corner of t.-p. missing, with slight loss of text on verso.

Ridpath was proprietor of the Flying Post, a Low-Church writer supported
by the Whig Junto, and one of Pope's 'dunces' often 'cudgell'd' for his
views (Dunciad, variorum, 1729, 2:141). He is taken to task by Charles
Leslie in The good old cause, further ... (q.v., p. 28-30). Here Ridpath
argues against Sacheverell's "perils" and "false brethren" and the doctrine

of non-resistance (e.g. p. 8), and defends occasional conformity (p. 17),
with page references to Sacheverell's sermon, and historical examples
citing scripture and the writings of noted churchmen.

  NUC(Pre-1956)494:371; BM(to 1955)202:866 & 210:786; Morgan,BBH:L356;
Rothschild:1757; Madan(Speck):75.

SACHEVERELL, Henry, 1674?-1724.

The communication of sin: a sermon [on 1 Tim. 5:22] preach'd at the
assizes held at Derby, August 15th, 1709. By Henry Sacheverell, D.D. ...
chaplain of St. Saviour's, Southwark. Publish'd at the request of the
gentlemen of the Grand-Jury. London: printed for Henry Clements, at the
Half-Moon in St. Paul's Church-Yard, 1709. 16 p. 8° 20 cm.(unbd.)

  Third of five 1709 editions in Madan, and the 1st 8° edition, with the
last line of t.-p. beginning: "in St. Paul's".

  Dedication "To the Right Worshipful George Sacheverell, Esq; High-
Sheriff of the the [sic] County of Derby", to whom Henry was "oblig'd by
the Relation I have the Honour to bear to your Family": p. [2], verso of
t.-p.

  Answered (in part) by: An answer to Dr. Sacheverell's sermon preach'd ...
5th of November 1710 [i.e. 1709]. London, 1710 (p. 7 refers to the Derby
sermon), and (as to the 4 articles of impeachment raised by the 1710 trial)
by A vindication of the last Parliament. In four dialogues ... London,
1711 (cf. Madan(Speck):108 & 1026).

  This is the text of the first of the two sermons by Dr. Sacheverell (his
The perils of false brethren ... preach'd ... 5th of November, 1709, q.v.,
being the 2nd) which lead to his impeachment and a vigorous crossfire of
pamphlets (though this was really a continuation of the contest of earlier
in 1709, between Blackall and Hoadly, q.v., above; cf. Morgan,BBH, v.II,

The Communication of Sin :

A

SERMON

PREACH'D at the

Affizes held at *DERBY,*

AUGUST 15th, 1709.

By *HENRY SACHEVERELL,* D.D.
Fellow of *Magdalen-College, Oxon,* and Chaplain of St. *Saviour's, Southwark.*

Publifh'd at the Requeft of the Gentlemen of the
GRAND-JURY.

LONDON:

Printed for HENRY CLEMENTS, at the *Half-Moon*
in St. *Paul's* Church-Yard, 1709.

Title-page of the first of the two sermons in which Dr
Sacheverell tried to show that the Church of England was in
danger, and which resulted in his impeachment. The other
sermon was The Perils of False Brethren, also published in
1709.

The PERILS *of* FALSE BRETHREN, *both in Church, and State:*

Set forth in a

SERMON

PREACH'D

Before the Right Honourable

THE

LORD·MAYOR,

Aldermen, and Citizens of *London*,

AT THE

CATHEDRAL-Church of St. Paul,

On the 5th of *November*, 1709.

——— Haud Imprudenter Speculatus, Neminem celerius *Opprimi*: quam Qui *nihil timeret*, & Frequentissimum Initium esse *Calamitatis* SECURITATEM. *V. Paterc.* L. 2. c. 118.

——— *When they shall say* PEACE, *and* SAFETY, *then* Sudden De-struction *cometh upon them as* Travail *upon a* Woman *with* Child, *and they shall not escape*, 1 Thess. c. 5. v. 3.

By *HENRY SACHEVERELL*, D. D. Fellow of *Magdalen-College, Oxon*, and Chaplain of St. *Saviour's, Southwark.*

LONDON:

Printed for *Henry Clements*, at the *Half-Moon* in St. *Paul's* Church-Yard, 1709.

The title-page of the second of the two High-Church sermons (The Communication of Sin, 1709, was the first), preached as a warning of the Church's danger from papists, dissenters, and antimonarchists, and which lead to Dr Sacheverell's impeachment in 1710.

p. 58). The Act of Settlement was passed after Princess Anne's son (Duke
of Gloucester) had died, and it provided for a Protestant succession if she
or William and Mary left no heirs, through the person of Sophia, Electress
of Hanover, granddaughter of James I and mother of George Louis (George I).
But as Queen Anne's reign progressed, the Tories lost their interest in yet
another foreign monarch, and renewed their hopes for restoring the hereditary English line. "The Sacheverell Trial of 1709-10 was a kind of shadow
replay of the Revolution", for the Tories had become as effectively barred
from positions of influence under William and Mary as were the Whigs under
James II (Howard Erskine-Hill, "Alexander Pope: the political poet in his
time", Eighteenth-century studies, v. 15, no. 2, Winter, 1981-2, p. 175).
The trial loosed factional frustrations: the fury of the Tories, and the
profound unease of the Whigs. The present work sounds an alarm for the
safety of the established Church of England, by constitution the supporter of the heriditary right of its monarch, under the present strains. The
text of the sermon is from Timothy, and reads, in part, "neither be par-
taker of other men's sins". The sermon analyses "the ways whereby an
individual might become responsible for the sins of others" (Madan), such
as by approving or communicating heresy (Socinus, Hobbes, Spinoza, and Fox
are named), schism, immorality, false doctrine, lying misinterpretations,
false libels upon King and Church, and other blasphemies (p. 15-16).

   NUC(Pre-1956)513:281; BM(to 1955)210:782; Morgan,BBH:L363 (& 36 p., 4°);
Rothschild:1778; Madan(Speck):50.

_____.

The perils of false brethren, both in Church, and state: set forth in
a sermon [on 2 Cor.11:26] preach'd before the Right Honourable the Lord-
Mayor, Aldermen, and citizens of London, at the Cathedral-Church of St.

Paul, on the 5th of November, 1709. ... By Henry Sacheverell, D.D. ...
chaplain of St. Saviour's, Southwark. London: printed for Henry Clements,
at the Half-Moon in St. Paul's Church-Yard, 1709. 24 p. 8° 20 cm.(unbd.)

Fourth in time of numerous editions in Madan; issued 3 Dec. 1709, with
dedication: "To the Right Honourable Sir Samuel Garrard, Bar. Lord-Mayor of
the City of London" (verso of t.-p.), and the last line of text: "Our
Lord." (p. 24).

Transl. into French as: Les dangers où l'on est exposé de la part des
faux frères ... Londres, 1710, and Sermon du Dr. Sacheverell ... Amsterdam, 1711; and into Dutch as: Het gevaar van valsche broderen ... Amsterdam,
1710; and into German as: Sacheverellischer Unfug oder Umständliche Nach-
richt ... 1710 (Hanoverian); and other editions in these languages - cf.
Madan(Speck):71,74,303, etc.

Bibliographical footnotes.

In the Dedication (p. [2]-[4]), Dr. Sacheverell says he speaks "By Your
Lordship's Command" against the misrepresentations of the Church of England's
adversaries, to stop the "Encroaching Mischief" in "this Distracted Kingdom" (being "Summon'd ... by Your Lordship"), and to set Londoners right
"in their Notions of Government, both in Church, and State".

Answered by: George Ridpath, The peril of being zealously affected.
London, 1709 (q.v.), William Stephens, A modest reply. London, 1709 (q.v.),
and numerous other works (cf. Madan(Speck):75ff.).

This prints the second of the two sermons by Dr. Sacheverell (his The
communication of sin ... August 15th, 1709, London, 1709, q.v., being the
1st) which gave rise to the famous controversy, well documented in contemporary pamphlets (1160 items in Madan!), and resulting in Sacheverell's
impeachment by Parliament early the following year. It has been estimated
that 100,000 copies of Perils sold in Britain, as well as translations

abroad (cf. Downie, p. 116). The text from Corinthians names Paul's
sufferings in his journeyings, and "in perils among false brethren".
Sacheverell compares the schismatic plots in St. Paul's time against the
Church of Corinth, with the more recent ones against the Church of England:
the papist Gunpowder Plot, foiled 5th Nov., 1605 (the occasion of this
sermon), the execution of Charles I, 1649 (p. 5-7), and the views of dissenting False Brethren today who care not if the church be under presbytery
or episcopal rule (p. 9), nor see that absolute obedience to the king and
"the utter Illegality of Resistance upon any Pretence whatsoever" is the
"Express command of God" (p. 12). Their views are heresy and treason,
against church and state (as scriptural quotations demonstrate). In over-
coming the restrictions of the Conventicle Act (1664) by occasional conformity, our False Brethren mangle church doctrine (p. 17). The state
must support the church against this betrayal of both (p. 18), for the False
Brethren can never again be trusted, and should leave our church if they
cannot support its founding principles, thus restoring it to unity and peace.

NUC(Pre-1956)513:284; BM(to 1955)210:784; Morgan,BBH:L365; Rothschild:1779;
Madan(Speck):60.

[SHIPPEN, William], 1673-1743.

Moderation display'd: a poem. ... [quotation from "Lucret. lib. 5."]
By the author of Faction display'd. London: printed and sold by H[enry].
Hills [jun.], in Black-fryars, near the water-side. 1709. 16 p. 8°
17 cm.(unbd.)

Also attributed to Defoe (cf.Morgan & NUC), but Moore has only Defoe's
Moderation maintain'd, London, 1704 (Moore:73).

First pub. London, 1704.

Answered by his own: Moderation display'd: a poem ... answer'd paragraph
by paragraph. London, 1705 (cf. Morgan, but unfound in NUC or BM); and his

The sequel: or, Moderation further display'd, a poem. By the author of
Faction display'd. [London?], 1705.

   Faction display'd. A poem, London, 1704, was also pub. anon.

   Set in rhyming couplets, this is described in DNB ('Shippen') as a dreary
satire against the Whigs, "in which the Whig lords are portrayed under the
names of the leaders in Catiline's conspiracy". Shippen, a Jacobite, deplores the opportunity now given "to a New Sett of Men to Ruin both Church
and State with their New Politicks" (cf. Pref.).

   NUC(Pre-1956)544:132 (& 1704, 2 of 1705); Morgan,BBH:G434 (& 1704, 2 of
1705 not same as NUC). Cf. BM(to 1955)221:520 (1704, 1705, & 1717 eds.
only).

SMALRIDGE, George, bp. of Bristol, 1663-1719.

   A sermon [on Judg.19:30] preach'd before the Right Worshipful the Court
of Aldermen, at the Cathedral Church of St. Paul, London; on monday, January
31. 1708-9. Being the anniversary of the martyrdom of King Charles I. ...
London: printed by H[enry]. Hills [jun.], in Black-Fryars, near the water-
side. For the benefit of the poor. [s.d.; 1709?]. 16 p. 8° 18 cm.

   Title within black mourning border.

   Another edition: London, printed by G.J. for Jonah Bowyer, 1709 (q.v.).

   Request to publish, by Sir Charles Duncombe, Lord Mayor of London, appears on the t.-p., signed: Gibson [i.e. Edmund Gibson, Chaplain to Archbishop Tenison]. Author's acknowledgement of this request ("Testimony ...
that a Discourse against Rebellion is as acceptable in the City, as at
Court"): p. [2].

   Upper margin closely trimmed, slightly affecting text.

   The lesson from Judges reads, in part: "... all that saw it said, There
was no such deed done nor seen from the day that the children of Israel

came up out of the land of Egypt unto this day: consider it ...", and the

sermon compares "The barbarous Fact" referred to here (abusing a woman and

cutting her into 12 pieces), so obviously shocking, with the treason of

the regicides (p. 14); in both cases advice, consideration, and vigorous

repentence are necessary, and the murder should never be forgotten (p. 15) -

all in accordance with the High Anglican and Tory doctrine of non-resistance.

 BM(to 1955)223:799. Cf. NUC(Pre-1956)550:90 (G.J. for J. Bowyer, 16 p.);

Morgan,BBH:L377 (J. Bowyer, 26 p., 4°); London Library(Suppl.1920):679

(no printer given).

───────────.

 A sermon [on Judg.19:30] preach'd before the Right Worshipful the Court

of Aldermen, at the Cathedral Church of St. Paul, London; on monday,

January 31. 1708/9. Being the anniversary of the martyrdom of King Charles

I. ... London, printed by G.J. for Jonah Bowyer, at the Rose Ludgate-

Street. 1709. 16 p. 8° 20 cm.

 Title within black mourning border.

 Another edition: London, printed by H. Hills, [1709?] (q.v. for other

notes), has the same text.

 Request to publish, by Sir Charles Duncombe, Lord Mayor of London, appears

on the t.-p., signed: Gibson [i.e. Edmund Gibson, Chaplain to Archbishop

Tenison]. Author's acknowledgement: verso of t.-p.

 The lesson from Judges reads, in part: "... all that saw it said, There

was no such deed done nor seen from the day that the children of Israel

came up out of the land of Egypt unto this day: consider it ...".

 NUC(Pre-1956)550:90-91; BM(to 1955)223:799. Cf. Morgan,BBH:L377 (26 p.,

4°). London Library(Suppl.1920):679 (no printer given); Arber,3:614.

[SOUTH, Robert], 1634-1716.

A sermon [on Judg.19:30] preach'd on the anniversary-fast for the martyrdom of King Charles I. at Court. In the last century. ... London:
printed by H[enry]. Hills [jun.], in Black-fryars, near the water-side,
for the benefit of the poor, 1709. 16 p. 8° 18 cm.

Title within black mourning border.

First pub. under this title: London, 1708; previously pub. as: A sermon
preach'd before King Charles II. London, [1705?], but "there is considerable difference in text between these 2 editions" (NUC,557:442).

The lesson from Judges reads, in part: "... all that saw it said, There
was no such deed done nor seen from the day that the children of Israel
came up out of the land of Egypt unto this day: consider it ...". The
sermon compares the time of Judges, when there was no king in Israel and
"Every Man did what was right in his own Eyes", and when the awful deed of
the lesson was revenged by a civil war (p. 2), with the events of Charles
I's execution and since, a warning that accords with the Tory doctrine of
non-resistance.

NUC(Pre-1956)557:443; BM(to 1955)226:469. Cf. Morgan,BBH:K388 (1708, &
2d ed. [1708] only).

[STEPHENS, William], 1647-1718.

A modest reply to the unanswerable answer to Mr. Hoadly. With some
considerations on Dr. Sacheverell's sermon before the Lord Mayor, Novemb.
5. 1709. In a letter to a Member of the Honourable House of Commons.
London, printed for J. Baker at the Black-Boy in Pater-noster-Row. 1709.
Price 2d. 24 p. 8° 19 cm.(unbd.)

Dated (p. 24): Dec. 2. 1709.

A reply to: Charles Leslie, The best answer ever was made. London, 1709

(<u>q.v.</u> for other notes).

Leslie had defended Bp. Offspring Blackall's <u>The divine institution of</u> <u>magistracy</u>. London, 1709 (<u>q.v.</u>), which supported the High-Anglican doctrine of non-resistance to royal commands. Stephens is opposed to passive obed-ience and non-resistance (p. 17). Dr. Henry Sacheverell's sermon (<u>The</u> <u>perils of false brethren</u>. London, 1709, <u>q.v.</u>) is attacked, on p. 21-4, for its Popish and anti-Parliament views. (Sacheverell was later impeached for that sermon.)

NUC(Pre-1956)567:629. Cf. Morgan,BBH:L387 ("by a student of the Temple" inserted in title); Madan(Speck):89.

[TINDAL, Matthew], 1657-1733.

New High-Church turn'd Old Presbyterian. Utrum horum never a barrel the better herring. London: printed, and sold by B[enjamin]. Bragg, at the Raven in Pater-Noster-Row. 1709. Price two-pence. 20 p. 8°(in 4s) 20 cm.(unbd.)

Tindal, a Low-Church Whig, and one of Pope's 'dunces' who was "prompt at Priests to jeer" (<u>Dunciad</u>, variorum, 1729, 2:367), cites numerous histori-cal examples of the High-Church view that the **clergy** is subject to the magistrate (monarch), while Presbyterians hold that the magistrate and people are subject to the Church (p. 4ff.); "But now ... There is hardly a Book publish'd by ... [the High-Church] but is full of complaints of our <u>unchristian Laws</u> relating to the Church" (p. 9), with quotations supporting this 'Presbyterianism'. He concludes that High-Churchmen must drop "Passive-Obedience", and shake hands with the Old Presbyterians.

NUC(Pre-1956)594:623 (& a 1710, 16-p. ed); BM(to 1955)239:328; Morgan,BBH: L405 ("2d.").

TRIMNELL, Charles, bp. of Norwich, 1663-1723.

A sermon [on Col.2:6-7] preach'd at the parish-church of St. James's Westminster, on Sunday the 30th of January, 1708. By the Right Reverend father in God, Charles, Lord Bishop of Norwich, at his taking his leave of the said parish. Published at the request of the gentlemen of the vestry. London: printed for Tho. Chapman, at the Angel in Pall-Mall, over-against St. James's Square, 1709. 16 p. 8° 19 cm(unbd.)

Bibliographical footnotes, mostly to Biblical sources.

The lesson from Colossians reads, in part: "As ye have therefore received Christ Jesus the Lord, so walk ye in him: ... as ye have been taught, ... with thanksgiving". This is a Tory bishop's valedictory sermon as rector of St. James's, exhorting the congregation to preserve faith in Christ and to guard against corruption, hoping that his own ministry has aided them in this.

NUC(Pre-1956)601:463; BM(to 1955)241:438; Morgan,BBH:L411 (also 1709, 4° ed.).

AN ADDRESS to the Church of England clergy, concerning resistance.
London: printed and sold by S[arah]. Popping, at the Raven in Pater-Noster-
Row, 1710. Price Three Pence. 30 p. 8° 19 cm.

Historical instances, and present implications, carefully considered in
a reasoned Whig argument for the legitimacy of resistance to arbitrary
royal power, against the Tory doctrine of non-resistance.

NUC(Pre-1956)4:89. Cf. Morgan,BBH:M6(29 p. & variant title: in error?).

[ASGILL, John], 1659-1738.

The assertion is, that the title of the House of Hanover to the succession of the British monarchy (on failure of issue of her present Majesty)
is a title hereditary, and of divine institution. ... London, printed in
the year 1710. 1 p.l., 5-38, [2] p. 8°(in 4s) 19 cm.

Errata: p. 38.

Another edition, London, printed by J. Darby, 1710, has title: De jure
divino: the assertion is ... (cf. Morgan,BBH:M42 & Hazen(Walpole)89:2:3).

List of "Books sold by John Darby": 2 p. at end.

Further to: Henry Sacheverell, The answer of Henry Sacheverell. D.D. ...
[London?], 1710, and other works (cf. Madan).

Imperfect: half-title wanting.

A defence of the Hanoverian title to the English Crown, quoting extensively from scripture, by hereditary and divine rights (e.g. p. 27), but
rejecting the doctrine of non-resistance as implying criticism of the Crown
(p. 33). The argument is offered to Dr. Sacheverell, who had quoted
Asgill "as part of his Defence" against impeachment (p. 5).

NUC(Pre-1956)23:316; Morgan,BBH:M41 (& 3 other 1710 eds.); Madan(Speck):
560n. Cf. BM(to 1955)7:767 (variant imprint); London Library,1:127 (3d
ed., 1710).

[BOLINGBROKE, Henry St.-John, 1st viscount], 1678-1751.

A letter to the Examiner. [London,] Printed in the year, 1710. 16 p.
8° 18 cm.(unbd.)

Morgan, who quotes the Wrenn Catalogue (Austin, Tex., 1920) as attribut-
ing this to Defoe (unsupported in Moore), has the subtitle: "containing a
view of foreign and domestic affairs"; but this is probably an error de-
rived from the note in the NUC entry.

Reprinted in Somers tracts, 1815, 13:71-5, and The examiners for the year
1711, p. v-xvi (cf. Madan), and transl. into French as part of: Lettres et
memoires sur la conduite de la presente guerre ..., vol. 2. La Haye, 1712.

Answered by: contributions to the Whig examiner (London, 14 Sept. - 12
Oct., 1710), 21 Sept. and 5 Oct., 1710, issues.

St.-John welcomes the new journal, the Examiner (London, 3 Aug. 1710 - 26
July 1714, a Tory supporter edited for a time by Swift), and urges further
arguments against "the present State of War Abroad" (War of Spanish Succession), exposing the indignities and ill rewards suffered by Britain in
Europe (p. 5-8), and the tyranny of the Whig Junto which sits in judgment
on the Crown at home (p. 12-14). These are "the real causes which have

prolong'd the war" and given hope to the enemy, France (p. 16).

   NUC(Pre-1956)64:513 (French transl., 329:296); BM(to 1955)136:105;

Morgan,BBH:M82 (with subtitle: cf. above); Madan(Speck)591 (and 592:

another edition, same title).

[BOYER, Abel], 1667-1729.

An essay towards the history of the last Ministry and Parliament: con-

taining seasonable reflections on I. Favourites II. Ministers of state.

III. Parties. IV. Parliaments. and V. Publick credit. ... London:

printed for J. Baker at the Black-boy in Pater-noster-Row, 1710. (Price

1s.) 2 p.l., 72 [i.e. 70] p. 8°(in 4s) 19 cm.

   Authorship: NUC; NUC & Morgan also cite an attribution to Defoe, but this

is not recognized by Moore.

   First edition? NUC copy, with variant collation (see next note), is

called 1st ed. Reprinted in Somers tracts, 1815, 13:43-65.

   Pages 23-4 omitted in paging but the leaf D4 is wanting, presumably can-

celled in the press; the text is continuous. NUC copy lacks 33-40 in

paging (sig. F) as well as p. 23-4, but sig. F present in this copy: [A]^2,

B-C^4, D^3, E-K^4.

   Boyer is remembered for his periodical The political state of Great

Britain (q.v.; editor, 1711-29), the first such to report parliamentary

debates with reasonable impartiality, though he was himself a Whig; here

he hopes to trace the fall of the Whig Ministry that summer (1710) in the

same spirit of fairness, to help in "Allaying the present Heats and Animos-

ities" provoked by the change in ministries. Boyer deplores the abuse of

royal favours, happy that Queen Anne is too wise to reward arrogant favour-

ites and as with any prince "that hath any Spirit" she will "Root out

Faction" and find another Ministry (p. 2-9). One objection Boyer has to the change: the Whigs had prosecuted the war (of Spanish Succession) with

success, and so should have been allowed to conclude the peace (p. 9-10).

However the (Whig) Junto, seeing the bad effects of its insults to the

Crown, used its zeal to impeach Dr. Sacheverell (mentioned throughout,

though this title is not noticed in Madan), a "Son of the National Church,

for a piece of Pulpit Oratory" (p. 14). The next pages show how the "fer-

ment" of the trial led to the downfall of the Whig party, how it gave the

enemy (France) a prospect for returning the Pretender, and how the Junto

tried all manner of tricks to regain favour and power - but instead these

were bestowed by the Queen on Robert Harley (created Earl of Oxford in

1711) and the Duke of Shrewsbury, supporters of King William and the Revol-

ution (p. 26-32). Other members of the new Ministry are identified, as

are the corruptions of past governments controlled by "the Money'd Men"

(Whigs) while "the Landed Interest" (Tories) were neglected (p. 44-50).

The early actions of the new Ministry (in securing the succession especially),

and the great hopes for it and for good peace terms with France, are dis-

cussed (p. 51-7), and the pamphlet ends with a sketch of the mismanagement

of "Publick Credit" in the hands of the Whig Junto, with some explanations

and proposals (p. 58-72).

   NUC(Pre-1956)71:25; Morgan,BBH:M222; Rothschild:89; Kress:2659.

BURNET, Gilbert, bp. of Salisbury, 1643-1715.

   The Bishop of Salisbury his speech in the House of Lords, on the first

article of the impeachment of Dr. Henry Sacheverell. London: printed in

the year, 1710. (Price Two Pence.) 16 p. 8° 21 cm.

   First edition (cf. Rothschild), but Madan lists 3 other 1710 editions, in

one of which the last line, p. 3, begins: "Protection"; in the present iss-

ue, the last line, p. 3, begins, "on those laws".

Article I of the impeachment reads: "He, the said Henry Sacheverell, in
his said Sermon Preach'd at St. Paul's [Cathedral, London, 5 Nov., 1709],
doth suggest and maintain, That the necessary Means us'd to bring about the
said Happy Revolution, were Odious and Unjustifiable: That his late Majesty,
in his Declaration, disclaim'd the least Imputation of Resistance; and
that to impute Resistance to the said Revolution, is to cast Black and
Odious Colours upon his late Majesty, and the said Revolution." (cf. The
tryal of Dr. Henry Sacheverell, before the House of Peers, for high crimes
and misdemeanors; upon an impeachment ... London, printed for J. Tonson,
1710, p. 3).

Answered by: Edmund Curll, Some considerations humbly offer'd to the ...
Bishop of Salisbury. Occasion'd by his lordship's speech, upon the first
article of Dr. Sacheverell's impeachment. London, 1710, and at least 5
other works (cf. Madan(Speck):326-30, and Curll's The white crow, q.v.,
below).

Disagrees with Sacheverell's High-Church doctrine of non-resistance "in
any Case whatsoever, without exception" (p. 2); sketches the history of this
doctrine from before the Reformation, and of church/state relations from
biblical times. Bp. Burnet shows the doctrine's relation to the Civil War,
its revival afterwards (p. 10-11), its influence on James II who relied on
it despite Burnet's advice, and how it lead to the Revolution because of
resistance (p. 12-13). Thus "... this puts an End to ... Non-resistance in
any Case" (p. 16), and disproves Dr. Sacheverell's view in his St. Paul's
sermon (as cited in Article I) that there had been no resistance to James
II. The strong support of resistance expressed here is in contrast with
the views in Bp. Burnet's sermon of 1674, Subjection for conscience sake
(London, 1675, reprinted as The royal martyr ..., 1710), in which he advocated "absolute subjection to the higher powers" (cf. Madan,90). Curll

takes the Bishop to **task** in his Some considerations (cited above).

   NUC(Pre-1956)85:620; BM(to 1955)30:429; Morgan,BBH:M104; Madan(Speck):
319 (last line, p. 3: "on those laws"); Rothschild:533.

[CLEMENT, Simon], fl. 1695-1714.

Faults on both sides: or, An essay upon the original cause, progress,
and mischievous consequences of the factions in this nation. Shewing that
the heads and leaders on both sides have always impos'd upon the credulity
of their respective parties ... at the expence of the peace ... of the
nation. ... By way of answer to The thoughts of an honest Tory. ...
London: printed and sold by the booksellers of London and Westminster,
1710. 56 p. 8° 19 cm.

   Authorship: Downie, p. 121, but by "Clement, under the direction of [Earl
of Oxford, Robert] Harley"; BM(to 1955) agrees, and the attribution is acknowledged by Halkett & Laing, Hazen(Walpole), and London Library. Also
attributed to Robert Harley (Morgan,BBH), Richard Harley (Somers tracts,
1814; London Library; NUC; Hazen(Walpole); Halkett & Laing; Morgan,BBH;
Stonehill:1018), and Defoe (Morgan,BBH; London Library; Halkett & Laing),
but not confirmed in Moore (2d ed.).

   Transl. into French as: Fautes des deux côtez ... Rotterdam, 1711 (NUC)
and Cologne, 1711, and into Dutch as: Misslagen aan weerkanten ... Amsterdam, 1710 (Knuttel:15942, Cologne; & 15870, Amsterdam).

   Reprinted in Somers tracts, 1814, 12:678 ("... ascribed to ... Harley ...
The real author ... may have been De Foe ...").

   Page 49-56 set in smaller type sizes.

   A reply to: [Benjamin Hoadly], The thoughts of an honest Tory. London,
1710 (q.v.).

   Answered by: The thoughts of an honest Whig. London, 1710 (q.v.); A true history of the honest Whigs. A poem. London, 1710; and A letter from a

High Church-Man to a Whig. [London?], 1710 (no copy located, but reprinted

Edinburgh, 1710, cf. Madan(Speck):524-5), and other works: see Appendix I.

Although suspecting the earlier work to be by "A Crafty Whig" (p. 3),

the author says differences between honest Whigs and Tories over religion

and civil government are not so great that public tranquillity cannot be

restored (p. 4). There follows an interpretation of the rise of present

bitter divisions, in the Crown's struggle for waning power and the people's

for their rights (p. 11), aggravated by the loss of influence by the media-

ting peers since Henry VII's time. The author's early moderation becomes by p.

20, zealously Tory, and strongly critical of Whig fiscal policies, but

ends by stressing again party similarities (e.g. p. 46-50), showing "faults

on both sides", and the need for general goodwill - in this reflecting

Harley's long-time efforts to reconcile parties and factions (e.g. p. 55).

Clement, Secretary to the Earl of Peterborough, defends the Earl on p. 28-

30.

NUC(Pre-1956)231:275 (DLC; under Richard Harley; also 1715, 24-p. ed.);

BM(to 1955)71:303; Morgan,BBH:M284; London Library,1:1081. Cf. Rothschild:

85 (2d ed., but extensive notes).

[_____].

Faults on both sides: or, An essay upon the original cause, progress,

and mischievous consequences of the factions in this nation ... By way

of an answer to The thoughts of an honest Tory. ... The second edition.

London: printed and sold by the booksellers of London and Westminster,

1710. 56 p. 8° 19 cm.

Reprinted from same stand of type as 1st ed., but on somewhat heavier

paper, and insertion of 2d ed. note on title-page without extending the

type-page (ca. 17.7 cm.) was accomplished by adjusting the leading from
'By way of an answer' downwards. Slight increase in type batter, e.g.
sig. mark 'D' reversed, p. 49; mutilated catchwords, p. 49, 50; 'I hope'
compressed, start of l.27, p. 56; etc.

A reply to: [Benjamin Hoadly], The thoughts of an honest Tory. London,
1710 (q.v.).

Answered by: The thoughts of an honest Whig. London, 1710 (q.v.), and
other works.

(See entry for 1st edition for other notes.)

Bound in late-18th or early-19th-century half-calf with marbled boards,
and title label along spine.

Provenance: Gift of Dr. A.R.M. Lower, Kingston, 1965.

NUC(Pre-1956)231:275 (also 1715, 24-p. ed.); BM(to 1955)71:303; Morgan,
BBH:M284; London Library, 1:1081; Rothschild:85; Hazen(Walpole):89:2:4;
Kress:2662.

[CURLL, Edmund], 1675-1747.

The case of Dr. Sacheverell. Represented in a letter to a noble lord.
... London: printed in the year 1710. 1 p.l., 3-32 p. 8° 20 cm.

Authorship, and name of person addressed, inscribed in Curll's own hand
in the BM copy, one of 4 items inscribed by their author, Curll, on the same
subject, which came to the BM via George III: cf. Straus (Curll), p. 37n.,
and p. 211 under pub. date "Mar. 23", 1710.

Further to: Henry Sacheverell, The nature and mischief of prejudice. Oxford, 1704 (of which work p. 5-32 in Curll are little more than a garbled
or thinly-disguised reprint - cf. Madan, 22 & 107). Reprinted in Curll's
collection of Tracts relating to the impeachment of Dr. Henry Sacheverell.
London, 1710 (Madan,350), and as his A letter to his grace the Duke of

The view from the "Dial and Bible", against
St. Dunstan's Church, inside Temple Bar,
London, the bookshop of Edmund Curll from 1709.
(Taken from Ralph Straus, The Unspeakable
Curll, London, Chapman and Hall, 1927, opposite
p. 33, here reproduced with the publishers'
permission.)

Beaufort. London, 1711 (Madan,606).

Addressed to Henry Somerset, 2d Duke of Beaufort (1684-1714), a pillar
of the Tory party (cf. DNB, 'Somerset'), according to a note Curll wrote in
his own copy, says Madan; but Straus (Curll), p. 37, notes "It was addressed, Curll relates, to the Duke of Bedford" (i.e. Wriothesley Russell,
2d Duke, 1680-1711). Beaufort as the intended recipient seems confirmed
in the title of the 1711 edition, above. This is one of at least 4 anonymous essays on Sacheverell which Curll wrote and printed hurriedly with
"numerous misprints" and in flowery language and sentences so long "the
verb is occasionally lost" (Straus, loc.cit., but I think he exaggerates
the faults). This attempts to identify the sources of prejudice against
Dr. Sacheverell for his two 1709 sermons The communication of sin and The
perils of false brethren, "the Day of his Tryal drawing nigh" (p. 4), and
by extension against the High-Church Anglicans. Curll hopes his Lordship
will read John Goodwin's The obstructours of justice. London, 1649 (p. 32).
Straus (p. 38) says the "Well-worn platitudes" demonstrate nothing but
the "author's good intentions" towards Sacheverell, though he is a bold and
shrewd observer.

  NUC(Pre-1956)129:605; BM(to 1955)47:55 & 210:792; Morgan,BBH:M156;
Rothschild:710; Madan(Speck):107.

[_____].

The white crow: or, An inquiry into some more new doctrines broach'd by
the Bp. of Salisbury, in a pair of sermons utter'd in that cathedral, on
the V. and VII. days of November, 1710. And his lordship's restauration
sermon, last 29th of May. ... The second edition corrected. [s.l.; London?]
Printed in the year of grace, 1710. (Price 6d.) 2 p.l., 36 p. 8°(in 4s)
20 cm.

Authorship: "A handlist (1706-1746)" in Straus (Curll), p. 214, under date "Dec. 4", 1710, for 1st edition; but cf. Madan.

Half-title: same as t.-p., except: "... Bp. of Salisbury, &c."

First pub. between 5th and 7th Nov., with slightly varying title (and pagination errors, here corrected in the 2d ed. - cf. NUC 1st ed.), and later as A full view of the Bishop of Salisbury's principles ..., London, 1711, comprising the sheets of the 1st ed. with a new t.-p. (cf. Madan, but see Straus, above).

Bibliographical footnotes and references within the text.

Refers to the sermons of Bishop Gilbert Burnet (1643-1715, "that self-satisfied Whig" says Straus (Curll), p. 39): A sermon preach'd in the cathedral-church of Salisbury, on the 29th day of May ... 1710. London, 1710; and Two sermons, preach'd in the cathedral church of Salisbury: the first, on the fifth of November ...; the second, on the seventh of November ... London, 1710 (cf. Madan, 445 & 641), and is further to Curll's own Some considerations humbly offer'd to the ... Bp. of Salisbury ... London, 1710.

Addressed to Bishop Burnet, under the date: "Glascow, November 25: 1710", Curll undertakes to "offer my Free Thoughts upon these Discourses" (the 3 sermons), but will not here discuss the Revolution further than he has already in Some considerations (cited above), in which Burnet's 1675 non-resistance sermon Subjection for conscience sake (London, 1675, reprinted as The royal martyr ..., 1710) is contrasted with Burnet's support of resistance in The Bishop of Salisbury his speech ... on the ... impeachment of Dr. Henry Sacheverell (London, 1710, q.v., and cf. Madan 90 & 323). Here Curll revives his contention that Bp. Burnet is inconsistent, by citing passages referring to the rendering unto Caesar what is Caesar's - Matthew 22:21 (p. 6-12), the grounds of the contract between king and people (p. 15-19), the accountability of princes to earthly power, 1674 vs. 1710 views (p. 26-8), toleration of occasional conformity (p. 29), and the

apostolic validity of episcopal ordination (p. 30-34). He concludes with

resounding tributes to both the bishop and the Queen.

BM(to 1955)47:57(also 1st ed.) & 30:439, 'Burnet'); Morgan,BBH:M111

(also 2d ed. 1710, & 2d ed., corrected, 1712); Madan(Speck):646. Cf.

NUC(Pre-1956)129:607 (1st ed. only).

[DAVENANT, Charles], 1656-1714

Sir Thomas Double at court, and in high preferments. In two dialogues

between Sir Thomas Double and Sir Richard Comover, alias Mr. Whiglove: on

the 27th of September, 1710. Part I [and II]. ... [London,] Printed, and

sold by John Morphew, near Stationers-Hall. 1710. 112 p. 8° 18 cm.

Part 2 begins on p. 65; caption title: The second dialogue between Sir

Thomas Double and Sir Richard Comover. Part 2 also pub. separately - cf. BM.

Type size reduced: p. 111-2.

Madan describes this as the sequel to Davenant's The true picture of a

modern Whig. London, 1701, and Tom Double returned out of the country.

London, 1702 (Kress:2347).

Imperfect: p. 23-6 misbound between p. 28 and 29. Last 3 leaves foxed.

A discussion between a town businessman, Sir Thomas, highly placed in

the Whig Party (p. 11), and an old friend unmet since 1701, Sir Richard,

formerly also a town Whig (p. 9) but now a country Tory since accepting a

family title and estate (p. 4). The Whig has now gained wealth, a knight-

hood, favour at Court, and seeks further recognition in a peerage: now-

adays "Birth and Merit" are not "the only true Steps to Greatness", for

a better claim is great wealth, and Sir Thomas boasts of having the equi-

valent "Estate of two good Earls" (p. 11-12). He stresses the importance

of business and finance, the influence London has at Court, then invites

Sir Richard to join in the advantages available from maladministration, duplicity, and the distribution of favours - it cost Sir Thomas 8,000 pounds for his own title! (p. 14). He explains (with obvious irony) his past financial schemes, his crimes turned to profit (e.g. p. 17-18, 110-12), with many allusions to actual persons involved. This satire on the Whigs and contemporary events of church and state is enhanced by the laconic shrewdness of Sir Richard, the Tory, whom Sir Thomas at first called Mr. Whiglove. Davenant, a political economist, wrote earlier works with the names Thomas Double and Mr. Whiglove in their titles, and he was himself a Whig "till he obtained something" (DNB), but an Old (or Country Party) Whig, not one of the Modern Whigs (further to these distinctions see my Introduction, p. viii), which he attacked in his True picture (cited above); he was favouring the Tories by about 1701, when he was overseeing the literary efforts of Robert Harley, later Earl of Oxford (Downie, p. 2, 38, 54). Six days before the date on the title-page, 21st Sept., Davenant benefited from the then recent Tory victory by his reappointment as Inspector General of Exports and Imports (DNB).

NUC(Pre-1956)134:74; BM(to 1955)48:1216 & 55: 30-31; Morgan,BBH:M166; Rothschild:719; Madan(Speck):612; Kress:2656.

[DEFOE, Daniel], 1661?-1731.

A new test of the sence of the nation: being a modest comparison between the addresses to the late King James, and those to Her present Majesty. ... London, printed in the year 1710. 1 p.l., 91 p. 8°(in 4s) 17 cm.

First edition (cf. NUC). The 15 addresses to James II are the same as 15 of the 42 included in Defoe's A collection of the several addresses in the late King James's time (1710), and 6 of the addresses to Queen Anne are condensed in his A speech for Mr D[unda]sse Younger of Arnistown

(London, 1711), p. 7-9 (cf. Moore).

Imperfect: half-title wanting; lower margin closely trimmed with slight loss of text, p. 46 & 70, and loss of some catchwords and sig. marks.

Marginal ms. notes in a contemporary hand, listing names of the High-Sheriff and all members of the Grand-Jury who addressed the Queen from Shrewsbury, 3 Aug. 1710: p. 64-5.

Provenance: J. Bridgeman, 1710 (t.-p. autogr.).

The meaning of words, such as "swear to the Queen, and swear at the Queen" (p. 10), depends on custom, and means nothing at all; this is the "Sence of the Nation". In considering the doctrine of non-resistance and heredi-tary and parliamentary rights to the Crown, Defoe transcribes, side-by-side, loyal addresses from various persons and places to James II and Queen Anne, and concludes satirically that in the "Sence of the Nation", they signify nothing. In the Postscript (p. 79-91), Defoe says that his intend-ed irony is to show that "these addresses have no Tendency to any Good" for either side (p. 87). (Cf. Dick and Tom: a dialogue. London, 1710, q.v., below.)

NUC(Pre-1956)136:574; BM(to 1955)50:116; Morgan,BBH:M186; Moore (2d ed.): 188; Madan(Speck):725; Wright(Defoe), no. 117 (pub. 12 Oct., 1710); BPL (Defoe):97.

[_____].

A speech without doors. ... London, printed for A[nn]. Baldwin near the Oxford-Arms in Warwick-Lane. 1710. Price two pence. 20 p. 8°(in 4s) 20 cm.

Authorship: Moore (2d ed.).

First edition.

Advertisement (p. [2]) contends Dr. Sacheverell did not himself write the

speech he gave before the Lords, 7th March, 1710. It was widely distributed in a hasty abridgement, and to counteract this, and prepare the speech
for a different audience, the present work "is fitted both to the Pockets
and Understandings of the Doctor's Judges without Doors" (i.e. "A much Inferior Order" of person from the listeners at Westminster Hall, 7th March).

A reply to: Henry Sacheverell, Doctor Sacheverell's speech, to the honourable House of Peers ... in Westminster-Hall the 7th March, 1710. London,
1710. (This single folio leaf "could be a hurried impression ... It bears
little resemblance to the speech actually delivered" - Madan(Speck):247.)

Refers mainly to: Henry Sacheverell, The perils of false brethren. London, 1709 (q.v., above).

Defoe addresses the electorate, or those outside the doors of Parliament.
His target is Dr. Sacheverell's Perils sermon, specifically "That it is unlawful to resist our Kings upon any Pretence whatsoever", and Defoe contends that Sacheverell said this "with an Intention to cast odious Aspersions on ... [King William], and to blacken the Revolution". This is not
the doctrine of the Church of England, as established by law since the
Revolution (1688), by the Bill of Rights (1689), the Act of Settlement (1701)
and the Act of Union (1707), all securing the rights and privileges of subjects, and against Sacheverell's "Illegality of resisting" statement (p. 3-
5). Defoe draws examples of resistance from classical and modern history,
and in England from the Magna Carta (1215) on, when laws have been made by
kings, lords and commons, not the king alone (p. 6-11). He now applies
his argument to James II, who usurped many powers not rightfully his (p.
13-17), so was resisted; William of Orange was enthroned, and "thus we
gain'd the Revolution" and settled the succession, by resistance. William
and Mary, and now Queen Anne, hold their titles by the revolution principles. Is the Pretender's claim legitimate, then, under the doctrine of

non-resistance? (p. 19).   To preach obedience is to subvert the government, hence Dr. Sacheverell's impeachment, for such as he endanger church and state (p. 20).

NUC(Pre-1956)136:650 (& 28-p., Dublin; & 40-p., 1712, eds.); BM(to 1955) 50:135; Morgan,BBH:M190 (& 28-p., 1710; Dublin, 1710; 40-p., 1711; & 1712 eds.); Moore(2d ed.):168; Madan(Speck):375; Rothschild:741; Wright(Defoe), no. 113 (pub. 19 Apr., 1710); BPL(Defoe):165 (all 3 eds.).

DICK and Tom: a dialogue about addresses.   The second edition.   London; printed for B[enjamin]. Bragg at the Raven in Pater-noster-Row.   1710. Price two pence.   16 p.   8°   18 cm.

A copy of the 1st edition in Trinity College, Dublin, is inscribed "By the Revd Mr Stevens of Sutton in Surrey", i.e. William Stephens, 1647?-1718, but no confirmation discovered, and this title not mentioned in DNB, 'Stephens' - cf. Madan(Speck).

First pub. same year, with same title and imprint (cf. NUC).

Dick and Tom, upholders of the High Tory doctrine of non-resistance and passive obedience, discuss the town and country addresses of loyalty to the Queen, at the critical time of Dr. Henry Sacheverell's trial (see his The perils of false brethren, London, 1709, above), when mobs were aroused (they say) by Tory Lord Mayor Sir Samuel Gerrard in support of Sacheverell (p. 3). They begin to question the mischief caused by such zeal though (Butcher, why does your "Calf lay so quiet"? Because "I have taught him Passive Obedience ... [look] you will see that I have cut his Throat", p. 5-6), and Dick asks "if the Addressers were in earnest ... [in maintaining the revolution principles], why should they insist so violently upon the Hereditary Title"? (p. 8). Support of the "House of Hanover", says Tom, "which being a contradiction to the Hereditary Right, takes Peoples thoughts off from too serious a Consideration of the Succession of Prince Taffy" (the

Pretender) and Popery (p. 9). Later Tom observes that "necessary Resis-

tance ... made way for the late happy Revolution, together with the Queen's

Parliamentary Title" (p. 10). Dick asks: if the revolution principles

"which preserv'd the Church from Popery, and the Kingdom from Tyranny, were

Schismatical; how came the Bishops to concur with it"? (p. 14).

Addresses from St. Albans, Salisbury, etc., are examined, and their

declarations of loyalty found to be little more than empty flattery (p. 10-

13). The conversation concludes with the observation that there was no

need for any addresses of loyalty, since both the Queen's title and the

Church of England are "by Law establish'd" (p. 15). (Cf. Daniel Defoe, A

new test of the sence of the nation. London, 1710, q.v., above).

Madan(Speck):720 (1st & 2d eds.). Cf. NUC(Pre-1956)142:568; BM(to 1955)

52:213; Morgan,BBH:M201 (all 1st ed. only, same title & imprint).

[DISTAFF, John] pseud.

A character of Don Sacheverellio, knight of the firebrand; in a letter

to Isaac Bickerstaff Esq; censor of Great Britain. Dublin: printed and

sold by Francis Higgins, bookmaker; and to be had of A[nn]. Baldwin, in

London. Price two pence. [1710] 1 p.l., 3-16 p. 8° 19 cm.(unbd.)

Authorship: Morgan notes an attribution to Defoe (but this is not in

Moore) and to Swift (unfound in Teerink-Scouten), but enters under Richard

Steele, to whom this pamphlet is addressed. Signed, p. 16: John Distaff.

First pub. under title: Quixote redivivus: or, The spiritual knight

errant, in a letter to ... London: 1710 (signed: Jack Touchwood, 20 Jan.

1710; cf. Madan).

First edition under this title; "reprinted at Edinburgh in the year 1710"

(comma after "Firebrand", cf. Madan). The present work is dated (p. 16):

March 16. 1710; Post Man, 23-5 Mar.: "published this day".

A similar work but in verse, issued under the same pseudonym, is: Monarchy and Church as explain'd by Dr. Henry Sacheverel. London, 1710.

The author congratulates Bickerstaff (the pseudonym Richard Steele used as editor of The tatler) on the success of his writings in The tatler, and of their good effects in Ireland; but, he says with tongue in cheek, you haven't yet drawn us a character of a "Spiritual Knight Errant", the "reverse to the Temporal Don Quixote", since one works for the good, the other for the destruction of mankind (p. 4). The author then must "tantalize" Bickerstaff with the project of writing about "Don Henrico Furioso de Sacheverellio" (i.e. Dr. Henry Sacheverell), telling his story satirically in terms of Dr. Sacheverell as a modern Don Quixote, giving the actual date (5th Nov., Gunpowder Plot) and close title ("In Perils among false Brethren", for Sacheverell's The perils of false brethren, 1709, q.v., above) of Don Sacheverellio's "Audacious Plot" as another to the Gunpowder Plot. The transparent satire presents the characteristic Whig viewpoint of the Sacheverell affair, with the armoured knight mounted on his steed Faction, and (as Madan puts it) "charging imaginary hosts of false brethren [p. 12] and braving in their castles four giants: The Church [p. 13], the Toleration Act [p. 14], the Whig government [p. 14-15] and the Revolution" (p. 15).

   NUC(Pre-1956)144:587; BM(to 1955)53:599; Morgan,BBH:M669; Madan(Speck): 146; Rothschild:2197.

FAULTS in the fault-finder: or, A specimen of errors in the pamphlet, entitul'd Faults on both sides. The second edition. London: printed, and to be sold by A[nn]. Baldwin, near the Oxford-Arms in Warwick-Lane, 1710. (Price 3d.) 24 p. 8°(in 4s) 22 cm.

Authorship has been attributed to Robert Harley (Morgan,BBH), and an ms. note on the t.-p. of this copy reads: "by Richard Harley". Robert

Harley, the Earl of Oxford, was however involved in the authorship of

Faults on both sides, to which this replies.

First pub. same year, with same imprint (cf. NUC & BM) but 47 p. (cf.

Morgan).

A public accounts extract, 1697, signed J. Taylour: p. 16-20.

A reply to: [Simon Clement], Faults on both sides. London, 1710. For

other titles in this controversy, see Appendix A.

In this Whig rebuttal, the author says "Page 17. and the three or four

following ... Pages only I shall consider", of Faults on both sides (p. 4),

and these deal with British conduct in the War of the Grand Alliance (1688-

97, also called the War of the League of Augsburg), and British monetary

policies during the period, dominated by Whigs. The pamphlet defends the

Whig ministry's military policies, its customs duties and taxes.

NUC(Pre-1956)167:545; BM(to 1955)71:304; Morgan,BBH:M283 (& 1st ed.,

47 p.); London Library,1:810; Rothschild:88.

FORBES, William, fl. 1703-1730.

A letter from William Forbes advocate, to his friend in England a Member

of the House of Commons, concerning the law of election of Members of

Parliament; collected out of the acts and records of the Parliament of

Scotland, and the statutes of England and Great Britain, &c. [Edinburgh]

Printed by the heirs and successors of Andrew Anderson, printer to the

Queen's most Excellent Majesty; and to be sold at the shop of John Vallange

bookseller in Edinburgh, upon the north-side of the High-Street a little

above the cross, Anno Dom. 1710. 45, [1] p. 8° 18 cm.

Errata (called "Advertisement"): [1] p. at end.

Place of printing: cf. Plomer, p. 5-6.

Page 3 misnumbered 1.

Bibliographical footnotes (mostly Acts of Parliament).

Advert. at end includes errata and 3 other "Books written by William Forbes Advocate", sold by J. Vallange, Edinburgh.

A close comparison of the laws of Scotland with those of England as they apply to the election of peers and commons to Parliament; the Acts are cited by the enacting Parliament for Scotland, and the year of Sovereign's reign in England (cf. p. 1[i.e. 3]-4).

NUC(Pre-1956)177:468(NN).

[HOADLY, Benjamin, bp. of Winchester], 1676-1761.

Reasons against receiving the Pretender, and restoring the Popish line. Together with some queries of the utmost importance to Great Britain. London: printed and sold by A[nn]. Baldwin, in Warwick Lane. 1710. Price 2d. 16 p. 8° 19 cm.

Morgan says attributed to Defoe, but not listed in Moore (2d ed.).

First edition; also 1718 and 1751 eds., and (says Morgan) a French transl., 1710.

Argues that a Roman Catholic monarch cannot protect a Protestant Church and people against the tyranny of Rome, as witness James II, nor respect Parliament (p. 3-4). Eight such 'reasons' are given, then 18 questions posed against the doctrine of non-resistance and divine right, from the Whig, dissenting viewpoint.

NUC(Pre-1956)248:475; Morgan,BBH:M316 (all eds.).

[_____].

The thoughts of an honest Tory, upon the present proceedings of that party. In a letter to a friend in town. London, sold by A[nn]. Baldwin, in Warwick-Lane. 1710.   Price 2d. [2], 14 p. 8° 20 cm.

Advertisement (p. [2], 1st count) hopes that the author (unnamed) of the
pamphlet will not mind that it is "now Published by one, into whose Hands
it came", because its honesty is a credit to the Tories; its frankness is
because it was written in confidence to a friend. (Advert., doubtless
written by Hoadly.)

Reprinted in Somers tracts, 1814,12:672, and in Hoadly's Works (1773),
1:630.

Answered by [Simon Clement], Faults on both sides. London, 1710 (q.v.),
Hoadly's pamphlet started a long chain of publications: see Appendix A.

Provenance: official stamp of Harvard College Library (verso of t.-p.).

Hoadly, a Low-Churchman who supported the 'revolution principles', speaks
here as a pretended Tory, deploring the damage to "our cause" by Tory mismanagement of Dr. Henry Sacheverell's trial, and the Tory mobs raised
against the Whigs (p. 3). Tory Sacheverell is now despised by both sides,
and "will sink us in time" (p. 6). Hoadly then expounds upon lies "our
Agents" have told, and the dishonesty of passive obedience and the doctrine
of non-resistance held by "false Friends" (p. 7), who qualify these principles so that "we mean the same with the Whigs Parliamentary Right" (p. 13).
In the Postscript (p. 14), the author condemns the Tory pamphlet "just now
receiv'd": An impartial account of what pass'd ... [in Parliament], relating to the case of Dr. Henry Sacheverell ... [London?], 1710 (Madan(Speck):
459), written by "a celebrated Patron of our Cause", for favouring a "second
Restoration", Papists, and nonjurors.

NUC(Pre-1956)248:478; BM(to 1955)104:611 & 240:347 (& another 1710 ed.);
Morgan,BBH:M318; Madan(Speck):483; Rothschild:1141.

[_____].

The voice of the addressers: or, A short comment upon the chief things maintain'd, or condemn'd, in our late modest addresses. London: sold by A[nn]. Baldwin, in Warwick-Lane. 1710. 2 p.l., 5-31 p. 8° 19 cm.

Half-title: The voice of the addressers. Price three pence.

First edition, 17th May; another edition: 10th June, 1710, 16 p. - "A Dublin piracy" (cf.Madan; BM:16°). Also issued as no. 2 of 12 in A collection of several papers printed in the year 1710. London, James Knapton, 1718 (cf.BM,41:808).

Bishop Hoadly argues against the High-Anglican critics of the Whig discontents addressed to the Queen (p. 6), the main points of quarrel being: the Queen's title to the Crown (Hoadly says her Revolution title is lawful only if resistance to the monarch, e.g. James II, is lawful: p. 7); that the addressers' resistance is "a Popish-Republican Doctrine" (but 'Popish' means servitude to the Pope, and 'republican' means prefering a commonwealth while we must preserve our Constitution, so we cannot be either: p. 10-25); loyalty (but resistance is not disloyal: p. 26); toleration (both the Queen and the addressers espouse this: p. 27); dissolution of Parliament (yet the present House of Commons "hath shewn so ungrateful a sense of Public Liberty", while Whigs stand for liberty of the subject: p. 27-9). "The Protestant Succession, and the Cause of our Allies abroad, are infinitely indebted to them [the low-church Whigs] for such Addresses" (p. 31).

NUC(Pre-1956)248:478 (& 16-p. ed.); BM(to 1955)250:143 (title, but 41:808 acknowledges Hoadly); Morgan,BBH:M734 (but 32 p., & under title); Rothschild:1142; Madan(Speck):717 (& 16 p. ed.).

[THE JUDGMENT of] whole kingdoms and nations, concerning the rights, power and prerogative of Kings, and the rights, priviledges, and properties of the people: shewing, the nature of government in general, both from God and man. An account of the British government ... [and] of the Revolution; with the names and proceedings of ten bishops, and above sixty peers, concern'd in the Revolution before King James went out of England. ... Recommended as proper to be kept in all families, that their childrens children may know the birth-right, liberty and property belonging to an Englishman. Written by a true lover of the Queen and country, who wrote in the year 1689. in vindication of the Revolution, in a challenge to all Jacobites ... and ... in the year 1690. against absolute passive obedience ... who now challenges Dr. Hicks, Dr. Atterbury, Dr. Welton, Mr. Milbourne, Mr. Higgins, Mr. Lesley, Mr. Collier, Mr. Whaley of Oxford, and the great champion, Dr. Sacheverell, or any Jacobite in Great Britain to answer this book. The third edition corrected with additions. London: printed for, and sold by T[homas]. Harrison, at the west corner of the Royal-Exchange, in Cornhill, 1710. Price stitch'd 6d. and bound 10d. 2 p.l., [4], 71 p. 8° 19 cm.

Authorship: BPL(Defoe) assigns this to Defoe (but Moore omits, and see note on authorship from this source under The re-representation ..., 1711), noting that it has also been attributed variously to Lord Somers (DNB, 'Somers', doubts this, and Halkett & Laing call this an error), John Dunton (not in DNB's extensive list, 'Dunton'), Charles Povery (i.e. Povey? not in DNB's list), and Thomas Harrison (fl. 1683-1711), the publisher of this, and of "several tracts against Sacheverell" (cf. Plomer) and to whom NUC assigns the authorship of Political aphorisms (see next note) an earlier form of the present work; Harrison is therefore a prime candidate, and regarded as the probable author by Kenyon, in Revolution principles (p. 123-

4), where Political aphorisms and Vox populi are said to be the 1st and
2nd editions, yet also strangely related to other works (p. 209-10);
but NUC & BM enter under title.

First pub. "in shorter form" (BPL, Defoe) under title: Political aphorisms; or, The true maxims of government displayed, 31 p. (NUC gives authorship to Thomas Harrison). London, 1690 - thus agreeing with one date on
the t.-p., above (the other, 1689, work referred to on the t.-p. has not
been identified); this appeared as "another version" (BPL, Defoe) under
title: Vox populi, vox Dei: being true maxims of government, 40 p. (NUC,
under title). London, 1709.

Reprinted in State tracts, vol. 1, 1705 (cf. t.-p.).

Answered by: [Francis Atterbury], The voice of the people, no voice of
God: or, Mistaken arguments of a fiery zealot, in a late pamphlet entitl'd
Vox populi, vox Dei, since publish'd under the title of The judgment of
whole Kingdoms ... [London?] 1710. Note also "An Appeal to thy Conscience;
which they call an Answer to this Book", issued by "John How, Printer, and
John Baker, Bookseller" (both fl. 1680-1710; cf. Plomer), as partners, but
which "pretended Answer, hath not one Word of Answer" in it, and "was
printed above Sixty Years since" (cf.2d p.l.). This work is [Edward Fish-
er], fl. 1627-1655, An appeal to thy conscience ... [London? 1643], reprinted: London, 1710 (cf. NUC,173:605). Also answered by: The royal
family of the Stuarts vindicated, from the false imputation ... by Buchanan,
and maliciously reviv'd in a late pamphlet, intitul'd, The judgment of whole
kingdoms ... London, 1711.

Imperfect: upper margin closely trimmed, with loss of first 3 words of
t.-p., and part of top line of text in a few pages and page numbers of many;
2d leaf of Contents misbound before the 1st.; 2d p.l. bound with its text
as a verso.

Begins with the usual arguments for the Revolution: that rulers are con-

fined by God to governing for the welfare of those whom they rule, that

in departure from this divine law the magistrate ceases to serve his god-

ordained purpose, dissolving his contract with the people - who have no

right to extend his powers beyond the limits set by God. Next, the author

states that civil government began with the unit of family and servants,

the father being the supreme power - the old patriarchal view. However,

after the "abominable Disorders" of the Deluge (resulti.g from the lack of

a civil constitution), when the rules of government were introduced, God

instituted magistracy with powers absolute except for the civil necessity

to govern for the good of the governed, the people freely submitting to

the ruler but retaining the right to define the public good. All the

rights and privileges of the Revolution principles follow from this, and

Britain above all countries has preserved them (p. 1-8, item 1-6; cf.

Charles Leslie, The finishing stroke, for a full presentation of the pat-

riarchal theory, but as leading to the absolutist position). The author

then reviews classical, Biblical, and Western literatures, and English

literature and history from Saxon times to date, with extensive quotations,

in support of his presentation, in a series of 191 "political aphorisms"

(cf. 1690 edition title), including the terms of the Bill of Rights, 1689

(p. 31-2, item 83), and the invitation and welcome addresses to Prince

William, 1688-9 (p. 47-55, items 124-47, ending with "People can never be

of one Mind, without his [God's] Inspiration ... Vox Populi, est Vox Dei"

- cf. title of 1709 edition). The pamphlet ends (item 191) with pointed

arguments against the "Billingsgate" of Dr. Sacheverell's two 1709 ser-

mons, Communication of sin and Perils of false brethren (q.v.), which the

author says were delivered "to blacken the Revolution". Morgan states that

"The original printer [of Vox populi], John Matthews, because of it was drawn on a sledge as being guilty of high treason".

NUC(Pre-1956)286:185 (22 eds. & issues to 1810); BM(to 1955)119:626
(9 eds. to 1717 under this title); Morgan,BBH:L105 (under Defoe, Vox
populi, title of 1709 ed.); London Library,1:1305 (title, but Defoe &
Somers queried); BPL(Defoe):66 (under Defoe).

[LESLIE, Charles], 1650-1720

Best of all being a student's thanks to Mr. Hoadly. Wherein Mr. Hoadly's
second part of his Measures of submission (which he intends soon to publish) is fully answer'd. If this does not stop it. ... In a letter to
himself. Which he is desir'd to send ... to ... Mr. Stoughton the state-
haranguer in Ireland. The third edition. London printed and sold by the
booksellers of London and Westminster, 1710. 32 p. 16°(in 4s) 19 cm.

First pub. London, 1709.

Refers to: Benjamin Hoadly, The measures of submission to the civil magistrate consider'd. ... in a sermon preach'd Sept. 29, 1705. London, 1706.
A 3d (and 4th) ed., perhaps the 'second part' Leslie anticipates, appeared
in 1710, with substantial additions. Leslie further defends his High-Church,
Tory position in The finishing stroke. London, 1711 (q.v.).

Hoadly had maintained that St. Paul (Romans 13) only required people to
obey rulers who governed for their good. Leslie disputes this by showing
the origin of government to be in the family, and where there is no higher
authority, the head "wou'd be King in his Family, with Power of Life and
Death, &c." (p. 23). The King is similarly "Father of all his Subjects",
and not one of the 3 estates, "but Sovereign to them all" (p. 30).

NUC(Pre-1956)328:210(NN); BM(to 1955)135:688; Morgan,BBH:L223.

[_____].

The good old cause, further discuss'd. In a letter to the author of The

Jacobite's hopes reviv'd. ... [Quotations from Psal. 31:13 and 2 Sam. 1:20]

London printed: and sold by the booksellers of London and Westminster.

1710. 32, [4] p. 8°(in 4s) 20 cm.

A "Postscript" (last 4 p.) discusses critically Robert Walpole's Four

letters to a friend in North Britain, upon the ... tryal of Dr. Sacheverell.

London, 1710 (pub. anon.).

A further reply to: Benjamin Hoadly, The Jacobite's hopes reviv'd ...

[in a reply to Leslie's work] entitled, The good old cause: or, Lying in

truth, &c. [by Misodolos, pseud.] London, 1710. Leslie's 1st reply was:

Beaucoup de bruit ... being a tryal of skill betwixt The Jacobite's hopes

reviv'd, and The good old cause. By a true Trojan. London, 1710 (pub.

anon.).

Imperfect: corner of last leaf wanting; paper restored, text supplied by

hand.

A leading Tory pamphleteer and High-Church Jacobite supporter of the doc-

trine of non-resistance to the commands of the monarch, Leslie here refutes

Hoadly's Whig arguments passage by passage, and accuses Hoadly of placing

government over the Queen (p. 16, 18, etc.). In spite of this further ex-

planation, and claims that he does not write against the government (p. 5),

a warrant was issued for Leslie's arrest for (so argued Hoadly) calling

Queen Anne a usurper. Abel Boyer, in An essay towards the history of the

last Ministry and Parliament (1710, q.v.), quotes (p. 54n) from Leslie's

earlier work of similar title: The good old cause: or, Lying in truth (1710):

"Hereditary Right, and the National Allegiance due to it, is a stubborn

Thing, and will not bend even to an Act of Parliament, nor to a Thousand

Usurpations! Page 35" (of Leslie). It's plain, says the author of An essay,

that by 'usurpation' Leslie means the Revolution settlement. Leslie was
one of the most outspoken of all the nonjurors! Towards the end of his
present pamphlet, Leslie comments on John Tutchin's Whig journal The observator (p. 26-8), and on George Ridpath, proprietor of the Whig's The
flying-post (p. 28-30).

   NUC(Pre-1956)328:214 (32 p. only); BM(to 1955)135:692; Morgan,BBH:M373;
Madan(Speck):451.

A LETTER to a new Member of the Honourable House of Commons; touching
the rise of all the imbezzlements and mismanagements of the Kingdom's treasure, from the beginning of the Revolution unto this present Parliament.
With an account ... of the many oppositions the House of Commons met with
about redressing the said publick grievances. And lastly, a proposal ...
how to prevent the like miscarriages for the future. To which is added,
a parallel account of the national expences, from November 3. 1640. to
November 1659. And from November 5. 1688. to Michaelmas 1700. Amsterdam:
printed in the year 1710. 1 p.l., 3-28 p. 4° 20 cm.(unbd.)

   Authorship: Signed (p. 20): "W.L.", and dated: Braintree, Feb. 19. 1705.

   Title not to be confused with: A letter to a new Member of the ensuing
Parliament ... London [1715?]. Caption title: A letter from a commoner
of England, to a new Member of this Honourable House of Commons.

   First (?) edition: reprinted in The Harleian miscellany, 1810, 11:140-61.

   Possibly a false imprint (unfound in Knuttel), but watermarks (fleur-de-
lis and "FH") unidentified in Briquet (close to, but not, 7095/6).

   Signature A2 signed A3.

   The 'Letter' extends from p. 3 to 20; 'A parallel account' from p. 25-28.

   Imperfect: outer margin of p. 27-8 closely trimmed, with partial loss of
half a single column of figures on p. 27, most if not all zeros.

Under the pretence of explaining to a new Member the implications of
Queen Anne's reference in the House to public debts, the author sketches
a history of "Miscarriages and Imbezzlements of the Publick Monies" from
King William's time, with the ostensible purpose of helping the Member
find a way, at the Queen's request, of preventing future misapplications.
Though everyone has complained, from 1701 "to this present Year 1710",
they have not been prevented (p. 4). Details of peculation and of attempts
to stop it are given, with its persistence despite all efforts to instit-
ute accountability. A Junto was set up in opposition to the Court Party,
to press for an enquiry, says the author; and several pages of tables item-
ize the naval expenses, showing the extent of embezzlement: almost 11 million pounds in 5 years. Perhaps vigilance at last will bring justice to
the common cause (p. 18), but punishment at the start would have deterred
later offenders - thus "W.L." concludes his letter, with the date 1705,
despite the 1710 date earlier. The lesson for the new Member continues
though, with emphasis on the Low-Church Party, those who "fleece the Government of the Publick Treasure", with 5 measures for a "Publick Remedy"
(p. 21-4). The "Parallel Account" of the title concludes the work. The
'commoner' author is evidently a Tory.

   NUC(Pre-1956)329:37; BM(to 1955)136:100; Morgan,BBH:M367; Kress:2667
(all have this ed. only).

THE MODERATOR: or, Considerations propos'd; in order to end the unsea-
sonable debates concerning the legality of the late happy revolution. By
a country minister of this Church of England, zealously devoted to her
doctrine and discipline ... London: printed for J[ohn]. Morphew, near
Stationers-Hall, 1710. 2 p.l., 5-30 p. 8°(in 4s) 19 cm.

The preliminary leaves are half-title and title.

A twice-weekly journal, The moderator, nos. 1-50, 22 May - 10 Nov., 1710
(cf. NUC & Rothschild:1523) was also sold by John Morphew.

Deplores the "violently excited" division into "High-Church, and Low-
Church", and sets out to show that both uphold the doctrines of the Established Church, as did the 'Glorious Revolution' which placed William and
Mary, and now Anne, upon the English throne (p. 7). The author says it
may be "Charitably Conjectur'd" that resistance to the King (James II) is
justified in "extraordinary Cases": to prevent bloodshed (p. 8), and to
restore ancient liberties (p. 9); but even the doctrine of non-resistance
is preserved when the king abdicates (p. 12). Thus, the rights of princes
and the rights of subjects are reconciled (p. 16). Scriptural warrant is
adduced for recent history, to moderate the opposing view points.

   NUC(Pre-1956)388:547; Morgan,BBH:M432 (& 2d ed., corr. & augm., 26 p.,
1710). Cf. BM(to 1955)161:744 (2d ed.).

THE OXFORD decree: being an entire confutation of Mr. Hoadley's [sic]
book, of the original of government; taken from the London Gazette, published by authority. London: reprinted in the year, 1710. 8 p. 8° 19 cm.

Reprinted from the London Gazette, 23-6 July, 1683, no. 1845, originally
printed Oxford, 1683 (cf.NUC) in both English and Latin texts. Editions
of each appear as WingSTC:0891(2) and 0893(4), under the respective titles:
The judgment and decree ... July 21, 1683. [Oxford], 1683, and Judicium &
decretum ... July 21, An. 1683. [Oxford], 1683. WingSTC:0872-3, Decreti
Oxoniensis, [Oxford], 1696, are another version.

   A reply to: Benjamin Hoadly, The original and institution of civil government. London, 1710 (BM(to 1955)104:611).

Reprints The judgement and decree under date of its presentation to His
Majesty (Whitehall, July 24. 1683), which lists 27 "Propositions contained
in divers Books and Writings, published in the English, and also the Latin

Tongue, repugnant to the holy Scriptures ... and also destructive of the
Kingly Government ..." (p. 2-3), all judged "to be false, seditious, and
impious" (p. 6), and threatening to Charles II. These were used as evidence by Dr. Sacheverell at his trial, but sentenced to be burnt along with
Sacheverell's two sermons (cf. Rothschild:1146). The last page carries an
address from Cambridge University, Whitehall, 25 July [1683], to Charles II,
expressing horror at the danger to the king and his brother (later James
II), condemnation of their enemies' "ungodly Principles and bloody Practices", and prayers for their punishment and the king's welfare. The
"Advertisement" (p. 8) warns Hoadly that if he doesn't recant his "Seditious
Principles", he may expect the same censure from the two universities.

Cordeaux & Merry:1129 (giving different Hoadly title). Cf. NUC(Pre-1956)
160:547 (1st leaf mutilated); BM(to 1955)104:611; Rothschild:1146 (all
under: An entire confutation ...); Morgan,BBH:M308 (under The entire ...).

PHILALETHES, Eugenius, pseud.

Some modest animadversions and reflexions upon a sermon preach'd before
the Honourable House of Commons, by Doctor West, on Monday, the 30th of
January, being the day appointed to be kept, as the day of the martyrdom
of the blessed King Charles I. In a letter to the abovesaid doctor.
By Eugenius Philalethes. ... London: printed, in the year, 1710. 52 p.
8°(in 4s) 19 cm.

Authorship: There are points of style and phraseology in this reminiscent
of the writing of Charles Leslie (1650-1722), for example, in his The best
answer, London, 1709, and The good old cause further discuss'd, London,
1710; and Leslie also used the pseudonym Philalethes, in his journal The
rehearsal, 1704-9 (see Appendix C.).

Page 47 misnumbered 07.

Proclamation, dated 25 Jan. 1660, by Charles II, "For Observing of the
Thirtieth Day of January, as a Day of Fast and Humiliation, acording [<u>sic</u>]
to the late Act of Parliament for that Purpose", to mark "the execrable
Murder of Our Royal Father Charles the first" (in black letter): p. 24-8.

A reply to: Richard West, <u>A sermon preached before the Honourable House</u>.
<u>of Commons ... Jan. 30, 1709/10</u>. London, 1710 (<u>q.v</u>., below).

Bound in a modern blue, pebbled, plastic-coated cloth.

Provenance: Indiana University Library (t.-p. perforated stamp).

The author, a staunch supporter of the doctrine of non-resistance and
passive obedience, disputes Dr. West's arguments against the annual obser-
vance of 30th January in memory of Charles I, on this "Day of Humiliation,
the present [Ecclesiastical] Year 1709" (p. 4). For example, he shows that
Dr. West's scriptural text (<u>Jeremiah</u> 31:297) does not support resistance,
for the king was good and his subjects bad, so they had no grounds for resisting the supreme power (p. 4-6). The author describes and deplores the
"Train of frightful Consequences" that must result from resistance to the
king, as happened after the execution of Charles I (1649), which event must
therefore never be forgotten (p. 8-9). Dr. West's arguments are refuted
point by point (and, p. 41-51, page by page), relating each statement to
scripture, to the great danger of resistance, which doctrine is against
state and church law (authorities cited, p. 24-38), and to the absolute
need for passive obedience for peace and order. You "insinuate, that there
were Faults on both sides [cf. Appendix A to this Catalogue]; but all I
can find ascribed to King Charles I. by any impartial Historian, was his
Goodness, Lenity, and too great Condescention to his Enemies for Peace
Sake" (p. 14).

NUC(Pre-1956)455:260; BM(to 1955)188:728; Morgan,BBH:M510: Madan(Speck):
177.

A REFUTATION of the doctrine of passive obedience and non-resistance.
Written by J.P. one of the laity of Marlborough. London: printed and
sold by S[arah]. Popping, at the Raven in Pater-Noster-Row, 1710. Price
two pence. 15 p. 8° 19 cm.

Argues against the use of Romans 13:2 ("Whosoever therefore resisteth
the power, resisteth the ordinance of God: and they that resist shall
receive to themselves damnation") as a foundation for the High-Church doctrine of non-resistance and passive obedience: it may have relevance under
tyrannical rulers (p. 7-10), but by Romans 13:3-4 such do not have rightful
power (O.T. examples given, p. 12-14), so there is no basis for this "idle
Doctrine" to be found in that so-oft-cited scriptural text (p. 15).

NUC(Pre-1956)485:444; Morgan,BBH:M494; Madan(Speck):663.

REMARKS on a letter from a Cambridge gentleman to the Reverend Dr.
Sacheverell, occasion'd by his sermons and sentence against him. London:
printed for J. Baker at the Black Boy in Pater-noster Row. 1710. Price
2d. 16 p. 8° 19 cm.

Bibliographical footnotes.

A reply to: A letter to the Reverend Dr. Henry Sacheverell. On occasion
of his sermon and late sentence ... By a Cambridge-gentleman [Rev. Dr.
Rawson? cf. Madan:409], London, 1710, which condemns Sacheverell's sermon
The perils of false brethren ... 5th of November, 1709. London, 1709 (q.v.,
above).

The writer defends Dr. Sacheverell by saying (p. 3) that his friends re-
joiced at his sentence not because they thought it could be more severe,
but because "he was pronounc'd Innocent by so many of his Noble Judges"
(69 'guilty'; 52, including the Abp. of York, 'not guilty'), and by many
refutations page-by-page, such as that Sacheverell had said 'Volpones' not

Henry Sacheverell, 1710, by A. Russell,
mezzotint engraved by J. Smith.
(From The Trial of Doctor Sacheverell,
Courtesy of the author
Professor G. Holmes.)

'Volpone' so could not have referred to the Minister (Lord Godolphin),
since the plural cannot signify a single person (p. 13; but Swift, in The
history of the four last years of the Queen (London, 1758, in edition of
Herbert Davis, Oxford, Blackwell, 1973, p. 9), referring to this incident,
says that Godolphin "became a thorow Convert [to the Whigs] by a perfect
trifle").

   NUC(Pre-1956)488:43; BM(to 1955)210:795; Morgan,BBH:M603; Madan(Speck):
428.

SACHEVERELL, Henry, 1674?-1724.

Collections of passages referr'd to by Dr. Henry Sacheverell in his
Answer to the articles of his impeachment. Under four heads ... The
second edition. London: printed for H[enry]. Clements, at the Half-Moon
in St. Paul's Church-Yard. 1710. 32 p. 8° 19 cm.

   Refers to: Henry Sacheverell, The answer of Henry Sacheverell, D.D. to
the articles of impeachment ... [s.l.; London?] 1710.

   Upper and outer margins closely trimmed; partial loss of some page numbers
and of some marginal glosses.

   Transcribes passages by archbishops, bishops (including Burnet and Wake,
who spoke against Dr. Sacheverell at his trial), and scholars, and sacred
and profane texts, all here brought together in support of the sermons and
statements of Sacheverell. Printed while the trial was still in progress
(11 March, 1710), a copy was burned 25 March by order of the House of Commons for contempt (cf. Madan).

   NUC(Pre-1956)513:281; BM(to 1955)210:781; Madan(Speck):238. Cf. Morgan,
BBH:M574 (has "A collection of passages ...").

_____.

The speech of Henry Sacheverell, D.D. made in Westminster-Hall, on
Tuesday, March 7, 1709/10. London: printed for J. Baker, at the Black Boy
in Pater-Noster-Row, 1710. Price two pence. 16 p. 8°(in 4s) 20 cm.

Authorship: Daniel Defoe contended that Dr. Sacheverell did not himself
write this speech, based on the evidence of a comparison with the doctor's
sermons; but he named no other writer. See: Defoe, A speech without doors.
London, 1710, p. [2].

The 1st ed. has on the t.-p. after D.D.: "upon his impeachment at the
Bar of the House of Lords", before the words "in Westminster-Hall"; this
issue has 10 ornaments on t.-p. and "in Season" on p. 16 (cf.Madan).

Answered by: Sir John St. Leger, The managers pro and con. London, 1710
(q.v., below).

Sacheverell's defence, given at his trial before the Lords and Commons
at Westminster Hall, where he was impeached for his two sermons, The communication of sin ... August 15th, 1709. London, 1709, and The perils of
false brethren ... 5th of November, 1709. London, 1709 (both q.v. above).
He says his trial is really directed against all "who maintain the Doctrine
of Non-Resistance" (p. 2), and claims his sermons have been misrepresented,
providing instances: applying this Doctrine to the Revolution, when I had
not the least thought of this (p. 4); ignoring the sources of my Doctrine:
the Gospel, and the Homilies of the Church [set forth in Edward VI's
reign], "established by the Thirty Nine Articles", confirmed under Queen
Elizabeth (p. 5); that I oppose laws favouring dissenters, when I oppose
only their abuses (p. 5-6); that my warning of the Church's peril means
it is endangered by the Queen's administration, when my "printed expressions" (quoted at length) attest to my loyalty (p. 7-11); the Protestant
succession is subverted by my sermons, though I said nothing to support

this (p. 12-13). If I inadvertently gave grounds for misinterpretation,
under provocation, I hope these "shall not be deemed High Crimes and Mis-
demeanours", but that my grief at this bar is sufficient punishment so I
may be acquitted, for all my doctrines are agreeable to scripture and the
Church (p. 13-15). The trial was reported in Howell's State trials, v. 15,
cols. 1-522 - cf. Rothschild, v.2, p. 481.

   NUC(Pre-1956)513:285; BM(to 1955)210:787(& 24-p., fol.); Rothschild:1782;
Madan(Speck):252. Cf. London Library,2:783 (1st ed.).

[ST. LEGER, Sir John], fl. 1710.

   The managers pro and con: or, An account of what is said at Child's and
Tom's coffee-houses for and against Dr. Sacheverell. ... The fifth edi-
tion. London: printed, and are to be sold by A[nn]. Baldwin in Warwick-
Lane. 1710. Price six pence. 48 p. 8°(in 4s) 20 cm.

   Reprinted in Somers tracts, 1814, 12:630-52.

   Transl. into Dutch as: De advokaten pro en contra den Dr. Sacheverell.
Amsterdam, 1711; and into French as part of: Les avocats pour et contre le
Dr. Sacheverell. Amsterdam, 1711.

   Appendix (p. 42-8) comprises State tracts, vol. 1, p. 539-40 (in which
King John cedes powers to his barons should he breach the peace and libert-
ies of the realm), and "Reflections on a late pamphlet, entitled, Priest-
craft in perfection" (caption title), which is a reply to [Anthony Collins],
Priestcraft in perfection. London, 1710 (Rothschild:649 says 1st ed., but
Morgan,BBH:L85 has 1st ed. as 1709).

   A reply to Henry Sacheverell, The perils of false brethren. London, 1709
(q.v. above).

   Answered by: A letter out of the country, to the author of The managers
pro and con ... London, 1710.

Provenance: Robert Blackburn Jonathan Chadorto (?) (t.-p. autogr.).

The author says Dr. Sacheverell intended to subvert the government, "the Protestant Succession as by Law established ... and [to] condemn the late Happy Revolution" (p. 3) in his 1709 Perils sermon. In this answer to "the Doctor's evasive and prevaricating" Speech ... made [at his trial] in Westminster-Hall ... March 7, 1709/10 (London, 1710, q.v.), in which Sacheverell and his Council "seem'd to be the Managers for the Pretender", the author seeks to inform those whose passions may have affected their judgment (p. 4). Criticism follows, of 4 assertions in Sacheverell's Perils sermon at St. Paul's, purportedly presented by "The Managers of Tom's Coffee-house" (Whigs) and "The Managers at Child's" (Tories; e.g., p. 5-6), but in fact a dissenting Whig attack on the 4 High-Church beliefs, that: 1. resistance is illegal; 2. the Toleration Act, 1689, is false; 3. the Church of England is in danger; 4. dissenters are destroying Church and state, aided by some of the Church's own sons. (Page references are given to both sermon and speech of Sacheverell.) The ringing conclusion is: Let toleration, the Union, the Hanoverian Succession, resistance, Church, Queen, and state prevail! (p. 41).

NUC(Pre-1956)514:651 (& 1st-4th eds.); BM(to 1955)211:483; Morgan,BBH: M619; Madan(Speck):388; Rothschild:1803.

THE THOUGHTS of an honest Whig, upon the present proceedings of that party. In a letter to a friend in town. London: printed in the year, 1710. 16 p. 8° 20 cm.

Authorship attributed to Benjamin Hoadly in Stonehill:2427, but this work is opposed to Hoadly; Joseph Trapp is a more likely author.

A reply to: [Benjamin Hoadly], The thoughts of an honest Tory. London, 1710 (q.v.). For other replies, and successive works in this controversy, see Appendix A.

Imperfect: lower margin closely trimmed, with bottom line of text, p. 3-4, and of catchwords, p. 13-14, lost, but all supplied in facsimile.

Although supposedly writing a private letter as one Whig dissenter to another, the author "cannot but say, that the violent Heats and Indiscretion of many of our Friends, instead of making our Condition better, have render'd it much worse" (p. 3), for our (Whig) harshness in promoting the doctrine of resistance (to unlawful royal commands) has provoked Tories "to Unite in defence of their Darling Doctrines of Non Resistance and Passive Obedience" (p. 4). By a critical 'self' analysis of Whig and dissenting activities (and a supporting reference to Dr. Henry Sacheverell, p. 5), the author points up the evil of disturbing the national tranquillity by pressing devisive and lying arguments: in the weekly The observator and The review (p. 11), and by such as Abraham Gill, Daniel Defoe, and others (esp. p. 7-11) - "Can't a Man be a Dissenter, but he must forfeit his Understanding"? (p. 14). The writer returns a borrowed copy of Thoughts of an honest Tory (by Hoadly, who in fact supported the doctrine of resistance), by one who "Writes in Favour of the Whigs", thus "defiling his own Nest" (p. 16).

NUC(Pre-1956)593:59 (also London,1720); BM(to 1955)256:397; Morgan,BBH: M699; Madan(Speck):486.

[TOLAND, John], 1670-1722.

The Jacobitism, perjury, and popery of High-Church priests. ... London; printed for J. Baker at the Black-Boy in Pater-noster-Row. 1710. 15 p. 8° 19 cm.

Authorship: NUC, BM, DNB, & Carabelli; also attributed to Defoe (but not in Moore) and to Matthew Tindal (Madan).

The author, another of Pope's 'dunces', "prompt at Priests to jeer"
(Dunciad, variorum, 1729, 2:367); views the High-Church oaths of allegiance
to William III, yet belief in the hereditary right to the throne of James
II, as perjury (p. 4-5). He names many High-Church divines whose principles
(non-resistance, passive obedience, de jure succession) he opposes, pointing up their compatibility with Jacobitism rather than with the Revolution
(p. 11).

  NUC(Pre-1956)596:324 (but "Price one penny"; & Edinburgh, 1710); BM(to
1955)239:720; Morgan,BBH:M706; Madan(Speck):157 (Tindal; also variant imprint); Carabelli:145.

A TRUE and faithful account of the last distemper and death of Tom. Whigg,
Esq; who departed this life on the 22d day of September ... 1710. Together
with a relation of his frequent appearing since ... to the great disturbance of Her Majesty's peaceable subjects. ... Part I. London: printed
in the year 1710. 2 p.l., 34 p. (incl. engraved front.) 8°(in 4s) 19 cm.

  Morgan cites the Wrenn Catalogue (Austin, Tex., 1970) attribution to Defoe,
but this is not supported by Moore.

  First edition, pub. before 10 Nov., 1710; "... the second edition, corrected", was pub. between 17-20 Nov. (cf. Madan,635-6).

  Bound with: A true and faithful account ... Part II. London, 1710 (q.v.).

  Madan has provided a comprehensive note on the subject of the text. "Tom
Whigg's death symbolises the demise of the Whig party, said to have begun
about 5 November 1709, the date of Sacheverell's St. Paul's sermon, when
Tom fell ill. The distemper worsened on 14 December when, egged on by Harl-
equin (Harley), Whigg fired a cannon from Westminster Abbey across the
river (see frontispiece) at a merlin (Sacheverell) perched on a pinnacle
of St. Mary Overy (St. Saviour's Southwark). This was the day when he was

Tom Whigg being treated for his infected tooth, from the
frontispiece to <u>A True and Faithful Account of the Last
Distemper and Death of Tom Whigg, Esq. ...</u> Part I.
London, 1710. For an explanation, <u>see</u> the Madan note in
    the annotation to this title, in the Catalogue.

summoned to appear before the House of Commons. Whigg accused him of
frightening the Queen's canaries, of being a bird of ill omen, importing
danger to the Church; of opposing the toleration of the rooks (dissenters)
and of insubordination to the Archbishop of Canterbury. When all efforts
had failed, and after twenty-one sleepless nights - the duration of the
trial - Whigg was visited by the Queen's physicians, who directed the removal of an infectious tooth - a reference to the dismissal of Sunderland
in June. His cries are said to have been heard by Messrs Pettecum and Buys
in Holland - evidently the men seen through the curtain in the frontispiece - whereupon they sent over their own physician, who visited Whigg
and tried to reconcile Aurelia (Anne) to him. The drawing of another
tooth (the dismissal of Godolphin in August), which led to the loosening of
others, led to a temporary rally, but then the illness grew worse, and
Whigg died on 22 September (the day after the dissolution of Parliament).
He was buried at St. Peter's Poor (Hoadly's church) and the sermon was
preached by Kennet", presumably White Kennett (1660-1728), Bishop of
Peterborough.

  BM(to 1955)256:392 (2 pts. in 1); Morgan.BBH:M760 (2 pts. in 1); Madan
(Speck):635. Cf. NUC(Pre-1956)602:574 (2d ed. only).

  A TRUE and faithful account of the last distemper and death of Tom Whigg,
Esq; ... Part II. London: printed in the year 1710. 2 p.l., 56 p. 8°
(in 4s) 19 cm.

  Half-title: A true and faithful account of Tom Whigg, Esq; Part II.

  First (and only?) edition (cf. BM & Madan). This has the same title and
imprint as Pt. I (above), except no period after 'Tom' and different Latin
sentence after title, but t.-p. type reset. For possible 2d ed. of Part II,
cf. NUC (cited below).

Imperfect: outer margin p. 13-14 closely trimmed, with loss of a few letters, but not of the sense.

Bound with: A true and faithful account ... Part I. London, 1710 (q.v. for other notes).

This continues the story from Pt. I of Tom Whigg, and using the same lampooning imagery, tells "a fantastic story of an imposter, claiming to be a resuscitated Tom Whigg, posing as a contestant at the parliamentary election in Kent" (Madan). Finally he addresses a horrified Kit-Kat Club as a ghost in a Roman Toga, whereupon the Club resolves that Tom Wigg still lives and will win his seat in Maidstone and "take the Reins of the World into his Hands" (p. 56). On p. 11 the author attempts to review his tale in verse, but after 3 lines gives up, content to leave poetry to "the Incomparable Author of the City Shower", Swift (The tatler, no. 238, Oct. 1710 - cf. Rothschild), whose "Wit is alone equal to the Work".

BM(to 1955)256:392 (2 pts. in 1); Morgan,BBH:M760 (2 pts. in 1); Rothschild:80; Madan(Speck):637. Cf. NUC(Pre-1956)602:574 (2 pts. in 1, 2d ed. - of both pts.?).

[WARWICK, Sir Philip], 1646-1710, supposed author.

Rules of government: or, A true balance between sovereignty and liberty. Written by a person of honour, immediately after the late civil war. And now published, to prevent another. London: printed for Bernard Lintott at the Cross-Keys, between the Temple-Gates, in Fleetstreet. 1710. 1 p.l., [6], 70, [1] p. 8°(in 4s) 20 cm.

"Wrongly attributed [e.g. by BM & Morgan] to --- Lund": Halkett & Laing. "... written by a person that had been bred and liv'd long in a Court", who had suffered during the civil war, and had "in his private Retirement

made these Reflections"; now published [evidently for the first time] to
meet present needs: Pref., p. [1]-[2], 1st count. The Sir Philip in DNB
(1609-1683) is also a likely attribution.

Running title: A True Balance between Sovereignty and Liberty.

First (?) edition.

The Contents (detailed): p. [4]-[6], 1st count. Advertisement for two
titles (one just pub., one in the press), both printed for B. Lintott:
[1] p. at end.

A study of the history and literature of the relations between sovereign
or princely power and freedom, and the need for defence of the people's
laws and liberties, with a criticism of Thos. Hobbes' Leviathan (p. 35-7).
The author concludes that "A Prince's Politicks will be as improsperous as
his Oeconomicks are, who loves to spend freely, and yet never to look
upon an Account" (p. 70).

NUC(Pre-1956)649:417; BM(to 1955)209:153; Morgan,BBH:M749 (& 79 p., 12°,
same imprint).

WEST, Richard, 1671?-1716.

A sermon [on Jer. 31:297] preached before the Honourable House of Commons,
at St. Margarets Westminster, on Munday [sic], Jan. 30, 1709/10. Being
the anniversary of the martyrdom of King Charles I. By Richard West, D.D.
Prebendary of Winchester. London, printed for J[ohn]. Churchill, at the
Black Swan in Paternoster-Row, 1710. 30 p. 8°(in 4s) 20 cm.

Order to print, dated 31 Jan. 1709 (1710 N.S.): p. [2].

Bibliographical footnotes.

Answered by: Some modest animadversions ... upon a sermon ... by Doctor
West ... 30th of January ... By Eugenius Philalethes. London, 1710 (q.v.,
above), and Remarks on Dr. West's sermon ... 30th of January, 1709-10. London,1710,

and also part of Edmund Curll, A search after principles ... Wherein

... Dr. West [and others] ... sermons ... are consider'd. London, 1710.

Madan notes that this sermon was often referred to in the Sacheverell

controversy.

Provenance: John Edwards (t.-p. autogr.).

The text from Jeremiah reads: "In those days they shall say no more, The

fathers have eaten a sour grape, and the children's teeth are set on edge".

The sermon develops the theme that "the Influence of the Sins of Fathers

upon their Children" (p. 4) has operated since Old Testament times; so,

resistance to Charles I (executed 30 Jan. 1649) causes many today to hold

the doctrine of non-resistance in expiation of "the Guilt of Royal Blood".

Damage to the Church (p. 17), liberty (p. 20), the Revolution spirit, and

internal divisions (p. 23) are results. Dr. West urges a new humility,

caution in placing blame, avoidance of sowing discontent, regard for gov-

ernors and governed, and respect for religion; then "we shall remain a

happy People" for ever (p. 30).

NUC(Pre-1956)657:159(& Dublin reprint, 1710); BM(to 1955)255:784;

Morgan,BBH:M754; Rothschild:2541; Madan(Speck):175.

WHALEY, Nathaniel, 1637?-1710

The gradation of sin both in principles and practice. A sermon [on 2

Kings 8:13] preach'd before the University of Oxford, at St. Mary's, on

the thirtieth of January, 1709/10. Wherein one of Mr. Hoadly's principal

arguments against the doctrine of non-resistance of the supreme powers is

occasionally consider'd. ... By Nathaniel Whaley, M.A. Fellow of Wadham-

College in Oxford. Imprimatur, Guil. Lancaster, Vice-Can. Oxon. Febr.

22. 1709-10. London, printed, and sold by H[enry]. Hills [jun.], in Black-

Fryars, near the water-side, 1710. 16 p. 8° 18 cm.

Refers to: Benjamin Hoadly, The measures of submission to the civil magistrate. London, 1706.

The text from 2 Kings reads: "But what, is thy servant a dog, that he
should do this great thing?" Here Hazael, King of Syria, refuses to believe
the Prophet Elisha's prediction that Hazael would cruelly destroy Israel.
But, says Whaley, men become in time accustomed to evil actions which they
abhorred in their unperverted state (p. 3); so (on this anniversary of
Charles I's martyrdom) good men reconciled themselves to habits of sin from
1641 to 1649 (p. 9), and the execution of their king. First they requested
an exception to absolute non-resistance, and today they insist that it is
lawful to resist any tyranny in a king (p. 9-11). This doctrine of resistance advocated by Mr. Hoadly (p. 14) has no scriptural basis, and his
Measures of submission is based on misinterpretation (p. 15).

    NUC(Pre-1956)658:563 (& Oxford, 1710, 17 p.). Cf. BM(to 1955)256:151
(2d ed., Oxford, 1710, only).

THE WHIGGS address: exploding their republican principles. London:
printed in the year, 1710. Price one penny. 1 p.l., 8 p. 8°(half-sheet)
19 cm.

Authorship: no attributions have been discovered, but probably written
by a Low-Church or Dissenting Whig, though possibly by a Scottish Presbyterian (cf. p. 6).

First (and only?) edition.

The author of this mock address to Queen Anne hopes "the loud Complaints
of the Church is in Danger" from the "False Brethren" (as Sacheverell had
cried), will cease (p. 4); he draws attention to the Queen's enemies, who
have as "their great Patron the French King" (the Jacobites; p. 5); he
deplores the principles of George Hickes, Charles Leslie, and Henry Dodwell

(nonjurors; p. 6), and other sycophants; and he warns against those hypo-
crites who take all oaths and declare for the Hanover succession, while
plotting the restoration of church lands as they were in "Holy Times before the Whiggish Reformations, Magna Chartas, Revolutions, Moderations"
and other affronts to the Queen (Roman Catholics? p. 7). All such are
against her "most grateful inferior Clergy, who are so exemplary in their
Lives, and so zealous for the Dr. [Sacheverell?] and Your Majesty"; they
(the enemies) have "the Doctor's Sentiments of the Hereditary Right ...
of Hanover" but not "such foolish Low Church Notions, as to imagine any
other right Jure Divino"; etc. The author concludes that they know nothing of toleration, but complain of blasphemy while in their taverns and
bawdy houses, pretending to be doing good for church and state (p. 8).
The Queen is flattered at great length by this author, and in thickly-
satirical and rambling sentences (only 6 in all), of dubious logic.

NUC(Pre-1956)659:351; BM(to 1955)256:397; Morgan,BBH:M761; Madan(Speck):
768.

WITHERS, John, fl. 1707-1724.

The history of resistance, as practis'd by the Church of England: in
which 'tis proved ... that ... since the Reformation ... the said Church
hath aided ... such subjects as have defended themselves against the
oppressions of their tyrannical, tho' natural princes. Written upon the
occasion of Mr. Agate's sermon at Exeter on the 30th of January; and in
defence of the late Revolution, the present Establishment, and the Protestant succession. ... Entred according to Act of Parliament. London:
printed for J[onathan]. Robinson, in St. Paul's Churchyard: and sold by
A[nn]. Baldwin, near the Oxford-Arms in Warwick-Lane. 1710. Price three-
pence. 24 p. 8°(in 4s) 18 cm.

First edition; NUC, BM, and Morgan note 2d to 4th & 6th eds., all 1710; reprinted in Somers tracts, 1814, 12:248.

Bibliographical footnotes, mostly secular.

All margins closely trimmed, with slight loss of text.

One in a series of exchanges between Withers and John Agate during at least 1708-15 (cf. NUC & Morgan). Withers' well-documented review of re-sistance in ancient Rome and more-modern Europe, from the Nonconformist and Whig viewpoint as opposed to the High-Church doctrine of non-resis-tance, was further argued in Daniel Defoe's A defence of Mr. Withers's History of resistance. London, 1715 (1st pub. as A new test of the Church of England's loyalty, 1702, q.v.; cf. Moore (2d ed.):44).

NUC(Pre-1956)669:694; BM(to 1955)259:812; Morgan,BBH:M767.

1711

AN ACCOUNT of the Charity-Schools in Great Britain and Ireland: with
the benefactions thereto; and of the methods whereby they were set up,
and are governed. Also a proposal for encreasing their number, and adding some work to the childrens learning ... The tenth edition, with large
additions. London, printed and sold by Joseph Downing in Bartholomew-
Close near West-Smithfield, 1711. 59, [1] p. tables. 4° 23 cm.

"Advertisement" (verso t.-p.) invites errors to be reported for correction "in the next Impression", to the printer (who might therefore have
also been the compiler?).

First pub. 1704 (? cf. Morgan; Kress:2534 says 1706); see also 1708, 1712
eds.

Includes list of Charity-Schools: p. 11-43, 47.

List of books sold by Joseph Downing: 1 p. at end.

Bound with: Robert Moss, The providential division. London, 1708 (q.v.),
and 3 other works, in a vol. lettered on spine: Pamphlets on Charity Schools.

Provenance: stamp of Mercantile Library, Philadelphia: p. 27.

NUC(Pre-1956)2:559 (London, 1706-10); Morgan:BBH:G4 (1704-17); Kress:
S1278 & S2512.

THE BALLANCE of power: or, A comparison of the strength of the Emperor
and the French King. In a letter to a friend. ... London; printed for
A[nn]. Baldwin near the Oxford-Arms in Warwick-Lane. 1709 [i.e. 1711].
(Price two pence.) 1 p.l., 3-15, [1] p. 8° 19 cm.

This title not to be confused with similar ones, e.g. the anonymous Essays
upon : 1.   The ballance of power (London, 1701), by Charles Davenant.

In the roman imprint date M.DCC.IX on the t.-p., the terminal letters IX
may have been transposed, because the last page of text is dated: Nov. 10.
1711. However, 1709 may be the unchanged date of an earlier version, because Morgan lists a 1709 edition; the possibility of error remains though,
for Morgan has this printed for "R. Baldwin ... in Warwick-Lane", and
Richard Baldwin died early in 1698 (N.S., cf. Plomer), the business being
continued at the same address by his widow Ann, publisher of the 1711
edition.

"In a few days will be publish'd" (refers to the 2d ed. of A letter to a
member of the October-Club - cf. Morgan,BBH:N269: 4 eds in 1711) and "Just
publish'd" (list of titles on war and peace, including a sermon preached
before Marlborough, Sept. 9, 1711, thus confirming pub. date of present
work): last page.

Further to: A letter to a member of the October-Club (attributed to Francis Hare etc. - cf. Rothschild:1111).

Answered, in part, by: Jonathan Swift, Some advice ... to the members of
the October Club. London, 1712.

Discusses balance-of-power principles, with contemporary European examples
during the War of the Spanish Succession, and the Whiggish implications for
trade and for peace. In the balance between Louis XIV of France and the
Holy Roman Emperor (in 1711 Joseph I, then Charles VI), Swift's arguments
(in the Examiner) are opposed (p. 3, etc.), as is the yielding of Spain to

the Duke of Anjou for peace (p. 11); Austria and Spain under the Emperor
will _not_ outweigh the power of France: a balance could always be maintained
by the intervention of England or Holland on either side (p. 13-14).

NUC(Pre-1956)32:400; Morgan,BBH:L26 (1709 and 1711 eds.)

[BENSON, William], 1682-1754.

A letter to Sir J——[_i.e._ Jacob] B——[_i.e._ Banks], by birth a Swede, but
naturaliz'd, and a M——r[_i.e._ Member] of the present P——t [_i.e._ Parlia-
ment]: concerning the Minehead doctrine, which was establish'd by a certain
free parliament of Sweden, to the utter enslaving of that kingdom. ...
London; printed for A[nn]. Baldwin in Warwick-Lane. 1711. 2 p.l., [4],
40 p. 8°(in 4s) 19 cm.

Half-title: A letter to Sir J- B--, concerning the late Minehead doctrine.
The surname of Sir Jacob Banks concealed in the title is variously spelled
in the bibliographies (Bankes, Bancks), but though unfound in _DNB_ it is
consistently 'Banks' in BM. **Variant** title: _A letter to Sir J- B-, by Birth_
_a S- ..._, also 1711 (cf. BM,10:1144 & 14:1419). First pub. under title:
The history, or present state of Sweden. In a letter to Sir J--- B---- ...
London, 1711 (cf. NUC & Rothschild). Transl. into French as: _Lettre au_
chevalier Jacob Banks, contre le pouvoire absolu et l'obeissance passive.
Cologne, P. Marteau, 1711 (but called a fictitious imprint in NUC: "probably printed in Rotterdam by Fritsch and Böhm" - though not so noted in
Knuttel:15943).

At least 11 'editions' appeared in 1711, and "100,000 copies in all are
said to have been sold" (_DNB_, 'Benson').

"Advertisement" (list of books sold by A. Baldwin, all relating to peace,
war, and treaties): p. [4] at front.

Includes printed marginal references to sources cited, with page numbers.

Answered by: [Sir Jacob Banks], A letter from Sir J. B--ks to W. B--n,
Esq; S.O. By birth an Englishman; but unnaturaliz'd and turn'd Swede ...
London, 1719, and by his Some remarks by way of an answer to a late pamph-
let, intituled, A letter to Sir J.B. ... London, 1711 (both in NUC,BM);
also: [Johann Georg Burchard], supposed author, The letter to Sir J[acob].
B[anks]. examined: the false ... quotations ... exposed ... By Irenaeus
Philalethes ... London, 1711 (NUC,84:472). These prompted: A second
letter to Sir J- B-, by Benson. London, 1711 (2 issues, about April &
May - cf. Madan).

The 'Minehead doctrine', that rulers are answerable to God alone and subjects owe them unquestioning obedience (cf. DNB, 'Benson'), was presented
in an address at Minehead, Wilts., 30th May, 1710, by Sir Jacob Banks, who
was M.P. for Minehead (1695-1714) and Sheriff of Wiltshire (1710). Sir
Jacob, born in Sweden, strongly supported passive obedience, while Benson,
just returned from Sweden (p. 3), reviews the history of that country and
Denmark, and the struggle against Church domination of the monarch, now
lost to the doctrine of his accountability only to God (p. 16). Benson
shows the injustice, greed, and cruelty engendered, he says, by that doctrine, and the powerlessness of Swedes and Danes against them for the same
reason, each "in eternal Bondage to a Tyrant" (p. 26). It is even possible
because these nations educate their clergy at Oxford, that their pernicious
doctrine began in Britain (p. 27)! Benson extols the Romans for their love
of liberty, and concludes with praise for Queen Anne, and warnings against
passive obedience, Catholicism, and their evil effects as he has shown them
working in Sweden and Denmark. "The parallel with modern English political
history is everywhere implicit and often made explicit" (Madan).

Swift called this Letter libellous (the Examiner no. 30, 1st Mar. 1711),
and on the complaint of the Swedish ambassador about this pamphlet, Benson

was called before the Privy Council, "but nothing followed" (DNB).

   NUC(Pre-1956)47:290 (latest ed. is 11th, 1711); BM(to 1955)14:1419 (variant title only, to 11th ed., 1711); Morgan,BBH:N57n.; Madan(Speck):470
(to 12th ed., 1711); Rothschild:361.

[BOYER, Abel], 1667-1729.

   The political state of Great Britain: containing, an impartial account
of the changes in the ministry, civil, military, and ecclesiastical preferments. With the characters of persons advanc'd ... the proceedings in
Parliament ... also, faithful abstracts of papers and pamphlets relating
to state affairs. In a letter, from a secretary to a foreign minister,
who has resided twenty one years in England, to his friend at the Hague.
To be continu'd monthly. This is for January, 1710/11. London: printed
for J. Baker, at the Black Boy in Pater-Noster-Row, 1711. Price one
shilling. 1 p.l., [6], 70 p. 8°(in 4s) 19 cm.(unbd.)

   First issue; The publisher to the reader (p. [1]-[6]) refers to this as
"a New Undertaking". The journal ran under Boyer to October, 1729, in 38
six-monthly vols., till restraint was threatened by the printers holding
the monopoly on parliamentary reporting (cf. DNB, 'Boyer'), but publication
continued in other hands till Dec. 1740, by then in 60 vols. The 1st 8
vols., 1711-14, reprinted under title: Quadriennium Annae postremum; or,
The political state ... (vol. 8 has title: Quadriennium Georgii; or, The
political state ...), London, 1711-14; 2d ed., improved and enlarged, with
indexes, 1718-20.

   Page 40-1 and sigs. F4^v-G1^r follow, but catchword and sense don't.

   Transl. into French as: Etat politique de la Grande-Bretagne ... Janvier,
1710/11 and Février, 1710/11. Amsterdam, [1711?] (cf. Morgan).

   This serial reported current events and both sides of political issues,

Cupola House, where Daniel Defoe resided in Bury St.
Edmunds, Suffolk, to recuperate after imprisonment.

attempting impartiality and "the Healing [of] our unhappy Divisions",

through abstracts of publications and personal observations (cf. "To the

Reader"). It was "the first periodical ... which contained a parliament-

ary chronicle, and in which parliamentary debates were reported" with fair

regularity and accuracy, drawing cn personal contacts, and using full names

whenever possible (cf. DNB, 'Boyer'). The present issue describes events

in Parliament, changes of officials, municipal happenings, Jacobite and

church/state affairs (including Dr. Sacheverell, p. 15), with transcripts

of addresses and letters.

    NUC(Pre-1956)464:44; BM(to 1955)185:742; Morgan,BBH:V252; London Library,

2:593 (complete work); Kress:2732 (all).

[DEFOE, Daniel], 1661?-1731.

    The secret history of the October Club: from its original to this time.

By a member. London: printed in the year, 1711. Price 1s. 1 p.l., 86 p.

8°(in 4s) 18 cm.

    First edition, pub. 19 Apr. (cf. Moore), 1st issue? (cf. NUC: 2d issue,

p. 34 begins: "From this small original", while in the present issue it

begins "the October Club"); 2d issue pub. 10 May (cf. Moore).

    In 3 parts: Pt. II begins p. 35; Pt. III begins p. 69, paging continuous,

caption titles. A later Pt. II appeared 23 Jun., 93 p. - cf. Moore (2d ed.):

207, BM(? imperfect), and NUC.

    Provenance: Kelly 1711 (ms., head of p. 15).

    Swift's Journal to Stella, 18 Feb. 1711 entry (2 months before this work),

complains of a group of over 100 country M.P.'s called the October Club,

who meet at a tavern near Parliament to drink October ale and "drive things on

to the extreams against the Whigs". These ultra-Tories, opposed to the

moderate Harley ministry, got their name Defoe says mockingly (p. 68) from their password 'October', taken from the month of the first foxhunting

season's meet. Pt. I traces the Club's source from the 1688 Revolution,

when its members were nonjurors and Jacobites, to the High-Flyers and Tack-

ers of Queen Anne's reign; Whigs became divided into Old and Modern Whigs

(p. 12-14), the Old now favouring the Tories. Pt. II parodies the customs

of the Club, describing the origin of its secret name and password. Pt.

III lists the Club's grievances against the ministry and means of redress,

and again satirizes the origin of the Club's name (p. 77-9). This is a

fine example of Defoe's gift of literary impersonation.

   NUC(Pre-1956)136:643 (also 86-p., & 93-p. Pt. II, bound together);

Morgan,BBH:N156; Moore (2d ed.):204; Hazen(Walpole):1608:9:2; Wright(Defoe),

no. 123; BPL(Defoe):151.

[Drake, James], 1667-1707.

   The memorial of the Church of England: humbly offered to the consider-

ation of all true lovers of our church & constitution. Now first publish'd

from a correct copy. To which is added an introductory preface, wherein

is contain'd the life and death of the author, and reasons for this present

publication. [London?] Printed in the flourishing year of the church. 1711.

1 p.l., xii, 57, [1] p. 8°(in 4s) 19 cm.

   Authorship: The author of the Preface, evidently close to Dr. Drake,

learned "from [Drake] himself some time before his Death" (1707), that he

was the author, assisted by Henry Poley, M.P. for Ipswich, "in the Law-Part"

of the pamphlet (p. iii). For notes on other author attributions, see 1705

ed., above.

   First pub. 1705; this (2d?) ed. includes the 1705 text, with some dash

words in text and marginalia completed or rendered more complete, thus re-

vealing 1705 anonyms; others are disclosed in the Preface. Further notes on editions appear in the 1705 ed., above.

The Preface (includes the circumstances behind the writing of the work, here reprinted posthumously only as a reminder of what the church has "miraculously escaped"; the proceedings in Parliament to which it gave rise; the search to identify the author; and, a life of James Drake): p. i-xii. Advertisement (listing 7 current pubs., with prices): last p.

For answers to this title, and description of the text, see the 1705 ed., above.

NUC(Pre-1956)375:319 (1705 and 1711 eds.); Morgan,BBH:G379 (both, & others; under: Wm. Pittis); Carabelli:116n (unspecified ed.); Rothschild: 1560 (both; under: Wm. Pittis).

[HARE, Francis, bp. of Chichester], 1671-1740.

The negociations for a treaty of peace, in 1709. Consider'd, in a third letter to a Tory-Member. Part the first. ... London: printed for A[nn]. Baldwin near the Oxford-Arms in Warwick-Lane. 1711. 1 p.l., 50 p. 8°(in 4s) 20 cm.(unbd.).

First edition; "... The second edition" has same imprint and collation.

"Postscript" (p. 50) attacks the "Ignorance and Malice of a Mercenary Scribler" in the Examiner (probably Swift), no. 4 in particular (cf. Rothschild), who had been insolent to the Duke of Marlborough says the author; but he will leave the riposte to the "Ingenious Writer" of The medley - almost certainly Arthur Maynwaring (1668-1712), who founded that Whig journal especially to pursue the Examiner (cf. DNB, 'Mainwaring').

Answered by: Remarks upon Dr. Hare's four letters to a Tory Member ... London, 1711 (NUC, 488:86), and An examination of the third and fourth letters to a Tory Member. London, 1711 (Rothschild:2202). This is further to Bishop Hare's The management of the war. In a letter to a Tory-Member. London, 1711, and his The management of the war. In a second letter ...

London, 1711, each issued in several editions (cf. NUC, 231:79). It was

followed by at least 2 more of his letters in this series: The negotiations

for a treaty of peace ... consider'd in a fourth letter to a Tory-Member.

Part II [to "Part the first", above]. London, 1711 (q.v., above), and The

reception of the Palatines vindicated: in a fifth letter ... London, 1711

(cf. Rothschild:1104 & 1105; note also his: The management of the war; in

four letters to a Tory-Member. London, printed for E. Sanger, 1711 - cf.

NUC,231:79). The letters were transl. into French as part of: Lettres et

mémoires sur la conduite de la présente guerre ..., 2 vols. La Haye,

1711-12 (cf. Morgan,N273n.).

Bound with his The negotiations for a treaty of peace ... a fourth letter

... London, 1711.

Dr. Hare was familiar with his subject from his appointment as Chaplain-

General to the British forces in the Netherlands in 1704, and he writes

here ostensibly to inform his cousin, George Naylor of Hurstmonceaux Castle,

under the date: "Decemb. 22. 1710". In tracing the close details of the

failed attempts at peace with France over the last two years, with his

criticisms and suggestions, Bishop Hare seeks to exonerate the Duke of Marl-

borough from the charge of "having contributed unnecessarily to prolong-

[ing] the War" of the Spanish Succession (p. 49).

NUC(Pre-1956)231:79 (50 p. only; also: "2d ed.", else same); BM(to 1955)

169:493 (Pt. I & II together, as above); Morgan,BBH:N273 (49 p. only; also

2d ed., 50 p., 1711) & M280 (given as 2d ed.; 1st ed. 1710, bd. with 4th

letter; another ed.: sold by E. Sanger [pub. of a work cited above], 1711);

Rothschild:1103 ("Part the first" is separate; given as 1st ed., with "Post-

script" p. 50, notwithstanding Morgan); Knuttel:15947 (2d ed.).

[_____].

The negotiations for a treaty of peace, from the breaking off of the conferences at the Hague, to the end of those at Gertruydenberg, consider'd,
in a fourth letter to a Tory-Member. Part II. ... London, printed for
A[nn]. Baldwin, near the Oxford-Arms in Warwick-Lane. 1711. 2 p.l., 72,
[2] p. 8°(in 4s) 20 cm.(unbd.)

Half-title: A fourth letter to a Tory-Member. Morgan notes "Same as
Management of the war in a fourth letter", which title has not been identified and may be confused with Hare's The management of the war; in four
letters to a Tory-Member. London, 1711 (cf.NUC,231:79).

Title list of Dr. Hare's 1st 3 letters, "Sold by E[gbert]. Sanger in
Fleetstreet": verso of half-title; list of "Books sold by E. Sanger ..."
(many of them treaties): 2 p. at end.

Answered by: Remarks upon Dr. Hare's four letter to a Tory Member ...
London, 1711 (NUC,488:86), and An examination of the third and fourth letters to a Tory Member. London, 1711 (Rothschild:2202).

Bound with his: The negociations for a treaty of peace ... in a third
letter ... London, 1711 (q.v. for other notes).

Written with the apparent motive of informing his cousin George Naylor
"of what has been done in relation to Peace" from 9th June, 1709 to 25th
July, 1710, under the date: Jan. 10. 1710/11 (p. 1). Bishop Hare provides
details and dates of conferences and communications between the parties involved in the Spanish Succession War (including the Duke of Marlborough
and the Duc d'Anjou), and vividly describes the waxing and waning of hopes
and fears in the long and bitter process of hammering out the elusive terms
of peace. He concludes by defending Marlborough from "groundless ... malicious Aspersions" of prolonging the war (p. 65ff.).

NUC(Pre-1956)231:80 (72 p. only); BM(to 1955)169:493 (Pt. I & II together); Morgan,BBH:N272 (72 p. only); Rothschild:1104; Knuttel:15948.

THE LAITY'S remonstrance to the late representation of the Lower H. of C--n [House of Convocation]: with a turn of the tables. ... London printed in the year 1711. (Price 6d.) 1 p.l., 45 p. 8°(in 4s) 20 cm.

BM and Morgan have the bookseller (publisher) as: J. Baker, but this information not found in present edition.

A reply to: Canterbury, England (Province). Convocation. A representation of the present state of religion, with regard to the late excessive growth of infidelity, heresy, and profaneness: as it passed the Lower House of Convocation of the Province of Canterbury ... London, 1711 (variant imprints and pagination, cf. NUC,25:214, under Bishop Francis Atterbury, and 94:183, under Canterbury. NUC,312:191 indicates Laity's remonstrance is a reply to "A representation of the present state of religion. 1711", but elsewhere NUC has this title with 5 variant subtitles, all 1711; that cited above is the only one to correspond with the description on p. 1 of the text: brought forth by the Lower House, without "the Seal of Both Houses".

The Convocation's Representation had documented the growth of infidelity, heresy, and 'profaneness' with numerous examples, and the writer comments on many of them throughout. For example, the Representation had said that infidelity was caused by the Rebellion (1640s and 50s), but the writer sees its origin in High-Church oppression, the "Doctrine of Arbitrary Power", Divine Right, and "Obedience without Reserve" (p. 3, 29). Other complaints in the Representation are examined (Gospel morality is undervalued, p. 10; the stage is licentious, the Lord's day neglected, p. 14-15; public impiety is rampant, p. 21; too much printing of 'loose' poems, p. 24; and

of sleeping in church, sporting with fasts, and excess in worship, p. 20,
37; country ministers inadequately paid, p. 40, are examples), and each is
challenged or resolved, from the viewpoints of dissenters, Whigs, and the
Revolution principles. There are many allusions to contemporary writings;
e.g., "the great Doctor Burnet's Archaeologia Sacra", p. 11 (probably refers to Archaeologiae philosophicae, by Dr. Thomas Burnet, 1635?-1715,
concerning the Creation, as the text suggests, p. 11); The rehearsal, a
periodical, p. 22, and also The good old cause, 1710, p. 27, both published in London, and the work of Charles Leslie, 1650-1722.

   NUC(Pre-1956)312:191; BM(to 1955)64:2747; Morgan,BBH:N341.

[LESLIE, Charles], 1650-1722.

The finishing stroke. Being a vindication of the patriarchal scheme of
government, in defence of the Rehearsals, Best answer, and Best of all.
Wherein Mr. Hoadly's examination of this scheme in his late book of The
original and institution of civil government, is fully consider'd. To
which are added, remarks on Dr. Higden's late Defence, in a dialogue between the three H-'s London: printed and sold by the booksellers of London
and Westminster. 1711. 1 p.l., [13], 239 p. 8° 20 cm.

   Page 110 misnumbered (at inner margin) 170.

   Defends Leslie's own High-Church, Tory arguments as published in his
journal The rehearsal (Aug. 1704 to Mar. 1709, repub. 4 fol. vols. 1708-9,
by Philalethes, pseud.); in The best answer ever was made [to Hoadly].
London, 1709 (q.v.); and in Best of all; being the students thanks to Mr.
Hoadly. London, 1709 (q.v.).

   A reply to: Benjamin Hoadly, The original and institution of civil government. London, 1710, and, William Higden, A defence of the View of the
English Constitution. London, 1710 (which defended Higden's own A view of

the English Constitution. London, 1709).

Caption title, p. 125: A battle royal between three cocks of the game.
Mr. Higden, Hoadly, Hottentote. As to the state of nature and of government. By a Man of Leasure. This continues, with running title: "A Battle
Royal, &c." to p. 239; running title to p. 123: "The Finishing Stroke, &c."
but paging, signature marks, and catchwords are continuous. Also pub.
separately: A new farce; represented in a battle royal ... London, 1716
(NUC(Pre-1956)328:216, but cf. also 328:214, The finishing stroke, London,
1716, with A new farce ... appended, separately paged, with special t.-p.).

"Just Publish'd. Obedience to Civil Government clearly Stated ..."
(cf. Morgan,BBH:N454 - London, printed for George Strahan, 1711): p. 239.

Bound in contemporary calf, blind-tooled in English-style panels.

Leslie's own defence discusses Hoadly's work point by point. DNB, 'Leslie', describes this as "probably the most plausible presentation ever made
of the older form of the patriarchal theory of the origin of government",
so it is presented here in some detail. After defining his terms (a modi-
fication of those in Patriarcha; or, The natural power of kings, by Sir
Robert Filmer (d. 1653), London, 1680), Leslie goes back to Adam, when Eve
and their children were subjects, and this first civil power was absolute,
none on earth being superior to it, and even commanded life and death (e.g.
Abraham and Isaac, p. 11). The authority of men over wives, children, and
servants having its origin in God, is supreme in the family (till Locke
made spouses equal, p. 9), extending through large families to small towns
etc. (citing scripture, history, the classics, and arguments in his journal
The rehearsal, of which Queen's University has complete holdings, 1704-09).
Mr. Hoadly says this is marital and paternal authority only, but his whole
argument, basing authority in the people, is in vain "till he proves the
Paternal not to be a Civil Authority" (p. 14). There follows a page-by-page

critique of Hoadly's argument, with telling wit and humour (Leslie had
studied in law), through the Old Testament from Adam to the Flood (Noah
governed his children, it was not a state of nature), Babel, the tribes,
to nations when primogeniture becomes hereditary right of succession, but
subject to forfeit to God for vice - but <u>not</u> to the mob (p. 86). If
<u>people</u> are the origin of authority then power <u>ascends</u>, from subject to
King to God (p. 87), and the equal power between individuals must lead to
anarchy (p. 25-6, 36); but primogeniture as a birthright (p. 78-86) ass-
ures the uncontested continuance of power (p. 27-35), and thus is not Hoadly's <u>marital</u> authority (what of a ruler's over his own mother? p. 77).
Leading into the doctrine of resistance to royal authority, Leslie says
that even the worst tyrant will not ruin his nation but preserve it from
anarchy and attack (p. 103-8); he then presents the usual arguments for non-
resistance to absolute power, calling this treatise "the finishing stroke"
to all arguments for resistance (p. 95; cf. also <u>The judgment of whole
kingdoms</u>, published the previous year, for the argument <u>for</u> resistance developed from the same patriarchal theory of civil government origins).

Following this (from p. 125), for the amusement of readers, the Higden
work is attacked in a dramatic farce, "A Battle Royal", beginning with a
narrative Prologue. In the farce, Whigs Hoadly and Higden are placed in
mock opposition to each other, with "Hottentote" (man in the state of nature) against both - cf. Leslie's <u>The best answer</u>. London, 1709, p. 16ff.
(<u>q.v.</u>, above).

NUC(Pre-1956)328:213 (& 1716 ed.); BM(to 1955)135:691; Morgan,BBH:N347
(123 p., thus omitting The battle royal, which is attributed to Henry
Gandy's authorship).

THE OLD and new ministry compar'd, as to these three grand points: I. Bribery and corruption from France. II. A partition of the Spanish monarchy. III. The plea of the prerogative of the Crown, in making peace, war, and alliances. ... London: printed for A[nn]. Baldwin, near the Oxford-Arms in Warwick-Lane. 1711. Price 6d. 1 p.l., 39 p. 8°(but in 4's, with turned, i.e. horizontal, chain lines) 20 cm.

Further to: Charles Davenant, Essays upon: 1. The ballance of power. London, 1701, and Edward Chamberlayne, Angliae Notitia; or, The present state of England. London, 1669; 23d edition, 1710.

Imperfect: small hole in p. 5-6, with loss of 2 or 3 words, but supplied in ms. Lacks half-title.

Rejoices at the new ministry in power (Tory), allaying fears that the old (Whig) ministry would have made "a bad Peace for Us and Our Allies" by adding Spain to the Empire and increasing the power of France, under French bribes, and would have made peace without the consent of Parliament (p. 1-3; War of the Spanish Succession). Regarding the latter, the author quotes extensively (with marginal citations) from Charles Davenant's Essays (see above), which shows that "from the Time of William the Norman downward" England has not made war, peace, treaties, etc., "without Advice of Parliament" (p. 13). English records are reviewed from Henry II to Charles II (with copious marginal sources) to see if there is any historical basis for the royal prerogative claimed (see t.-p.), and none is found (p. 13-38). The reader is invited to determine between the records of Dr. Davenant, and the contrary arguments in Dr. Edward Chamberlayne's work (see above).

NUC(Pre-1956)429:149; Morgan,BBH:N459; Rothschild:95.

THE RE-REPRESENTATION: or, A modest search after the great plunderers
of the nation: being a brief enquiry into two weighty particulars, necessary at this time to be known. I. Who they are that have plundered the
nation. II. Why they are not detected and punished. London, printed in
the year, 1711. Price one shilling. 2 p.l., 3-88, [8] p. 8° 19 cm.(unbd.)

Authorship: attributed to Daniel Defoe by William P. Trent (1862-1939),
the great American Defoe collector, who included this title in his contribution on Defoe to the CBEL. This attribution is accepted by the Boston
Public Library (in BPL (Defoe), cited below), which institution purchased
Prof. Trent's Defoe Collection, and by NUC (not LC cataloguing) and Stonehill - but not by Halkett & Laing and Moore; BM equivocates (see citations
below). In doubting Defoe's authorship I have kept in mind John Alden's
admonition in his Preface to BPL (Defoe) that collector Trent's ascrip-
tions were often made on "subjective and stylistic grounds", while bibliographer Moore made use of "objective and external evidence".

Half-title: same as t.-p., except: "... A modest search, &c."

Another edition (issue?) pub. the same year (cf. BPL(Defoe):115); this
present issue uncorrected, having: 'aganst', p. 11, line 25, and 'publitick',
p. 20, line 12.

List of "Books printed for J. Baker at the Black-Boy ..." (contemporary
religious and political titles): 6 p. at end. This list is absent from the
collation in the bibliographies checked, but the signatures (H4) are continuous.

A denunciation of 'plundering' ("a violent robbing the Innocent, under
Protection of Power, or of the Law"), with numerous examples, mostly amongst "People entrusted by the Nation" to handle "the public Treasure" (p. 4).
Bribery, breach of trust, peculation, arrogation, all are presented, with
dark allusions to recent historical instances: victualling in the navy

(p. 17), over-mustering in the army (p. 18-19), the selling of Dunkirk
(p. 25), padding the Estimates (p. 32), misappropriation to meet exigencies
of the war (p. 38-49). These corruptions often occur without representation (complaint) to proper authority, allowing the guilty to go unpun-
ished, or else the representation is simply against lack of fore-knowledge
(p. 50). The work ends with an apologue, the Commonwealth of the Brutes
(p. 79-88). Kress notes that this work is an "Attack on John Smith, Chancellor of the Exchequer, 1708-10, and other Ministers".

   NUC(Pre-1956)136:584 (under Defoe); BM(to 1955)50:126 (Defoe; & 50:127,
a variant with 'viz.' after 'known') & 201:198 (under title); Morgan,BBH:
L102 (1st ed. & "another ed.", 1711, both under Defoe); Rothschild:749
(under Defoe); BPL(Defoe):115 (under Defoe); Kress:2746 & S2557.

[TRAPP, Joseph], 1679-1747.

   Most faults on one side: or, The shallow politicks, foolish arguing, and
villanous designs of the author of a late pamphlet, entitul'd Faults on both
sides, consider'd and expos'd. In answer to that pamphlet: shewing, that
the many truths in modern history, related by the author of it, do not make
amends for his many falsehoods in fact, and fallacies in reasoning. ...
London: printed for John Morphew, near Stationers-Hall, 1711. 1 p.l.,
3-70 p. 8° 16 cm.

   Running title: An answer to Faults on both sides.

   Second edition; 1st pub. 1710, 63 p.; 3d ed. 1711, 63 p.

   Page 22 wrongly numbered 12.

   "Postscript" (a reply to: [Daniel Defoe], A supplement to the Faults on
both sides, London, 1710; not seen by Trapp till he had nearly finished his
text; "Whigish Eloquence" refuted as nonsense and lies, page by page):
p. 61-70.

A reply to: Simon Clement, Faults on both sides. London, 1710 (q.v.);
also to Defoe's Supplement: see preceding note.

Answered by: Simon Clement, A vindication of the Faults on both sides.
London, 1710. For other related works, see Appendix A.

Dr. Trapp, a High-Church Tory, says Faults on both sides is a whimsical,
"motly, party-colour'd, in-and-out Piece"; the Whigs being caught in a net,
are twisting into all shapes to escape, and although the author exposes
the Whigs (Clement wrote for Robert Harley) he does so to appear impartial, to cover his main design: to press for a coalition; the Whigs being
unable to rule alone, their next effort is for a share. The author (Clement) is a friend to dissenters and enemy to the Church, and in answering
The thoughts of an honest Tory (London, 1710; a satirical title by Whig
Bishop Benjamin Hoadly, q.v., above), he is unsure if that author is on
the same side as himself (and perhaps Dr. Trapp himself should have had
the same concern about his author, Clement) (p. 1-6). Trapp then embarks
on an ultra-conservative, paragraph-by-paragraph (page numbers cited) critique of Clements' (and Harley's) attempt to reconcile the parties (p. 6-
58). Dr. Trapp winds up his long refutation by explaining the need to dis-
entangle the fallacies from the "perplex'd Sentences" of this "very bad
Writer" who is nonetheless no fool: his moderation Trapp interprets as cunning, to be treated with contempt; and though he (Trapp) has argued against
the Whigs, he concedes that many honest people have at some time been so
called, so by Whig Trapp means only those who hold the principles he has
condemned in this author (p. 58-60).

NUC(to 1956)600:44 (InU; & 1710, 63 p., & 1711, 63 p.); BM(to 1955)71:304
(& 1710, 63 p.; 1711, 63 p.); Morgan,BBH:M713 (? has "1711" only). Cf.
Rothschild:2447 (1st ed.).

A VINDICATION of the present M--y [ministry], from the clamours rais'd against them upon occasion of the new preliminaries. ... London, printed in the year 1711. 52 p. 8°(in 4s) 19 cm.

Moore (2d ed.) disagrees with Stonehill and BPL's attribution (and Morgan's conjectural one) to Defoe's authorship; BPL suggests Richard Steele or John Asgill, while Morgan thinks Bolingbroke is possible (though the Harley-Bolingbroke Ministry is ridiculed).

BPL identifies two 52-p. variants: 1. Page 6, line 17 reads "Triffling" in one, "Trifling" in the other; p. 38, line 32 reads "Let" in one, "let" in the other. The present copy has "Triffling" and "Let". Both pub. 1711, and BPL says there were several editions in that year, one of 24 p., while Morgan notes a French transl. (Utrecht, 1712, nothing further discovered), and a 1713 ed.

The "new preliminaries" of the t.-p. are the preliminary articles of peace being negotiated with France, in the War of the Spanish Succession, and the author judges from their ambiguity and other anomalies that they are spurious (p. 5): could terms so favourable to France and so repugnant to English honour, be the work of the new (Tory) Ministry, "the best and wisest this Nation was ever bless'd with?" (p. 12). The intricacies of issues, alliances, barriers, and trade between the belligerents, are presented in rambling detail, as related to the negotiations and as exposing the falsity of the new articles (e.g. allowing the house of Bourbon to retain possession of Spain and the West Indies, p. 15): though some ministers defend them, yet were they genuine, the ablest pens would spring to their defence - such as that of "the ingenious Writer of the Tale of the Tub" (Swift; p. 30). Only with great deference to the Examiner can we now believe wrong what for so long we thought right (p. 33). This satire on the Harley administration becomes more explicit towards the end: if our good ministry <u>does</u> ignore my arguments and regard the articles as

genuine, then "we have a sure Refuge in the P--t" (Parliament; p. 51).

   NUC(Pre-1956)638:416 (52-p. ed. only); BM(to 1955)249:302; Morgan,BBH:

N163 (Defoe? Also 1711 24-p. ed., French ed., 1712, and 1713 ed.); BPL

(Defoe):183 (2 variant 1711 52-p. & 1711 24-p. eds.).

[WAGSTAFFE, Thomas], 1645-1712.

A vindication of K. Charles the martyr: proving that His Majesty was

the author of 'Eikon Basiliké. [Transliterated from Greek.] Against a

memorandum, said to be written by the Earl of Anglesey. And, against the

exceptions of Dr. Walker and others. To which is added a Preface, wherein

the bold and insolent assertions published in the passage of Mr. Bayle's

Dictionary, relating to the present controversy are examined and confuted.

The third edition, with large additions; together with some original lett-

ers of King Charles the First under his own hand, never before printed, and

faithfully copied from the said originals. ... London: printed for R[ich-

ard]. Wilkin at the King's-Head in St. Paul's Church Yard, 1711. 1 p.l.,

iii-xl, 163, [1] p. 4° 20 cm.

   Errata: p. 163.

   Running title: A vindication of King Charles I. &c.

   Third edition; 1st pub. under title: <u>A vindication of King Charles the</u>

<u>martyr</u>. London, 1693 (but cf. <u>Restitution to the royal author; or, A vin</u>-

<u>dication of</u> ... 1691; Arber,2:370).

   Pages 102-103 incorrectly numbered 103, 102, respectively.

   "Books lately printed for Richard Wilkin ..." (mostly religious): last p.

   A reply to: Anthony Walker, <u>A true account of the author of a book in</u>-

<u>tituled Eikon Basiliké</u> [transliterated]. London, 1692.

   Answered by: John Toland, <u>Amyntor</u> (see below). London, 1699.

The publications referred to on the t.-p. are Eikón Basiliké [translit-
erated; Greek: 'royal image']. The pourtraicture of his sacred majesty in
his solitudes and sufferings. [The Hague, 1648] (many reprints London,
1648), and Pierre Bayle (1647-1706), Dictionaire historique et critique.
Rotterdam, 1697 (1st English transl.: An historical and critical dictionary ... London, 1711, 4 vols.).

Bound with his: A defence of the Vindication of K. Charles the martyr.
London, 1699.

Provenance: Lieut James Macdonald late 2d Battn 84 Regt London April 1784:
t.-p. autogr.

The Preface criticizes Bayle and his Dictionaire for misrepresenting
John Milton's Eikonoklastes [transliterated; Greek: 'broken image'], in
answer to a book entit'd Eikón Basiliké [transliterated], the portrature of
his sacred majesty ... [London?], 1649 (in which Milton charges plagiar-
ism and insinuates doubt as to the King's authorship - cf. DNB, 'Milton'),
and John Toland's Amyntor: or; A defence of Milton's life. Containing ...
A complete history of ... Icon Basilike, proving Dr. Gauden, and not King
Charles ... the author of it: with an answer to all the facts alledg'd by
Mr. Wagstaf to the contrary; and to the exceptions made against ... Anglesey's Memorandum, Dr. Walker's book, or Mrs. Gauden's narrative ... London, 1699 (Carabelli:54; the title clearly indicating Toland's intentions),
as evidences against Charles I's authorship of Eikón Basiliké. In the
text Wagstaffe, a nonjuror, wants to weigh the evidence on both sides of
the controversy, he says as to whether Dr. John Gauden (1605-1662), Bishop
of Worcester (1662) or Charles I wrote Eikón Basiliké, and "to assign the
true Author of this Book, and repudiate the false one" (p. 1). First he
considers the signed ("Anglesey") Memorandum (cf. t.-p.) supposedly by
Arthur Annesley, 1st Earl of Anglesey (1614-1686), which states that Char-

les II and the Duke of York (later James II) both assured Anglesey "that

this was none of the said King's [Charles I's] compiling, but made by

Doctor Gauden, [then] Bishop of Exeter" (p. 1). Wagstaffe denounces this

undated, unwitnessed note as false (to p. 24), and then systematically dis-

mantles and discredits the whole body of evidence supporting the author-

ship of Bishop Gauden, particularly that of Dr. Anthony Walker (fl. 1660-

1692), Gauden's former curate (p. 25-6; not Sir Edward Walker, 1612-1677,

Charles I's Secretary - cf. p. 73), and of Mrs. Elizabeth Gauden, the

Bishop's widow (p. 47-8), while assembling a structure of testimony favour-

ing King Charles' authorship. Many contemporary manuscripts are trans-

cribed throughout, and the text concludes with a catalogue of editions "of

King Charles ... Book, Intituled, Icon Basilike", 30 without the concluding

prayers (1648-81), 27 with them (1649-86): p. 138-40. The letters of

Charles I in the Appendix (p. 140-63) are dated 12th July - 30th December,

1648, and several persons are referred to by number, e.g. Marlborough is

51, and King Charles himself is 39 (p. 145).

   NUC(Pre-1956)644:665 (1st-3d eds.); BM(to 1955)37:41 (under: King Char-

les; 1st-3d eds.).

[_____].

   A defence of the Vindication of K. Charles the martyr; justifying His

Majesty's title to '`Eikon Basiliké [transliterated from Greek]. In ans-

wer to a late pamphlet intituled Amyntor. By the author of the Vindication.

London, printed by W[illiam, the elder]. Bowyer, at the White Horse in Litt-

le Britain; and sold by most booksellers in London and Westminster. 1699.

1 p.l., 96 p. 4° 20 cm.

   First (and only?) edition.

   A reply to: John Toland, Amyntor: or, A defence of Milton's life. Con-

taining ... A complete history of ... Icon Basilike, proving Dr Gauden,
and not King Charles ... the author of it ... London, 1699, itself a reply to Wagstaffe's A vindication of King Charles. London, 1693 - see the
3d edition, 1711, below, for other notes.

Bound with his: A vindication of K. Charles the martyr. London, 1711
(the reason for including this 1699 work, otherwise too early for the
Catalogue).

A continuation, and largely a repetition, of Wagstaffe's evidence and
conclusions in his Vindication, intending to show Charles I and not John
Gauden as the author of the Eikoń Basiliké (transliterated from Greek),
The Hague, 1648. Here, marginal references are given to sources and page
numbers, particularly with reference to Vindication. Wagstaffe, a nonjuror,
is at pains to defend his work against the alleged misinterpretations of
Toland, who supported the Revolution Settlement.

NUC(Pre-1956)644:664; BM(to 1955)37:40.

1712

AN ACCOUNT of Charity-Schools in Great Britain and Ireland: with the
benefactions thereto; and of the methods whereby they were set up, and
are governed. Also a proposal for adding some work to the childrens
learning. ... The eleventh edition, with large additions. London,
printed and sold by Joseph Downing in Bartholomew-Close near West-Smithfield, 1712. 73, [2] p. tables. 4° 23 cm.

"Advertisement" (verso of t.-p.) invites errors to be reported for
correction "in the next Impression", to the printer (who might therefore
have also been the compiler?).

First pub. 1704 (? cf. Morgan; Kress:2534 says 1706); see also 1708,
1711 eds.

Includes lists of Charity-Schools: p. 11-14, 17-54, 57-9.

Bound with: Robert Moss, The providential division. London, 1708 (q.v.),
and 3 other works, in a vol. lettered on spine: Pamphlets on Charity
Schools.

Provenance: bound in vol. with bookplate of Mercantile Library Company,
Philadelphia.

Imperfect: p. 11-14 (B2-3) wanting.

NUC(Pre-1956)2:559 (London, 1706-10); Morgan,BBH:G4 (1704-17). Cf.
Kress: 2534 (1707), S1188 (1708), 2644 (1710), S1278 (1711).

ALL at stake Hannover or Perkin, in a letter to a country clergy-man.
London, printed for J. Baker, at the Black-Boy in Pater-Noster-Row, 1712.
(Price 3d.) 1 p.l., 3-24 p. 8°(in 4s) 19 cm.

Signed (p. 24): E.S. Authorship has not been determined.

First edition; 2d ed., under title Abel's alarm, has same imprint but:
15 p., 16°, & in verse (cf. BM & Morgan).

Concerns the terms of the Act of Settlement (1701), by which the throne
was to pass to Electress Sophia of Hanover (granddaughter of James I) or
her Protestant descendents - "Hannover" of the title-page refers to her
husband the Elector, while "Perkin" refers to the (Old) Pretender, Prince
James. Addressed to "Reverend Sir" (p. 3), the (Whig) author complains
that during a recent visit to him in the country he found him praying for
the Church before the Queen, head of that Church (p. 6-8), and he observed other seditious and near-treasonable offences, more agreeable to the
Church of Rome than to the English Church (p. 9-11). The country has social crudities too, but more intolerable are sentiments there against the
Revolution, King William, and the Protestant succession, expressed by those
who supported the "Notion of Abdication" by James II, and swore allegiance
to William and Queen Anne (p. 12-19). The author denounces the clamour
against the Dutch allies, just because the Barrier Treaty (1709, England
guaranteeing forts against the French) helps defend the Protestant succession (p. 19-20); the toasts to "the Chevalier: The Young Gentleman on
the other side, the Royal Exile" and other disguises, encouraging the Pretender; the abuse of the bishops, who uphold the Revolution; and "Defaming
the late Administration" (Whig), which is no compliment to the Tories, who

follow similar steps. The country people will be found, at last, to be

"a Pack of Designing K-ves" (knaves).

NUC(Pre-1956)9:17 (this ed. only); BM(to 1955)210:419 (1st & 2d eds.);

Morgan,BBH:0593 (under: S.,E.); Rothschild:1776.

[BURNET, Sir Thomas], 1694-1753.

The history of ingratitude: or, A second part of antient precedents for

modern facts. In answer to a letter from a noble lord. ... [London? for

J. Baker?] Printed in the year 1712 (Price 6d.) 1 p.l., 3-37, [2] p.

8°(in 4s) 18 cm.

Imprint suggested by "Books lately printed for and sold by J. Baker at

the Black Boy in Pater-noster-Row" (list; does not include the Letter from

a noble lord, so presumably supposed to have been a private letter): 2 p.

at end.

"A Letter to Mr. B- -", evidently Burnet ("not knighted until November

1745" DNB), unsigned but with the complimentary close "Your Obliged Friend,

and Humble Servant": p. 3-4. The author of this letter (if other than

Burnet) has not been discovered. "The Answer to the Letter. My Lord,"

begins on p. 5, and is signed: "My Lord, Your Lordship's sincere Friend

...", p. 37. This is a sequel to Burnet's Our ancestors as wise as we:

or, Ancient precedent for modern facts, in answer to a letter from a noble

lord ... London, A[nn]. Baldwin, 1712.

The opening "Letter to Mr. B- -" thanks Burnet for "your last to satisfy

my Curiosity" (evidently Our ancestors above), and asking for more "Exam-

ples of base Ingratitude and Folly", not in Britain this time, but from

other countries, which might parallel "the turning out of the D. of M."

(Marlborough had been dismissed by Queen Anne, 31 Dec. 1711): was there

ever in Greece and Rome such malice in repayment for such "Eminent Ser-

vices"? (Swift had attacked Marlborough in the _Examiner_ for prolonging
the war to satisfy personal avarice.) Burnet, a scholar and a Whig, responds with a 'history of ingratitude', from the Greek general Miltiades
(d.489 B.C.; in Herodotus and Thucydides - marginal sources given throughout) to Belisarius (ca.505-565; p. 25), general under the Roman Emperor
Justinian I, concluding (p. 30-37 with personal reflections on envy and
ingratitude, of which he says there is no parallel in history to the present case.

  NUC(Pre-1956)85:665; BM(to 1955)30:458; Morgan,BBH:0115 (all 1712 ed.
only, but Morgan has 34 p.).

GT. BRIT. Parliament, 1712. House of Commons.

The humble representation of the House of Commons to the Queen. With
Her Majesty's most gracious answer thereunto. London: printed for Samuel
Keble at the Turk's Head in Fleet-street, and Henry Clements at the Half-
Moon in S. Paul's Church-yard. 1712. Pr. 2d. 1 p.l. [3]-15 p. 8°
18 cm.

  Morgan has a 4-p. folio ed. of 1711, otherwise same imprint, price 2d;
NUC has a similar imprint but "1711 [1712]", price 3d, 32.5 cm., p. 121-6.
The present edition, price 2d, may not be the 1st, but BM, and NUC's
heading, agree on 1712 as date 1st pub.; in Jan. 1712, peace negotiations
began at Utrecht.

  Order of House of Commons to be printed by Keble and Clements, and no
other, signed "W. Bromley [,] Speaker": p. 15, last paragraph.

  Closely trimmed; the page no. of p. 3 may have been cropped, for it is
missing.

  The object of the representation is to argue for the conclusion of the
war (of the Spanish Succession) expeditiously and honourably, "procuring a

safe and lasting Peace" (p. 4), and to present Queen Anne with observations
and advice to this end. As background, King William's reasons for embark-
ing upon the war are given (the terms of the Grand Alliance, 1701: mainly,
to prevent the union of the thrones of France and Spain), with a survey
of the war from its 1702 start, emphasizing the unreasonably large burden
of manpower and treasure borne by England (e.g., over 8 million pounds
required for the current year, p. 5), to the unfair profit of the States-
General and Austria. The Emperor has gained large new territories, yet his
contribution falls short of that agreed upon in the original treaties (p.
10-11). The Commons seeks an equitable distribution of the burden, peace
but only a just one, and some recompense to England in the peace terms.
These ends were not furthered by the Barrier Treaty (1709, when Britain
guaranteed 19 forts to protect the Netherlands from France), which already
threatens English commerce (p. 12-14). The Queen's "Most Gracious Answer"
(p. 15) reassures the Commons: "I will give such Orders, as shall effect-
ually answer what You Desire of Me in every Particular"; she was as good as
her word: England withdrew from the war in July, 1712.

   NUC(Pre-1956)214:560 (& 1711 & Edin. 1712); BM(to 1955)63:1198 (3 1712
eds., 2 of 1715); Morgan,BBH:N312 (1711 ed. only, 4-p. folio).

[LESLIE, Charles], 1650-1722.

   Salt for the leach. In reflections upon reflections. Il lupo perde il
pelo, ma non il vitio. The wolf cannot conceal his voracity in the sheep's
cloàthing; and the butcher does but awkwardly act the shepherd. A view
of the Pontificate, p. 560. London: printed in the year 1712. 1 p.l.,
21 p. 4° 21 cm.

   Authorship: "By Charles Lesly" in an old ms. hand on t.-p., supported
by NUC and Morgan, and reference to himself ('Lesley') on p. 12.

Caption title, p. 1: Evil Be thou my Good. The subtitle reflects a similar image in Leslie's The wolf stript of his shepherd's cloathing. London, 1704, and The second part of The wolf stript ... London, 1707.

First edition? Morgan has "1710?" (before the 1712 work to which it replies!), and 3d ed., 1712; but NUC has a 1712 imprint with no edition statement, and "The 2d ed.", 1712. The present work has no edition state-ment. However, "P.S. to the Author" (of Reflections, hoping that his "late Sickness" had brought him to repentence, but in vain), p. 21 is dated: March 26. 1712 (i.e., the 2d day of the new year 1712, O.S.), so this is 1712 in both Julian and Gregorian calendars.

A reply to: Reflections upon the present posture of affairs: with relat-ion to the treaty of peace ... London, 1712 (q.v.; dealing with the strength of the dissenters), signed "M.N.", and attributed variously to William Wotton and Sir Richard Steele (cf. NUC,485:324).

A High-Church viewpoint and a satire against Whigs and dissenters - par-ticularly Presbyterians, from the words of one of whom the caption title is taken (p. 1), and whose book Reflections is identified (p. 2). Leslie assails the truth of statement after statement quoted from Reflections, citing page numbers, showing all that author's 'good' to be evil (cf. cap-tion title). Leslie defends the peace negotiations (War of the Spanish Succession), while the Whigs block them by crying for the impracticable: "no Peace without Spain" (p. 7-8); and the Occasional Conformity Act (1711), which the Whigs had long opposed along with the Low-Church bishops (p. 12; but which the Whigs passed to gain Tory support against the Peace). The satirical tone concludes: having found the cause of the 'disease' to be the Revolution, you should remove the leach; without salt to the leach soon, the nation will die.

NUC(Pre-1956)328:218 (1712, & 1712 2d ed.); BM(to 1955)212:43 (one "1712" only); Morgan,BBH:M376 (1710?, & 3d ed., 1712).

A LETTER from a Tory freeholder, to his representative in Parliament, upon Her Majesty's most gracious speech to both Houses, on the subject of peace, June 6. 1712. Giving an account of several conversations on that head. ... London: printed in the year, 1712. (Price six-pence.) iii, 4-42 p. 8°(in 4s) 17 cm.

First edition? Dated (p. 38): July 12. 1712, 6 days after the Queen's speech. Morgan notes another ed., 42 p., 1713.

"The Table" (an alphabetical index which appears to be quite unreliable): p. ii-iii; "Postscript": p. 39-42.

Imperfect: small holes in p. 35-42, with slight loss of text.

The author poses as a beleaguered Tory trying to defend his party against Whig charges, but finding defence difficult he writes his Tory Member for help. I was told, he says for example, that when it suited the Tories we dethroned James II; I replied as best I could, with care not to fall in with the Jacobites, who condemn the Revolution, implying the Queen is a usurper (p. 5). The author enters into a mock defence of the Tory stance in such current issues as: the royal prerogative (p. 6); Spain and peace with France (Spanish Succession War), quoting from several works of Dr. Charles Davenant, with titles and page numbers (p. 6-11); the peace terms and the Pretender, the Barrier Treaty (1709), and the Tory preference for the French plans in disregard of the Queen's speeches from 1701, and of the resolutions of Parliament from 1703, to 1711 (p. 13-26); the unfavourable preliminary peace terms of 1709, and the Tory wish for a separate peace - which (I said) had been answered by (Swift's) <u>The conduct of the Allies</u> (1711, in favour of peace; p. 30). The text concludes with a hollow defence of the Protestant succession from the Tory view. The Postscript continues the 'Tory' arguments for the Pretender and the Jacobites.

NUC(Pre-1956)328:675 (CtY; & 36-p. 1712 ed.); Morgan,BBH:0397 (& 1713 ed.).

MR. WALPOLE'S case, in a letter from a Tory Member of Parliament, to his friend in the country. ... The second edition corrected. [London,] Printed in the year, 1712. (Price sixpence.) 2 p.l., 44 p. 8°(in 4s) 17 cm.(unbd.).

Authorship: DNB attributes to Robert Walpole; Morgan considers this possible, but NUC, and BM (under Walpole as subject) have title entry; unlisted in Halkett & Laing and Stonehill. Also attributed to William Wagstaffe (cf. Morgan).

Half-title: The case of Mr. Walpole.

First edition was also pub. 1712, 44 p.; another ed., London, 1739, 36 p.

The letter ends on p. 24, where it is dated: London, June 5. 1712. The depositions of witnesses follow to p. 33. "Postscript" (a sequel, after Walpole was "re-elected [as MP for King's Lynn] and again expell'd", charged by nonjurors and Jacobites, against his rights, the rights of his electors who may choose their own MP even if he is a prisoner in the Tower, and of Parliament whose Members are not in office at the pleasure of the Ministry - expulsion does not incapacitate for re-election, else this is "an additional Punishment to the being expell'd", for which there is no reason nor legal precedent): p. 34-44.

Imperfect: p. 19-22 wanting; supplied in facsimile.

The author, who speaks with legal precision and rather in the voice of a Whig than a Tory MP, states that the House of Commons resolution against Walpole of "Breach of Trust, and Notorious Corruption" (in connection with forage contracts for troops in Scotland) means nothing if it can't be proved. As to the first, no Member concurred with this after Walpole had spoken in self defence and withdrawn from the House (p. 1-3). The author then reviews the circumstances and evidence, and demonstrates that the charge was never substantiated. As to "Notorious Corruption", this charge was based

on a "bare suspicion" only (p. 8), and the case against Walpole here too
is systematically demolished, with numerous quotations from the testimony of witnesses. The author is thus convinced that Walpole was not guilty of either charge (p. 18), and he could never "consent, to a five Months
Imprisonment" in the Tower, a heavy fine, expulsion from the House, and a
blackened record - excessive even if the charges had been proved. (Morgan
suggests the possibility of this being written in his own defence by Walpole while in the Tower.)

   BM(to 1955)252:425 (1st, 2nd, & 1739); Morgan,BBH:0717 (1st, 2d, & 1739);
London Library,2:1229 (1712); Kress:2796. Cf. NUC(Pre-1956)387:589 (1st
& 1739).

   A NEW project, dedicated neither to the Q---n [i.e. Queen] nor the Lord
T------r [i.e. Treasurer], nor any of the Houses of P--------nt [i.e.
Parliament] but to the Unbelieving Club at the Grecian. ... London:
printed for the booksellers, 1712. Price 4d. 1 p.l., 3-23 p. 8°(in 4s)
20 cm.

   First (and only?) edition.

   Includes bibliographical foot- and marginal-notes, mostly to the classics.

   Evidently addressed to the members of the (Whig?) Grecian Club in London,
the author says those labouring for the public good should find substantial
recompense, not just titles, which won't feed and clothe them! So, government ministers should be rewarded and encouraged by "Honourable Salaries",
and the author's 'project' is to accomplish this "without putting the Nation to One Farthing Charge" (p. 1-9). After vilifying Louis XIV with
satirical excess, warning that he would have all Britons his slaves, and
goading Whigs into mock attacks (p. 10-18), he unfolds his project: that
pensions for the English ministry be exacted from the French King (hinting

this should be part of the peace treaty, p. 20). Thus would Louis be
stung with his own weapons, and villany deserves no better; such 'bribes'
cannot corrupt true Englishmen, but will beggar our enemy, even if Louis
should gain control of Spain and its American wealth! All of which is
given with instances and precedents from Greek, Roman, and some later
history.

   NUC(Pre-1956)413:291 ("A political satire"); Morgan,BBH:0494 (both have
this ed. only).

REFLECTIONS upon the present posture of affairs: with relation to the
treaty of peace, now on foot. In a letter to a friend. London: printed
for J[ohn]. Churchill, at the Black-Swan in Pater-Noster-Row. 1712. Price
6d. 1 p.l., 3-44 p. 8°(in 4s) 18 cm.

   Attributed by Halkett & Laing to Dr. William Wotton (perhaps confusing
with his Reflections upon ancient and modern learning, London, 1694),
but signed (p. 44): Feb. 11. 1711 [O.S.]. Your very affectionate Friend
and Servant. M.N.

The Reflections, purporting to respond to the friend's request for information, concern the events of the Spanish Succession War, and the domestic
conditions for peace, on the occasion of the opening of peace negotiations
at Utrecht, Jan. 1712 (p. 3). Suspicions of a separate English peace are
heightened by the ungrateful discharge of the Duke of Marlborough, but
these must be groundless rumours against the Queen (p. 7-8). Grave fears
that Spain and its American empire may fall under the power of France are
strongly expressed (p. 8-11): the restoration of the Pretender would assure
English favours for France (p. 12); the unanimity of the church against
James II is contrasted with the dissention now, yet rather Presbyterians
than a "Popish Prince" in power, who would give Spain to the House of

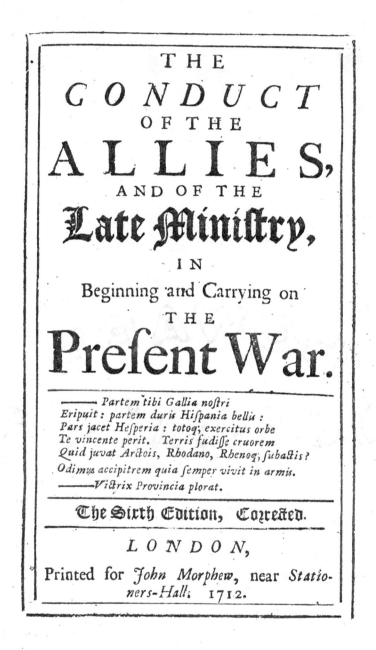

THE

CONDUCT

OF THE

ALLIES,

AND OF THE

𝕷𝖆𝖙𝖊 𝕸𝖎𝖓𝖎𝖘𝖙𝖗𝖞,

IN

Beginning and Carrying on

THE

Preſent War.

—— *Partem tibi Gallia noſtri*
Eripuit : partem duris Hiſpania bellis :
Pars jacet Heſperia : totoq; exercitus orbe
Te vincente perit. Terris fudiſſe cruorem
Quid juvat Arctois, Rhodano, Rhenoq; ſubactis?
Odimus accipitrem quia ſemper vivit in armis.
——*Victrix Provincia plorat.*

𝕿𝖍𝖊 𝕾𝖎𝖝𝖙𝖍 𝕰𝖉𝖎𝖙𝖎𝖔𝖓, 𝕮𝖔𝖗𝖗𝖊𝖈𝖙𝖊𝖉.

LONDON,

Printed for *John Morphew*, near *Statio-*
ners-Hall. 1712.

Here Jonathan Swift presents the 'official'
Tory policy regarding the War of the Spanish
Succession, and in defence of the peace
negotiations. He writes after regular consultation with Robert Harley, Earl of Oxford, and
he draws upon unpublished documents of state.

Bourbon (p. 13-18). Hopeful signs of concord between Low and High epis-
copalians are observed (e.g., passage of the Occasional Conformity Act,
1711), toleration and succession secured, and the Whigs tamed under Tory
rule (p. 21-3). It remains to settle the bitterness against nonjurors,
aggravated by Charles Leslie's pamphlets, and between the High and Low
bishops (p. 25-31). The case of Rev. James Greenshields (imprisoned in
Edinburgh for substituting English for Scottish episcopal liturgy, 1708,
but delivered by the House of Lords, 1711) is stated "at length", to show
the loyalty of the Low-Church bishops (p. 31-8). By such reconciliations,
come peace abroad and some measures against the mischief of scibblers
(Examiner, 24 Jan. 1711, cited in support), and the blessings of a good
Queen, peace at home may also be restored (p. 38-44).

   NUC(Pre-1956)485:324; BM(to 1955)200:109; Morgan,BBH:0487 (all have this
ed. only).

[SWIFT, Jonathan], 1667-1745.

The conduct of the Allies, and of the late Ministry, in beginning and
carrying on the present war. ... The sixth edition, corrected. London,
printed for John Morphew, near Stationers-Hall. 1712. 1 p.l., [2],
5-48 p. 8°(in 4s) 20 cm.(unbd.)

Authorship: all sources consulted are agreed on Swift's authorship, including Teerink-Scouten, and there are frequent references to it in Swift's
Journal to Stella throughout the autumn of 1711, though not by title till
28 Jan. 1712 (N.S.).

Also pub. under title: Good Queen Anne vindicated, and the ingratitude
... of her Whig Ministry and the Allies ... exposed, in the beginning and
conducting of the war ... By the author of the Dissertation on parties.
London, 1748 (also attributed to Lord Bolingbroke, supposed author of "A

dissertation upon parties", Craftsman, Oct. 1733-Dec. 1734, but in reality

a posthumous edition of Swift's Conduct, now to be read as critical of

Whig policy in the War of Austrian Succession; French transl., Apologie de

la Reine, Bruxelles, 1769).

Transl. into French as: La conduite des Alliez ... Liege, 1712 (with

other editions pub. here, in La Haye, and in Luxembourg); and into Spanish

as: Conducta de los Aliados ... Madrid, 1712.

First ed.: London, 1712 (i.e. 27 Nov. 1711, cf. BM, etc.; the date was

corrected in the 2d ed.), 96 p.; for the numerous subsequent editions, see

Morgan and Teerink-Scouten, but the H. David ed. of Swift's Works, "Politi-

cal tracts", vol. 6, p. ix, notes that a 2d ed. was required after 2 days,

which sold out in 5 hours whereupon a 3d was immediately printed; both had

small revisions by Harley and Swift who made final alterations 3d Dec. for

the 4th ed., after which Swift disclaimed responsibility for any changes.

There were 4,000 copies of the 5th ed., and by the 6th ed., sold out be-

fore the end of Jan. 1712, 11,000 copies had sold with a 7th ed. in the

press. Alarmed, the Whig Chief Justice Parker threatened Morphew in Dec-

ember for the name of the author, but nothing came of it - cf. Journal to

Stella, 13 Dec. 1711 and (for copies sold) 28 Jan. 1712 (N.S.).

Signature F2 signed F3.

Contents: "The Preface" (no reasonable person wants to continue the war

unless he profits from it, or ignores the cost in blood and treasure -

greater than we can bear, or is necessary; and after 10 years of victories,

how can a good peace be impossible?): [2] p. at front. After the text is

"Postscript" ("I have in this Edition [i.e. the 4th] explained three or

four Lines in the 21st Page", to remove the "Cavil" from my mention of

the succession - lines 37-40 of this 6th ed.; 4th ed., p. 27, lines 22 ff.):

p. 48.

Answered by: 1. [Francis Hare, Bp. of Chichester], The Allies and the late Ministry defended against France ... In answer to ... The conduct of the Allies. London, 1711/12 (4 vols. in 1), and French and Dutch transls.; this is probably the most comprehensive answer to Swift's arguments ever made (cf. H. David, op. cit. under edition note, above, p. xi). 2. Remarks on a false, scandalous and seditious libel, intituled The conduct of the Allies ... London, 1711. 3. Remarks upon remarks: or, The Barrier-Treaty and the Protestant succession vindicated. In answer to ... The conduct of the Allies. London, 1711. 4. A full answer to The conduct of the Allies: to which is added, some observations on the Remarks on the Barrier Treaty [also by Swift, 1712]. London, 1712, and Dutch transl. 5. The Dutch barrier our's: or, The interest of England and Holland inseparable, attributed to John Oldmixon. London, 1712, and French transls. 6. [Daniel Defoe], A further search into The conduct of the Allies ... London, 1712; also attributed to Swift himself (another 1712 ed. has title: A farther search ...); reprinted in Somers tracts, 1815, 13:182-205, where it is described as "a sort of continuation" of Swift's Conduct, but by an "inferior hand". 7. [Daniel Defoe], A defence of the Allies and the late Ministry ... Being a detection of the manifest frauds ... in ... The conduct of the Allies ... London, 1712. Most of these answers (and undoubtedly there are others) appeared in more than one edition; cf. NUC and Teerink-Scouten for further bibliographical details.

Further to this is 1. [Charles Leslie], Natural reflections upon the present debates about peace and war. ... London, 1712; also attributed to Richard Steele; besides Swift's Conduct, this refers to Defoe's A defence of the Allies and to A vindication of the present M--y. 2. "An appendix to The conduct of the Allies; and Remarks on the Barrier Treaty", by Swift, in the Examiner, vol. 3, no. 16, 16 Jan. 1713 (N.S.).

Imperfect: small strip detached from outer margin, p. 7-9, with slight

loss of text.

The Grand Alliance (1701) was formed, to prevent the union of the thrones

of France and Spain (which would upset the balance of power in Europe),

between England, Holland, the Empire, joined by Prussia, Hanover, the Pala-

tinate, and (1703) Portugal and Savoy; on the other side in this War of the

Spanish Succession (1702-13) were France, Cologne, and Bavaria. The "late

Ministry" of the title is the Whig one, in power in 1702 and dominant 1708-

10. Swift's tasks, as propagandist writer for Robert Harley (Earl of Ox-

ford), Lord Treasurer and Tory leader, were to dispose public opinion,

"half bewitched against a peace" (Journal to Stella, 30 Oct. 1711),

towards peace negotiations, and to defend the new Ministry as it began

(1711) unilaterally to end Britain's part in the war: the conference opened

at Utrecht Jan. 1712, and was signed there, 1713. Swift's pamphlet, imm-

ediately popular (see 'editions' note, above), was composed in consultation

with Harley and other Ministers (cf. Journal to Stella, autumn, 1711;

numerous meetings reported), in time for the new session of Parliament at

the end of November, and it was the 'official' statement of Tory policy

regarding the war. Most of the arguments had already appeared in the col-

umns of Swift's Examiner, the 'official' journal of the Tory perspective.

Swift opens by reflecting upon the various motives for war in general,

and the prudent conditions of peace in a confederate war. Present condi-

tions are plainly visible in his arguments, so that when he turns to

review specific English wars, his factional preconceptions are ready in

place: these wars yielded so little, for the great loss of blood and trea-

sure (p. 5-9). The Grand Alliance and the conduct of the ensuing war are

described in close detail, much of it drawn from hitherto unpublished state

documents to which Swift had special access: the Dutch needed a barrier

against France, the Emperor desired to recover the throne of Spain, Portugal needed naval protection - all had good motives, and good subsidies;
we saw (says Swift) only the danger to the balance of power in Europe if
France and Spain were united under the Bourbons; so, we went to war, as
principals, at the cost now of 60 million pounds (so we are worse off
than anyone, including our enemies), instead of as auxiliaries pursuing
our own ends (p. 12). Ten years of land war, with us bearing the major
costs, and now crippled by public debt, what use have our military victories been to us? As a maritime power we could have got the West Indies and
the trade of America, compelling France and Spain to peace on our terms;
instead, they have the trade, and our Allies have broken the treaties and
placed the war burden unfairly on us. Then comes an analysis of the various treaties, with Portugal, Holland, Prussia, the Emperor, etc. (p. 20
ff.), showing how the terms were all in favour of the other Allies, not
England, and how each has broken these terms (especially the Dutch, in
failing to keep their quotas) to suit themselves, and at England's cost.
Our Queen keeps paying, and while our Allies request ever more from us, they
gain new provinces from our victories. "If, after all our Success, we
have not made that use of it ... by what Motives ... we are thus become the
Dupes ... of Europe?" Is England safe in the hands of those who act by
such motives? (p. 31). Those in power got the profit, not the nation;
these "Monied Men" traded in stocks, and in loans at great interest, and
their "perpetual Harvest is War", so these Whigs must decline peace (p. 32-
3). They applied to the Queen not to change Ministers, but she was out
of patience: by such means "a G-----l [i.e. General, the Duke of Marlbor-
ough] during pleasure, might have grown into a G-----l for Life, and a
G-----l for Life into a King" (p. 34; intimates the Tory charge that
Marlborough sought to be Protector of a commonwealth). I address not those

who want peace only if Spain is restored to the Empire, but those, Whig or
Tory, who want "the Welfare of their Country"; for this condition on Spain
is a new one, created by Whigs, and not in "The Eighth Article of the
Grand Alliance" (which is then transcribed, p. 35-6; though Bp. Hare in his
answer - no. 1 above - called it a misleading translation), nor was it required in earlier treaties. Moreover, since the Emperor's death (Joseph
I, 1711), the views of many states in Christendom have changed, and so
should our view (p. 39); Swift then shows that the balance of power will
not be disturbed with Spain and France together). Though discretion and
danger held me from speaking sooner, our ruinous public debt make peace
imperative (the situation is then vividly portrayed as desperate); and
don't be misled that France is weak: Louis XIV has rallied from his defeats,
and the wealth of the West Indies has kept his debts light. Lastly (p.
46-8), consider the danger from the North, of England, Hanover, and Prussia
forced into a new war to maintain the balance of power in Scandinavia,
and the advantage this will give to France if the present war continues.
No, even though the Tories might gain a private advantage, it is better
for Britain to accept reasonable terms of peace "without adding Spain to
the Empire", than to risk a worse situation forcing upon us a worse peace.

NUC(Pre-1956)579:165 (1st-8th, & Edinburgh & Dublin eds., 1711, 1712,
etc.); BM(to 1955)233:440-41 (1st, 2d, 4th, 6th, 7th eds.); Morgan,BBH:
N569 (1st-5th, 1711; 6th, 7th, 1712; 8th, 1713; & many "corrected" eds.;
& 5 Dublin eds.; etc.); Teerink-Scouten:539 (all eds. & transls.). Cf.
Rothschild:2025-30 (1st, 2nd, 4th, 5th, & Dublin); London Library,2:1050
(5th ed.).

[TRAPP, Joseph], 1679-1747.

The character and principles of the present sett of Whigs. ... The
third edition corrected, and enlarged. London, printed for John Morphew,
near Stationers-Hall, 1712. Price 3d. 1 p.l., 3-23, [1] p. 8°(in 4s)
19 cm.

The 1st and "The 2d ed.": 1711, else same imprint, but 48 p. (cf.NUC).

List of "Books Printed for and Sold by John Morphew, near Stationer's-
Hall" (mainly political and religious): 1 p. at end.

The author, a Tory High-Church pamphleteer who aided Dr. Sacheverell at
his trial (some references to Sacheverell: p. 7, 11, 13), defines the kind
of Whig he addresses: he makes chaos by placing all power with the people,
who alone shall judge what is for the common good at any given moment:
"The Governed are the Governours", so there is no government at all (p. 5).
These Whigs, mostly upstarts without family or title, assert "all Honour
and Greatness [to] consist in nothing but in getting Money" (p. 7). Enemies to monarchy, they pretend patriotism while afflicting the nation with
debts, prolonging the war (of Spanish Succession), refusing to lend money
for it and thus alienating Spain (p. 8-10). Jacobites all, yet they accuse
Tories of Jacobitism, using the Revolution principles against Scripture
while seeking preferment in the Church (p. 16). They hate episcopacy and
its Courts, and the 2 universities, and are often deists, placing these
beneath their clubs and theatres (p. 21-3) - all illustrated with contemporary examples. They should "renounce the Pretender, as heartily as they
do our Saviour". DNB states that on 14 May, 1711, Swift took this pamphlet in manuscript to the printer and described it as "a very scurvy piece"
('Trapp').

  NUC(Pre-1956)600:43 (all 3 eds.); BM(to 1955)256:394 (all 3 eds.);
Morgan,BBH:N615 (1st & 2d eds., 1711); Rothschild:2448 (3d ed.).

[_____].

Her Majesty's prerogative in Ireland; the authority of the government

and Privy-Council there; and the rights, laws, and liberties of the City

of Dublin, asserted and maintain'd. In answer to a paper falsly **intit**-

uled, The case of the City of Dublin, in relation to the election of a Lord-

Mayor and sheriffs of the said city: A true state of this matter being ab-

solutely necessary, for the information of all Her Majesty's subjects in

Great Britain, as well as in Ireland. ... London, printed for H[enry].

Clements, at the Half-Moon in St. Paul's Church-yard. 1712. 1 p.l., 53,

[1] p. 8° 19 cm.

   Authorship: BM, DNB, and Halkett & Laing; 'attributed' in NUC.

   First (and only?) edition.

   List of "Books printed for H. Clements ..." (mostly religious): last p.

   A reply to: The case of the City of Dublin, in relation to the election

of a Lord-Mayor ... (cf. t.-p., but unfound in NUC, BM). It was earlier

presented to the Queen as a petition, and published while still under her

consideration (cf. p. 1).

   Dr. Trapp, a High-Church Tory and former Chaplain to Sir Constantine

Phipps, Irish Lord-Chancellor, 1711, here contends that the work he answers

does not speak for Dublin, but is a "prevaricating Representation of some

particular Persons" only (p. 2). He closely dissects the paper on Dublin

in the context of the New Rules of 1672 (p. 3) against Popery and insurr-

ection, for the support of the monarchy, and particularly for regulating

civil government and elections in the city, concerning which the author in-

dulges in much fine logic-chopping. Many instances are invoked to supp-

ort points of contention, from Queen Elizabeth's time (p. 16) to 1711. The

author supports monarchy, episcopacy, the constitution, and the Hanoverian

succession (p. 45), but condemns the faction in Dublin for disregarding

Council authority, infringing on royal prerogative, and "trampling upon

the Rights of our Fellow-Subjects" (p. 41). This is largely of ephemeral,

local factional interest, and includes the names of numerous civic off-

icials, especially that of Robert Constantine, Senior Alderman, and supp-

orter of the Protestant succession, who was passed over in the 1711 elect-

ion for Lord-Mayor (p. 51-2).

   NUC(Pre-1956)600:44; BM(to 1955)240:907; Morgan,BBH:036 & *0691a.

[WAGSTAFFE, William], 1685-1725.

The representation of the loyal subjects of Albinia. ... [s.l.; Lon-

don,] Printed in the year 1712. Price two pence. 1 p.l., 3-14 p. 8°

19 cm.(unbd.)

Authorship: Halkett & Laing, 5:98; also attributed to Defoe (cf. Morgan),

but this is not supported in Moore (2d ed.); and to Swift (cf. Teerink-

Scouten), considered likely by some (cf. DNB, 'Wagstaffe').

First edition; an NUC note to The second representation indicated a 3d

ed., 1712, and there was a Dublin reprint, 1712 (cf. NUC).

Further to this is his: The second representation of the loyal subjects

of Albinia. London, 1712 (q.v.), issued in a new edition (cf. BM) with

the title: A representation of the loyal subjects of Albinia, to their sov-

ereign, upon his concluding a treaty of peace with his foes. London [1715?

cf. BM, but could be 1714 from Peace of Utrecht date and gender of pronoun

in title]. Teerink-Scouten says this is another ed. of A representation

... 1712: (i.e., The representation?).

Set in epistolary form, this is addressed "Most Gracious Sovereign",

Queen Anne, her subjects probably being those of England (anciently called

Albion, though Albany was used for Scotland). Offering thanks for measures

that may soon end the long war (Spanish Succession), the writer, a High-

Church physician and hater of Whigs (cf. DNB) abhors the Whig opposition
to peace, and all who dispute the Queen's exercise of her prerogative as
an "Arbitrary Proceeding". What is the aim of this faction who advised
the war, conducted it with fraud, and would continue it for their gain and
our misery? (p. 3-6). If they opposed the peace as dishonourable (this
was a Whig argument), they might be excused; but knowing their terms are
impossible, they insist on them. Shall we rather be ruined by war taxes?
They fear exposure of mismanagement and loss of their plunder, and while
we do thank our General (Marlborough) for his victories, his embezzlement
must not be "screen'd from Justice". All must be held accountable. We've
suffered enough under the (Whig) Junto's taxes and mismanagement; we represent to your Majesty the (Tory) "Good Designs for the Common Cause"
(p. 11), and beseech you to guard against the rebels, who speak now as they
did when your royal grandfather was murdered. We hope for a secure Church,
taxes not embezzled, and a good peace - else war, but with prudent management; anyway, we submit to your Majesty as God's laws oblige (p. 12-14).

   NUC(Pre-1956)644:667 (CLU-C; & Dublin ed., 1712); BM(to 1955)251:573
(but 13 p.); Morgan,BBH:0712; Rothschild:2468; Teerink-Scouten:865.

[_____].

The second representation of the loyal subjects of Albinia. ... London:
printed in the year, 1712. 1 p.l., 3-15 p. 8° 18 cm.(unbd.).

   Authorship: NUC & BM; see also notes to Wagstaffe's The representation of
the loyal subjects of Albinia ([London] 1712), above.

   First edition; a subsequent edition (probably the 2d) has the title: A
representation of the loyal subjects of Albinia, to their sovereign, upon
his concluding a treaty of peace ... London: [1715? evidently after George
I's accession & Treaty of Utrecht, but could be 1714], 23 p., and a further

edition with the same title and no. of pages has the imprint (cf. NUC):
London [172-].

Further to his: The representation of the loyal subjects of Albinia. [London,] 1712 (q.v., above).

Addressed to "Most Gracious Sovereign" in epistolary form, as was the earlier Representation, this pamphlet appeals to Queen Anne in a sycophantic style for peace, in opposition to the Whig Junto who, in wanting to continue the war (of Spanish Succession), "have brought us upon the very Brink of Ruine" (p. 4). Wagstaffe, a physician and an enthusiastic supporter of the High-Church, continues his argument in the same tone as in his first Representation: a faithful Ministry seeks to "deliver Nations from Wars and Bloodshed", while the Whigs libel your Majesty by voting for the "Defence of Robbery" and by subverting the church - the very people on whom you have "bestowed the greatest Honours" (e.g. Marlborough) and whom you generously refrain from chastising (p. 6-9). There is no language to describe such people, nor punishment too severe for them, and your subjects, in "all the Provinces of Albinia", await "Your avenging Sword" (p. 10-12). We are sworn to protect your title while you live, against any Pretender, as also to support any of royal blood who succeeds you by law and your desire. "We know no other Obedience than what we owe Your Majesty", and your successors having the same authority shall have the same obedience. You have not sought war for conquest or encroachment; your aims are our trade, security, and liberty, the quiet possession of our rights, and the "Happiness of Your People"(p. 13-15).

NUC(Pre-1956)644:667 (all 3 eds.); Morgan,BBH:0713. Cf. BM(to 1955) 251:573 ([1715?] ed. only).

1713

AN ALARM to the people of England: sounded in an oration from the top of
St. Paul's Cathedral, London. By a Protestant of the Church of England.
... London: printed for J[ames]. Roberts, near the Oxford-Arms in Warwick-
Lane. [1713?] (Price Three-Pence) 1 p.l., 22 p. 8°(in 4s) 19 cm.

Imprint date: '1712' in NUC, '1712?' in Morgan; but referring to the imprint address, 1713 was the first year printer/bookseller James Roberts
operated in Warwick Lane (cf. Plomer).

Paper browned throughout.

A rhetorical warning that, though a glorious Queen reigns and the succession is secure, yet traitorous murmerings are abroad supporting the Pretender (James, Prince of Wales, the Old Pretender, 1688-1766), requiring
an alarm. Freedom was endangered before, but the people rallied, and were
saved by King William; threatened again, by powerful Jacobites, nonjurors,
and "Passive-Obedience Men", we must be alerted to the dangers of Popery
(p. 7-8). Formerly the press was restrained from alarms against Papal bondage; now, we don't need "the Approbation of the Examiner, or some other
such mercenary Tool, who is paving the Way for Popery and the Pretender"
(p. 11). Better to see valiant Marlborough calumniated than to lose the
freedom to give alarms, earn salaries, own goods, and to risk our lives;

so let's be ready for sacrifices, relying on the protection of a free
Parliament - tell your representatives that you want liberty and good Queen
Anne, not the Pretender. There's no proof he has royal blood, and anyway
we must prefer the greater good of the constitution to the hereditary
right and tyranny, whatever a recent impudent Templar (probably Charles
Leslie) has published (p. 16-19). Avoid "that Trumpeter of Popery and
Arbitrary Power the Examiner" as you would a mad dog, and pray for the
blessings of Queen Anne, and the House of Hanover thereafter, Amen (p. 20-
2).

   NUC(Pre-1956)6:625;. Morgan,BBH:P12 (this ed. only in both).

THE CHARACTER of a modern Tory; in a letter to a friend. By which it
is evident, that he is the most unnatural and destructive monster (both
in religion and politicks) that hath yet appear'd in any community in the
world. ... London: printed for T[homas]. Harrison, at the south-west
corner of the Royal Exchange, in Cornhill; and A[nn]. Baldwin, near the
Oxford-Arms in Warwick-lane, 1713. Price Three Pence. 1 p.l., 3-24 p.
8°(in 4s) 18 cm.

Although reluctant to disturb the quiet of his friend's retirement from
public life, the author responds to his request for a Tory character in a
lively, ranting manner, dividing them into those "deluded" (who thought
Church and Queen in danger from a Whig commonwealth with Marlborough as
Protector, and France and Spain under the Bourbons), and the modern "Rigid
Tories" (p. 1-12), his subject here. The modern Tory has "an English Face,
a French Heart, and an Irish Conscience", a monster with no brains, who
would be groom when Popery and tyranny are matched (p. 10-12). He would
destroy our constitution, religion, and laws: "Monarchy is Jure Divino",
so he prefers slavery to liberty, Magna Charta being seditious, and law

courts a waste of time (p. 15). He assails dissenters and cries for Dr.

Sacheverell, the surplice, the sign of the cross, and bowing at the word

Jesus, using a new language from the Examiner (Swift's journal), but fear-

ing God not so much as Parliament (p. 16-21). The work ends with "Verses

out of the 3d Volume of State-Poems, Page 422" (p. 22-4), which rail against

the Tories for fomenting strife.   Several arguments resemble those in Dr.

Sacheverell's picture drawn to life: or, A true character of a high-flyer,

London, 1710 (cf. Madan(Speck):488).

NUC(Pre-1956)103:660; Madan(Speck):1097 (both: this ed. only).

[DUNTON, John], 1659-1733.

Neck or nothing: in a letter to the Right Honourable the Lord ———[Ox-

ford] Being a supplement to the Short history of the Parliament. Also

the new scheme (mention'd in the foresaid History) which the English and

Scotch Jacobites have concerted for bringing in the Pretender, Popery and

slavery. With the true character or secret history of the present minist-

ry. Written by his grace John Duke of ------ [i.e. Marlborough]. ... Lon-

don, printed by T. Warner near Ludgate. 1713. 1 p.l., 3-60 p. 8°(in 4s)

18 cm.

Authorship: Halkett & Laing,4:161, gives Dunton's The life and errors of

John Dunton, p. 744, as source; there was an ed. of 1818 (cf. DNB).

Signed (p. 60): John Duke of ....

First edition, of many (cf. NUC, below); a letter within is dated 10 Oct.

1713: p. 53.

Page 44, 45 and 48 misnumbered 42, 47, and 46, respectively.

Includes bibliographical footnotes and references in the text.

This is not the same work as Samuel Wesley (1691-1739), Neck or nothing:

a consolatory letter from Mr. D-nt-n [i.e. Dunton] to Mr. C-rll [i.e.

Curll]. London, 1716. (In verse).

A reply to: Robert Walpole, A short history of that Parliament which committed Sir Robert Walpole to the Tower, expelled him [from] the House of Commons, and approved of the infamous Peace of Utrecht. London, 1763 (1st pub. 1713, q.v., below, under a shorter title). Morgan notes that the following titles by Dunton (and there are other 'Neck or nothing' titles still, in NUC) "are called parts of this pamphlet": Queen Robin: or, The second part of "Neck or nothing". London, 1713; NUC & BM: [1714]; The shortest way with the King: or, Plain English spoke to His Majesty (the 3d part). London, [1714?]; King George for ever; or, Dunton's speech ... London, [1715]; The neck-adventure; or, The case and sufferings of Mr. John Dunton. London, [1715]; The mob war; or, A detection of the present state of the British nation. London, [1715?]. Some information from NUC.

Clearly not written by Marlborough (cf. p. 59-60), and the many references to Dunton, usually flattering (e.g. p. 30, 55) are suggestive. Addressed by a Whig to several members of the Tory ministry. One in particular is the Tory leader Robert Harley: the title Rt. Hon. perhaps to him as head of the "Present Ministry" (t.-p.) and certainly as a peer (created Earl of Oxford May 1711); but the caption title of the 20th ed., [171-?] has "... a letter to the Earl of Ox-rd" (cf. NUC, 152:223), and other clues throughout support this attribution. Harley is condemned for "the late separate and Pernicious Peace" with France (Spanish Succession War), venturing neck or nothing in pursuit of private gain to the ruin of his country; so the author here ventures his neck to save his country, in defence of the Queen's "Just Title" to the throne, by "setting your Neck-Adventures ... in a true light" (p. 5-8). The other Tory minister particularly addressed is Henry St.-John (Viscount Bolingbroke), who negotiated the separate peace, 1712, at Utrecht, 1713, and privately with the Pretender. He is cruelly maligned

as "Leud Harry", a debauched drunkard, in a supposed letter of 2 Oct. 1713
(p. 25-38). After p. 31, Dunton's principal antagonists are referred to
as O---- and B----. The author is chiefly alarmed by the growth of Perk-
inism (p. 57) and a Jacobite plot (in Paris, p. 10; in Scotland, p. 21-2,
43, 51, 53) to return the Pretender, bringing Popery and slavery (p. 43,
etc). Dr. Henry Sacheverell is deeply involved in the plot (p. 9, 10, 18,
30, 41, etc), and Charles Leslie the noted nonjuror is tutoring the Pretender in readiness (p. 18). All this is proved in Dunton's journal Court-
spy, and other works cited, encouraged by French bribes (p. 10-12, 15n.),
the premature "Jacobite peace" (p. 19), the delay in demolishing Dunkirk
(p. 6, 13, and quotations on p. 43-7 [i.e. 45] from John Toland's Dunkirk
or Dover, 1713, q.v. below), all giving strength to France and upsetting
the balance of power (p. 17-18). There is much repetition of points of
contention throughout. At the end is an allusive passage on authorship,
stating that the writer, unlike "Robin and Harry" (Robert Harley and Henry
St.-John), has an entirely English heart and would never sell his religion
and country for "Luidores" (French bribes).

   NUC(Pre-1956)152:222 (& 20th ed., 171-?); BM(to 1955)117:423 (12°);
Morgan,BBH:P212 (& another ed., 3 pts., [1713]); London Library, 1:718.

[LESLIE, Charles], 1650-1722.

   The right of monarchy asserted; wherein the abstract of Dr. King's book,
with the motives for the reviving it at this juncture are fully considered.
... London: printed, and sold by John Morphew, near Stationers-Hall.
1713. 1 p.l., [14], 96 p. 8° 19 cm.

   First (and only?) edition.

   The 14 preliminary pages consist of The Preface (8 p.), A Hint to the
Reader (2 p.), and Contents (a page-by-page outline of the text, 4 p.).

A reply to: William King, <u>An answer to all that has ever been said ...</u>
<u>in favour of a Popish Pretender. Exhibited in an abstract of The state of</u>
<u>the Protestants of Ireland</u> ... London, 1713, itself an abridgement by other
hands (cf. Leslie's Pref.) of <u>The state of the Protestants of Ireland under</u>
<u>the late King James's government</u> ... London, 1691 ('late' referring to
his kingship; James II d. 1701).

The Whigs must be desperate to revive a 20-year-old legend "to refresh
their Drooping Cause", says Leslie, a nonjuror, and Abp. King won't thank
the new editors for waking it from its long sleep; evidently they haven't
read the answers, showing it to contain "many Errors". The Preface continues, setting the style and subject of the book: the "Presbyterian Inqui-
sition" against episcopal clergy in Scotland, 1688-9, was more persecuting
than anything James II did to the Church of Ireland, and the Catholic maj-
ority would have made it "more Just to set up Popery in Ireland, than Presbytery in Scotland".

In the text, Leslie applies his lawyer's mind to a page-by-page analysis
of the <u>Answer,</u> by William King, Archbishop of Dublin (Anglican). He separ-
ates principles from facts, first showing Dr. King's main principle as
that all power rests in the people, to whom kings are deputies (p. 2). All
the Whig Revolution principles stemming from this are examined, being cast
under Leslie's absolutist, <u>de jure</u> convictions; but he cleverly skirts
open disloyalty and Jacobitism, referring Abp. King's principles to scripture and history (p. 28-36). Turning to Dr. King's facts, Leslie argues
that the Protestants in Ireland fared worse under William III than under
James II, whose "Tenderness" and "strict Regard to Justice, could weigh
nothing ... with this Author", himself guilty of treason against his King
(p. 37-55). James II resisted Catholic pressure to repeal the Acts of
Settlement (Ireland:1652, 1662, 1665), and move against the Protestants,

but the author disregards this (p. 62-3). Only nonjurors have kept their

oaths of loyalty, says Leslie, referring to James rather than William.

After further counter arguments against Dr. King, with instances of King

James' mercy and moderation (e.g. at the Battle of the Boyne, 1690) and

resistance to French enticements, as against the ravages by King William's

men and other Protestants, of the Catholics (p. 69-84), Leslie concludes

with a defence of King James' policies in England ("Pepys Memoirs" prove

James did not allow the navy to decay, p. 85), asserting that whenever

James did what William and Protestants do it is misrepresented as tyranny:

"let Truth prevail"! (p. 84-96).

NUC(Pre-1956)328:218; Morgan,BBH:P343 (this ed. only).

A LETTER to the gentlemen and freeholders of the county of Dorset, con-

cerning the next election of Members of Parliament for the said county.

... London, printed for, and sold by A[nn]. Baldwin at the Oxford-Arms in

Warwick-lane. 1713. 2 p.l., 5-40 p. 8° 17 cm.

Half-title: A letter to the gentlemen and freeholders, &c.

First (and only?) edition.

Imperfect: upper margin closely trimmed, some page numbers wanting, all

or in part.

The author supports succession through Princess Sophia and her son George

Louis, Elector of Hanover (later George I); he opposes the Pretender, even

though it's heard he has renounced his Romish religion - a French trick!

(p. 8). All voters should inquire of those who might represent them in

Parliament whether they value Her Majesty, our constitution in church and

state, and the Hanoverian succession, etc., before voting for the 20 good,

moderate Members from Dorset (p. 9-11). Rampant poverty must be tackled,

perhaps by resettlement in Newfoundland ("our best Nursery for good Seamen") after the peace (p. 12). There follows a passionate remonstrance against

the tyranny of Popery, the dangers from it in England past and present,

the blessings of liberty, cautions against the Pretender, the restrictive

doctrines of the episcopal church (from absolution to absolutism; p. 14-

25), and other reminders (of personal qualities too) of considerations in

selecting representatives for a Parliament which must negotiate the peace

with a powerful and unscrupulous France. There are notes favouring Whigs

over Tories (p. 28-9), warnings against the Tory influence of the Examiner

(Swift's journal), and of Oxford (Robert Harley) and Bolingbroke (Henry

St.-John) with the Queen, all disposed towards the Pretender (p. 38):

"Let not the Influence and Threats of great Men in Power byass you in your

Choice" of representatives, for only Parliament can "retrieve the Glory

and Honour of the British Nation" (p. 39-40).

   NUC(Pre-1956)329:84 (CtY; this ed. only); Morgan,BBH:P354 (this ed. only,

but "12°").

   OBSERVATIONS upon the state of the nation, in January 1712/3. The second

edition. London: printed for John Morphew, near Stationers-Hall. 1713.

Price Six-pence. 1 p.l., 33 p. 8°(in 4s) 19 cm.

   Authorship: Halkett & Laing, 4:228, Stonehill:2014, and Morgan,P447 att-

ribute this to Daniel Finch, Earl of Nottingham, but DNB, 'Finch', says

this is not possible because the tract "maintains the ulta low-church view

of church government and doctrine"; also, the note to Somers tracts re-

print of The memorial of the state of England, in vindication of the Queen,

the Church, and the administration, by Nottingham [i.e., by John Toland,

q.v. above, 1705, and Carabelli:115] (which DNB, 'Finch', incorrectly states

is a re-issue of Observations upon the state of the nation, 1st ed., 1713),

points out that Observations attacks "the measures against occasional conformity, which the Earl of Nottingham had so actively furthered" (1814, 12:527; but cf. comment at end of the annotation, below). BM,219:716, states that Observations was "wrongly attributed to D. Finch, Earl of Nottingham", while in Hazen(Walpole)1608:14:7, Horace Walpole says this is unquestionably Nottingham's. Also attributed in Morgan to Dr. William Wotton, 1666-1727.

First edition also pub. 1713, as is evident from the date in the title; that ending the text (p. 33) is: Jan. 13. 1712/3.

Answered by: 1. George Sewell, Remarks upon a pamphlet entitul'd [Observations upon the state of the nation ...] London, 1713 (brackets enclosing Observations ... appear on the t.-p.); 2d ed., 1713; 3d ed., 1714 (cf. BM,219:716; & NUC,540:112). 2. Not——am [i.e. Nottingham] politicks examin'd, being an answer to a pamphlet intituled, Observations upon the state of the nation. London, 1713 (cf.BM,65:3860 and 73:132).

The author believes in loyalty to Queen and Ministry but the right of moderate dissent, then expresses his thoughts on this the eve of a separate peace treaty with France (concluded 11 April; Spanish Succession War), as Parliament is about to reassemble (Jan. 1713). He thinks the peace "may not produce those lasting good effects" for which the Tory Ministry hopes (p. 3). The great reason for peace on the present terms is that otherwise the balance of power in Europe would be upset by the union of the thrones of France and Spain; but consider: Emperor Charles V possessed the Netherlands, the large part of France called Burgundy, Spain and its empire, etc., while his subservient brother Ferdinand was "King of the Romans" and of parts of Germany; yet Francis I, ruler of only the rest of France, held Charles V at bay for a long period (p. 3-5). Similarly Henry VIII of England, with a smaller fleet than the Emperor's, controlled the balance of power; and England was weaker then, so Queen Anne has greater control (p. 7).

France and Spain will stand together anyway, whether or not their crowns
are united, because of close blood and trade relations, and to prevent
civil war (p. 16). The author is indignant at the abuse of the Dutch;
though our rivals in trade, they have opposed Spain and upheld Protestantism, as have "Hanover and Brandenburgh", and all must stay united against
France: yet, if any loyal Tory "declare against a peace with France" now,
he is vilified in print and declared a member of the 'Calves-Head Club'!
(formed late 17th century to ridicule Charles I, named for the calves'
heads used to represent that king on the anniversary of his execution;
suppressed 1735; p. 19-23). Confidence in everything Tory can ruin us, but
the Ministry is for the Protestant succession, against the Pretender: God
bless them for upholding the Church of England, monarchy, and episcopacy,
while the previous Whig Ministry failed to defend the Church (e.g., at
Dr. Sacheverell's impeachment, p. 25), and even allowed in print the work
of such freethinkers as Toland. Abroad, we have lost old friends without
gaining new ones, for France will not support the Church of England. In
Scotland half the Established Church ministers are busy nonjurors, while
juror's churches are deserted; Jacobitism flourishes, and Tory and Whig
mean only for or against the Pretender (p. 30). Parliament must remedy this
soon. The Act to prevent occasional conformity by dissenters was passed
(1711) with Whig support, showing they are friends of "our Church". With
the Protestant succession secured by Whigs and Tories, the Dutch will be
our friends. When peace revives us from the costly war we need not fear
France or the Pretender, and the Queen will listen to Parliament (p. 31-3).
(This does not appear to be "the ultra low-church view" of DNB, nor an attack on "the measures against occasional conformity" of Somers tracts noted
above. Evidently more has to be done in establishing authorship of this
work.)

NUC(Pre-1956)426:96 (2d & 3d eds., 1713); BM(to 1955)65:3860 (2d ed.
only); Morgan,BBH:P447 (2d only); London Library (Suppl. 1920):532 (2d ed.).
Cf. Hazen(Walpole)1608:14:7 & Rothschild:1474 (both 1st ed. only).

[RIDPATH, George], d. 1726.

Some thoughts concerning the peace, and the thanksgiving appointed by
authority to be observed for it. In a letter from an Elder to a minister
of the Church of Scotland. ... [s.l.; London?] Printed in the year 1713.
1 p.l., 3-31 p. 8°(in 4s) 18 cm.

First (or 2d?) edition; 3d ed., 1713, 39 p.

"Postscript" (if the war was just, then let's not be thankful till its
ends are met. Why be thankful for ruinous peace terms, even if some terms
are good? The Church cannot make judgments in civil affairs by calling for
thanksgiving, nor can anyone else till the terms are made clearer): p.29-31.

The author lists numbers of reasons why he "cannot join in a Thanksgiving
for the present Peace" with France (11 April 1713), as called for by the
Church, in 3 groups: those coming before and those during negotiations, and
those since the treaty. Among these reasons are: those who were most
against the war (of Spanish Succession) were Jacobites, enemies of the Revolution principles and the Toleration (Act, 1689), and of the Establishment of the Church of Scotland, who saw the power of the House of Bourbon
endangered; those who raised the rebellion against the Queen at the time
of Dr. Sacheverell's trial (p. 4); that "Oracle" of the Tory Ministry who
opposed the Hanover succession in The conduct of the Allies (Swift);
p. 7 & 12); the faction which deluded the Dutch by denying a separate English peace with France, then conducted such negotiations "more like Ministers of France, than those of Great Britain" (p. 8-9); those who oppress
Low-Churchmen for their toleration of dissenters who had lost their birth-

right to civil and military positions (p. 11). Ridpath then lists obnox-
ious articles 4 to 6 of the peace treaty (from the midwinter Abstract),
showing there is no security for the Hanover succession (after all, Louis
XIV promised to maintain the Pretender's title at James II's deathbed!),
nor for the separation of France and Spain (the treaty says only that they
may not be under the same king; p. 12-18). The 3d list, of events since
the treaty, includes the complaint of the Emperor that he is deserted,
the threats to the German, Scandinavian and Scottish Protestants from
France, and the sacrifice of British trade (p. 18-24). Ridpath then answers some anticipated counter-charges (p. 24-7), and says that as a good
Presbyterian he has no wish to divide parishioners in this matter of a day
of thanksgiving for peace (p. 28).

   NUC(Pre-1956)494:372 (31-p. [London?] & 39-p. [London] "3d ed.", both
1713); BM(to 1955)238:641 ([London?] 1713, & [London], Robt. Aldsworth,
1713); Morgan,BBH:P511 (31-p. London, 24-p. & 39-p. 'no place', eds., all
1713).

[SEWELL, George], d. 1726.

The clergy and the present ministry defended. Being a letter to the
Bishop of Salisbury, occasion'd by His Lordship's New preface to his past-
oral care. London, printed for J[ohn]. Morphew near Stationers Hall. 1713.
Price 6d. 1 p.l., 30, [1] p. 8°(in 4s) 20 cm.

   Lacks half-title; caption title: A letter to the Bishop of Salisbury
occasion'd by ... his pastoral care.

   First edition; 3d ed. has title: Sewell's answer to the Bishop of Salisbury's new preface ..., 1713; 4th ed.: Mr. Sewell's first letter to the
Bishop of Salisbury ... a full answer to his ... New preface to his pastoral care, [1713].

"Books sold by J. Morphew ..." (religious, 3 of 5 on Bp. Burnet): 1 p. at end.

A reply to: Gilbert Burnet, <u>A new preface and additional chapter, to the third edition of the pastoral care ... Publish'd singly, for the use of those who have the former editions</u>. London, 1713 (2d & 3d eds. entitled: <u>The Bishop of Salisbury's new preface to his pastoral care, consider'd</u> ... London, 1713, 43 p. & London, [1713?], 24 p., respectively, cf. NUC - unless these are <u>about</u> the former work). The 'pastoral care' originally appeared as <u>A discourse of the pastoral care</u>. London, 1692 (3d ed., London, 1713).

Dr. Sewell (M.D., Edinburgh, ca. 1725) was at this time "inclined to toryism", and though not yet half the Bishop's 70 years (p. 3), a bitter critic of Gilbert Burnet, Bishop of Salisbury, the present work being one of five pamplet diatribes against him, 1713-15 (<u>DNB</u>). Here Sewell assails the aged Burnet for his prevarication, equivocation, false doctrine, inconsistency, insincerity, and other personal qualities, with examples. He is sharply rebuked for being an unfair examiner of candidates for holy orders and for irresolute instruction (p. 8-12), for dangerously favouring Low-Churchmen, dissenters, and even popery (p. 14-21), for gentleness to nonjurors (p. 24-5), and for preaching but not practicing humility (p. 27). The falsity of your new Preface, charges Sewell, will have "many unfair Consequences" so should be retracted or proved, else "Remember the Woe against false Teachers, and Sowers of Sedition"! The overall effect is one of triviality and vindictiveness; Sewell's animosity (says <u>DNB</u>) even extended to Burnet's son.

NUC(Pre-1956)540:110 (this ed. only); BM(to 1955)219:715 (1st & 4th eds.); Morgan,BBH:P532 (also 3d & 4th eds., 1713); Rothschild:1827.

[TOLAND, John], 1670-1722.

Dunkirk or Dover; or, The Queen's honour, the nation's safety, the liberties of Europe, and the peace of the world, all at stake till that fort and
port be totally demolish'd by the French. London, printed for A[nn].
Baldwin, near the Oxford-Arms in Warwick-Lane. 1713. Price six pence.
1 p.l., 3-40 p. 8° 21 cm.

Evidence of Toland's authorship is noted in Carabelli, and is acknowledged
in John Dunton's Neck or nothing (1713), p. 43.

Running title: Dunkirk or Dover.

First ed.; reprinted 1713: "The Second Edition", otherwise the same (cf.
Carabelli).

A reply, in part, to: Reasons concerning the immediate demolishing of
Dunkirk ... London, 1713.

This is part of a considerable literature on the destruction of Dunkirk,
called for in the Treaty of Utrecht (11 Apr. 1713), but delayed by the Tories and clamoured for by the Whigs. With peace, says the Whig author, we
must be ever alert to the French, who are more dangerous as friends than
as enemies: undermining our ministers, trade, and allies. Honest people,
now aroused, call on the Queen to use her discretionary powers to execute
the 9th Article of the Treaty (p. 11: the demolition of the fort and harbour
of Dunkirk, p. 13) as she, and Louis XIV at first, had agreed in the 21st
Article of the preliminary treaty, 1709 (p. 14), or risk the dire consequences named on the title-page. This Article was an essential condition
of the peace, and at Utrecht it was agreed it would be effected at once,
at French expense, the fort never to be rebuilt (p. 17-20). "As soon let
the French fortify Dover" as fail in this (p. 32). Toland then exposes
French delaying tactics, encouraged by articles in the Examiner(Swift's
Tory journal), replies to which he leaves to The guardian (Whig, in which

Steele had called for immediate action, 7 Aug. 1713), and concludes with a page-by-page attack on the anonymous pamphlet Reasons concerning the immediate demolishing of Dunkirk (see note above), which truly should be called "Reasons for not demolishing of Dunkirk" (p. 33-40).

   NUC(Pre-1956)596:323 (1st ed.); BM(to 1955)57:442 (both eds.); Morgan, BBH:P608 (both eds.); Carabelli:167 (both). Cf. Rothschild:2442 (2d ed. only; conjectural attribution).

[WALPOLE, Robert, Earl of Orford], 1676-1745.

   A short history of the Parliament. ... London: Printed for T. Warner, near Ludgate. 1713. 2 p.l., [4], 9-31 p. 8°(in 4s) 20 cm.

   Authorship: Morgan says this is also attributed to Defoe (but not found in Moore) and Steele; but later editions carry Walpole's name on their title-pages (see editions note); authorship given to Walpole without qualification in DNB ('Walpole') and NUC.

   Half-title: A short history of the Parliament.

   Later editions, when the Whigs were back in power, had a longer title with author's name: A short history of that Parliament which committed Sir Robert Walpole to the Tower, expelled him [from] the House of Commons, and approved of the infamous Peace of Utrecht. Written by Sir Robert Walpole. London, 1763 (cf. NUC and Morgan).

   Morgan (1st ed.: 1713, T. Warner, 20 p.) & Kress are the only bibliographies consulted with a 1713, 31-p. ed. (though Morgan's only ed. with "T. Warner, near Ludgate" is: 1713, 36 p.); other eds. are: 19 p., 1713 (NUC, BM); 20 p., 1713 (Morgan); 33 p., 1713 (BM); 36 p., 1713 (BM,Morgan, & Kress); 2d ed., 24 p., 1713 (NUC, BM, Morgan; London Library - unpaged); 3d ed., 24 p., 1713 (NUC; Morgan - unpaged); 2d ed., 1763, 61 p. (NUC).

   Dedication (made satirically to a lord of the Tory Ministry, no doubt

Harley, Earl of Oxford, to whom (says Walpole) is due all honour expressed
in the text: the security of the Protestant succession, the balance of
power in Europe, the demolition of Dunkirk, etc., all are owed to your eloquence - and to the 12 peers (created to gain passage of the peace); thus
very few will deny you your just reward): [4] p. at front.

  Further to this is: John Dunton, Neck or nothing. London, 1713 (q.v.,
above), which calls itself a 'supplement' to Walpole's work, presenting a
similar Whig perspective.

  The satiric vein of the Dedication is modified in the text. Former
parliaments have been proudly loyal, but electors must ask whether Tory
loyalty may be more fitly applied to "Britain or the Parliament of Paris"
(p. 10). The Grand Alliance (1701) was formed to reduce French power and
subtract Spain and her American empire from the House of Bourbon, and to
settle the balance of power in Europe and the Protestant succession in
England. Yet the new Ministry seeks to end the Alliance and have a separate peace and friendship with France; the ruinous implications will become
clear when English eyes are opened again. A Commons address had already
(8 Dec. 1711) won the House to the view that no honourable peace could
leave Spain and France united; then, to teach the Commons a lesson, The
conduct of the Allies was published (anonymously, but by Swift, q.v., 1711),
and its creed, full of misrepresentations against our treaty Allies, was
embraced by Tories and all Friends of France. Spain, the last obstacle
to their peace, was given up by showing that we could not afford to continue the war; soon after, a separate peace was agreed to by the Commons
(p. 15). A Dutch protest was branded "Malicious Libel" (8 Apr. 1712).
Next, the Commons raised a furor about the misapplication of public funds
and large navy and general debts, all Whig explanations (here given in detail) being ignored by a Parliament whose purpose was to show a tax burden

so onerous as to warrant almost any peace terms (p. 16-22). Then Marlborough, who "had beaten France too often" to please the Tories, was disgraced
by implication in the public debt scandal (p. 23), and similarly with Towns-
hend, while Walpole was punished for defending the Whigs. Forced by public opinion to reject their treaty of commerce, the Tories then mockingly
congratulated the Queen on the terms of the peace (Commons, 23 June, 1713),
and the Queen graciously approving, they thanked her, thus confessing
approbation of their recent move of rejection. Walpole then sketches "the
Secret History of the Treaty of Commerce", showing how the Tory submission
to importunate France, inevitably ruining British trade, would have succeeded but for 9 votes (p. 26-9). Finally, though its demolition is stipu-
lated by the peace, Dunkirk still stands, with no move towards its destruction. All of which should warn English freeholders from voting again for
those who, bowing to France, can bring us only the Pretender, Popery, and
slaver,.

   Morgan,BBH:P644 (longer title; many eds., incl. 31 p., 1713). Cf. NUC
(Pre-1956)647:19 (19 p., 1713; BM(to 1955)63:1089 (19, 33 & 36 p., & 2d
ed., 24 p., all 1713); Kress: S1374 (19 p.), S1375 (31 p.), 2890 & S1376
(36 p., all 1713); S2641 (2d ed., 1713, 24 p.).

[WITHERS, John], fl. 1707-1724.

   The Dutch better friends than the French, to the monarchy, church, and
trade of England. In a letter from a citizen to a country gentleman. The
fourth edition. London, printed for John Clark, at the Bible and Crown in
the old Change. 1713. Price four-pence. 1 p.l., [3]-36 p. 8°(in 4s)
21 cm.

   First ed. pub. in same year.

   Bibliographical footnotes.

Provenance: Dawson (autogr., in 18th or early 19th-century hand): t.-p.,
p. 17, 20, & 21.

Cast in epistolary form, the author opens by setting royal approval upon
the burden of his title: the Queen has declared before the last session of
Parliament that her interest and that of the States-General are inseparable.
It is not surprising, says Withers to his correspondent, to hear "profli-
gate Scriblers" wheedle the illiterate mob into thinking the Queen's friends
are our enemies; but you sir, are educated, and I'm amazed that you are "for
aggrandizing of the French", and regard Holland as our enemy (p. 3).
Withers then lists 7 'Objections' made in the letter from the "Country
Gentleman" (clearly a Tory), each followed by his own (Whiggish) 'Answer'.
The Objections are (briefly stated) that: the Dutch are antimonarchical;
they are Presbyterians and thus against the (episcopal) Church of England;
they traded with France during the war (Spanish Succession); though we joined the war to relieve their distress, yet they soon threw the entire burden
upon us; the barrier (of forts) they want against France, is also a threat
to England; they are our rivals in trade, and if crushed world commerce
would be ours; they killed 5 or 6 Englishmen in the East Indian island of
Amboyna (the 'massacre' of 1623, Amboina, Indonesia). Each Objection re-
ceives an extensive rebuttal in favour of the Dutch, impressively footnoted
with numerous supporting sources (p. 4-35). "Thus Sir", epitomizes Withers,
"I have endeavour'd what I can to remove those causeless Prejudices you
have conceiv'd against the Dutch", to show it as against our interest to
war with our friends, after peace is obtained against our "tricking Enemies", the French (p. 36).

BM(to 1955)259:812(& 1st-3d eds., all 1713); Morgan,BBH:P675(& 1st-3d
eds.); Kress:2891 (36 p., 1713). Cf. NUC(Pre-1956)669:694 (1st-3d eds.).

1714

ASGILL, John, 1659-1738.

The succession of the House of Hannover vindicated, against the Pretender's second declaration in folio, entitled The hereditary right of the
Crown of England asserted, &c. ... Written by Mr. Asgill. London, printed for J[ames]. Roberts at the Oxford-Arms in Warwick-Lane. 1714. (Price
one shilling.) 1 p.l., 75, [1] p. 8°(in 4s) 20 cm.

First edition; "2d ed." has same imprint and pagination (cf.NUC).

"Preamble to the Duke of Cambridge's Patent" (transcript, in Latin and
English, of Queen Anne's document creating the Elctoral Prince of Hanover,
George Louis, the Duke of Cambridge): p. 72-5.

List of "Books written by John Asgill Esq;": 1 p. at end.

A reply to: George Harbin, The hereditary right of the Crown of England
asserted ... and the true English constitution vindicated from the misrepresentations of Dr. [William] Higden's View [of the English constitution,
1709] and Defense [of the View ..., 1710] ... London, 1713 (also attributed to Hilkiah Bedford; cf. NUC).

This is another in the spate of pamphlets published close to Queen Anne's
death, and the accession of the Elector of Hanover as George I, on the contentious matter of the succession. George Harbin had demonstrated in his

pamphlet that, by the last will of Henry VIII, the Crown devolved on that

monarch's younger sister, Queen of France, not on his older sister, Queen

of Scotland, thus making James I and his descendants usurpers – the argu-

ment presented with "Marginal Notes ... and Appurtenances belonging to a

Twelve-Shilling Folio" (p. 3-7). Asgill, a lawyer and an eccentric, then

takes his readers through Harbin's work, providing many quotations, and

also with references to Dr. Higden's work, with which Harbin's is in dis-

pute. Harbin, a nonjuror, held that the monarch rules by hereditary

right, not by de facto possession of the throne with Parliamentary limit-

ations – the view held by Higden and Asgill. In the play of argument and

counter-argument, historical precedents are freely drawn upon, from William

the Conqueror to Henry VII, wherein Higden's proof that in this period 12

non-hereditary kings ruled, is disproved by Harbin and re-proved by Asgill

(e.g., p. 11-12, 33, 41), who adds instances of the power of Parliament in

action. He ends with a short discourse on settlement and the Hanover Pat-

ents (p. 66ff.).

   NUC(Pre-1956)23:318 (1st & 2d eds.); BM(to 1955)7:770 (1st & 2d);

Morgan,BBH:Q44 (1st, 2d, & 2 other eds., all 1714). Cf. London Library,1:127

(2d ed.).

[ATTERBURY, Francis, bp. of Rochester], 1662-1732.

   English advice, to the freeholders of England. ... [s.l.; London?]

printed in the year, 1714. 1 p.l., 3-30 p. 8°(in 4s) 23 cm.

   Authorship: Somers tracts, 1815, 13:521-2, & NUC & BM; Morgan notes att-

ributions to 'C. Hornsby' (i.e. Chas. Hornby) and Defoe (but not in Moore).

   Reprinted in Somers tracts, 1815, 13:521-41 (also, 1751, v.4: Morgan &

BM).

   A reply to: Charles Povey, An inquiry into the miscarriages of the four last years reign. London, 1714 (q.v., below).

Answered by: 1. English advice to the freeholders of England. [London?]
1714 (NUC & BM may not have distinguished this from the Atterbury work;
information from Somers tracts, 1815, 13:542-59, imprint place not given;
in Somers this is described as a parody of Atterbury's work, following
"through the argument paragraph by paragraph, putting a Whig application upon
the rhetoric of the Prelate"; the texts have been compared and the differences, though apparently slight, I found to be indeed significant). 2. British advice to the freeholders of Great Britain: being an answer to a trea-
sonable libel intituled English advice ... London, 1715 (Morgan,R74).
3. Daniel Defoe, A reply to a traiterous libel, entituled, English advice
to the freeholders of Great Britain. London, 1715 (Moore,299). 4. Remarks
on a late libel privately dispersed by the Tories entituled, English advice
... shewing the traiterous designs of the faction. Paris [1715?] (Morgan,
R172, under Defoe, but not in Moore), transl. into French as: Remarques
sur le libelle intitulé English advice ... [Paris? 1715?] (BM, & Morgan,
R31). 5. Daniel Defoe, Treason detected, in an answer to that traiterous
and malicious libel, entituled, English advice ... humbly offer'd to the
consideration of all those freeholders who have been poyson'd with that
malignant pamphlet. London, 1715 (Moore, 292; 22d Jan. 1715), 2d ed.,
Feb. 1715.

Further to this is: Charles Hornby, The second and last English advice,
to the freeholders of England. London, 1722 (cf. NUC, 255:95).

Nicholas Tindal (1687-1774) has commented on this work in The history of
England, London, 1727-31, 15 vols. (transl. and edited from Paul de Rapin-
Thoyras, Histoire d'Angleterre, La Haye, 1724-27, 10 vols.), vol. 4, p. 414-
5 (cf. Somers tracts, 1815, 13:521-2). The late Tory ministry foresaw
trouble would result, says Tindal, from arranging its peace with France, and

sought ways to avoid it. Soon after, a "traitorous libel" appeared: <u>Eng-
lish advice</u> ...

> Nothing could be more full of malice and falsehood against the
> King's person and family, as well as against the whigs in gener-
> al, and the present ministry; and it was artfully contrived to
> raise discontents among the people against the government, and to
> possess them with an opinion, that the church was in danger by
> his majesty's administration. It was carefully dispersed through
> the country ... Upon which the government issued out a proclam-
> ation, promising a reward of one thousand pounds for the discov-
> ery of the author of the libel, and five hundred pounds for the
> discovery of the printer: But to no purpose.

The English electors are honest (says Bp. Atterbury in his text), resisting bribes from Whigs, who are more active in this and in inventing falsehoods than Tories are in publishing truths. They have the money now, profits from the war which only weakened the country Tories; money to destroy
the Church, landed interests, our liberties and security. This is the
situation the author will examine, to aid electors (freeholders) in making
the best choices of Members of Parliament, else it will be our last free
Parliament (p. 3-5). The Whigs can pack the House of Commons, leaving the
King (George I) "no Power to Act but as they direct"; they have an arbitrary Junto not subject to the King, yet quick to pronounce as arbitrary
whatever <u>they</u> can't dictate. With such insolence they treated the late
Queen (Anne). The Tory Parliament secured peace and the Treaty of Commerce
which, though not perfect, is 1000 degrees more in the English interest than
10 of Marlborough's campaigns, for it enabled the King's undisputed succession without civil war, and avoided further ruinous costs (p. 6-7).
Events at the start of George I's reign are then recounted, purporting to

illustrate the corruption and disloyalty of the Whigs, while placing Tory

actions in the light of reason: we do not oppose the Hanoverian success-

ion, says Bp. Atterbury (p. 17), but we do want peace, and the English

Church; the Whigs want war, profit, and destruction of the Church of Eng-

land; His Majesty was lately Lutheran, which is closer to Popery and not

episcopal (p. 18-20). The Whigs say the King may go abroad at will (this

gives themselves more power), and are not happy that he is obliged to join

the English Church (p. 23). The Whigs also want a standing army and, in-

fluenced by their kirk, they would invade the liberty of the press - be-

cause now they are in power, down with toleration! Under the Tories, only

2 or 3 writers were prosecuted, and one was a Tory! (p. 26-8). Lastly,

the Queen was barely dead (says Bp. Atterbury) when the Marlborough's cav-

alcaded in triumph, while her relations, even her servants, are left ill-

rewarded. Tories (the prelate concludes) are not all virtue; but the

Whigs are "Positively Bad, and the Churchmen Negatively Good" (p. 29). On

the last page are lists of the 8 merits of each party, Whig and Tory.

(That this pamphlet was a thorn in the side of the Whigs is evident from

the vigorous response, noted above.)

   NUC(Pre-1956)25:213; BM(to 1955)8:134 (8°); Morgan,BBH:Q47 (31-p., 4°,

& 32-p., 8°, 1714 eds.).

[BOLINGBROKE, Henry St.-John, 1st Viscount], 1678-1751.

   Considerations upon The secret history of the White Staff. Humbly address'd

to the E- of O-- [i.e. Earl of Oxford]. The sixth edition. London: printed

for A. Moore, and sold by the booksellers of London and Westminister. [1714]

2 p.l., [5]-35 p. 8°(in 4s) 18 cm.

   Authorship: attributed to Bolingbroke in DNB ('Saint-John'), accepted by

NUC, Stonehill, Halkett & Laing (from BM), and by BM whose copy of the 1st ed. has the t.-p. ms. note "By My Lord Bolingbroke".

Half-title: Considerations upon ... the White Staff, &c. Price six
pence.

A reply to: Daniel Defoe, The secret history of the White-Staff. London,
1714, q.v., below, for other notes.

Defoe's pamphlet had defended Robert Harley, Earl of Oxford, probably at
his patron's instance. Harley had been dismissed by Queen Anne (July),
mainly for his unpopular peace terms with France, and St.-John, another
Tory Minister, by the new King (George I, in Aug.) for his Jacobite lean-
ings. Defoe tried to show that Harley (the Staff) had resisted St.-John's
increasing Jacobitism. Here, St.-John addresses Harley, the author as
supposed from his "notorious Sincerity", intending to correct the unwary
"who may have drunk too deep of your Poison" - thus early revealing their
mutual detestation (I see nothing in the text inconsistent with St.-John's
authorship). Some agents may rise independently over their benefactors,
you say; but not in your case, for your never confided your view and
where you were supplanted, your contempt should be blamed (p. 9). Even before you held the Staff (symbol of the Treasurer's office), you preached
gloom (p. 10), and when in office you hoped for a coalition. The faction
against you (Whigs) did not expect the General (Marlborough) to be insol-
ently dismissed! We had had the Queen, the nation, and Parliament with us,
but your pride, "designing obscurity", and broken promises, failed us (p.
15). You were saved only by public sympathy when Guiscard attempted your
life (the anonymous author can't mention that he was the intended victim!);
with restored credit, you tried again for a coalition, but "there was no
Confidence" in you (p. 17). Instead of just Whigs and Tories, there were
many factions, including the High-Church October Club - but you did not
put an end to it, as you claim; nor did you purge the Schism Bill (1714,

against dissenters), for you were <u>silent</u> during the debate. Instead, you
give us a Secret History, to accuse others (<u>e.g.</u>, St.-John himself) but
clear yourself of interest in the Pretender (p. 23). Indeed, you assert
you defeated the others and secured the Hanover succession, whereas in
fact your "juggling" envoy was a farce who affronted the Hanover Court, who
were also aggravated by your delay in paying their troops (p. 24-8). You
advanced your relatives, made Swift (another Harley writer) a Dean, and
others bishops (p. 32-3). Then you say the Queen was reluctant to strip
you - no! it was the best act of her reign, and may teach you "to retrieve
your own Character before you attempt another Mans" (<u>i.e.</u>, St.-John's).
Next time the spirit to write a Secret History possesses you, get the Bishop to exorcise that Lucifer! (p. 35).

   NUC(Pre-1956)64:510 (1st-6th eds., all 1714); BM(to 1955)104:492 (1st,
4th, 6th eds.); Morgan,BBH:Q81 (1st, 2d, 1714; 4th, 1714?; 6th 1715?);
Kress:2898.

COOK, John, d. 1660.

   King Charles's case: or, An appeal to all rational men, concerning his
tryal at the High Court of Justice. Being for the most part that which was
intended to have been deliver'd at the bar, if the King had pleaded to the
charge, and put himself upon a fair tryal. With an additional opinion concerning the death of King James [I], the loss of Rochel [La Rochelle, 1628],
and the blood of Ireland. By John Cook, of Grays-Inn, Barrester. ...
London: printed for J.H. a friend to legal monarchy, but an enemy to mon-
archical tyranny; in the glorious year 1714. 1 p.l., [2], 5-43 p. 8°(in 4s)
20 cm.

   Caption title (p. 5): An appeal to all rational men that love their God,
justice and country, more than their honour, pleasure and money, concerning

the King's tryal.

First pub. under title: King Charls his case ... London, 1649 (though
the charge was pub. in the House of Commons Proceedings as: The charge of
the Commons of England, against Charls Stuart, King of England ... exhibited to the High Court of Justice by J. Cook, London, 1648 [O.S., Cook
bringing forward the charge 20 Jan., 1649, N.S.: DNB, 'Cook']; cf. BM,
43:534); transl. into Dutch as: Regis Carol Casus ... [Amsterdam?], 1649,
and as Regis Caroli Integritas ... t'Amsterdam, 1649 (NUC,BM; unfound in
Knuttel). Reprinted in Somers tracts, 1748, vol. 4 (cf. BM, 43:534) and
1811, 5:214-37; several other reprints: see locations notes below. Also
"copied out" by Col. Edmund Ludlow, pseud., and issued as a Letter (see
title of the answer by Samuel Butler, noted below) published within Ludlow's
Memoirs, Vivay [Switzerland], 1698-9, 3 vols.; 2d ed., London, 1720-21,
3 vols.; London, 1751, p. [3]-20; and 3d ed., Edinburgh, 1751, 3 vols.,
vol. 3, p. 323-67 (cf. BM, 146:85; NUC, 121:227; for other 'Ludlow' letters,
and replies, on the same subject, cf. NUC, 344:549-50, and BM, 146:84).
The London, 1751 ed. had the subtitle: ... To which is now added the Case
of the King Charles I [by Cook] (cf. BM, loc. cit., for this and later eds.)
Memoirs was transl. into French as: Les mémoires d' Edmond Ludlow ... Amsterdam, 1699 (and other eds., cf. NUC, 344:550 and BM, 146:85). Cook's
King Charles's case was reprinted, with other extracts from Ludlow's Memoirs, as: The imprisonment & death of King Charles I. ... Edited by J.T.H.
[i.e. J.T. Hornby]. Edinburgh, 1882 (Aungervyle Society reprints, 1st
series, no. 6, p. 81-117; cf. NUC, 344:550, under Ludlow with dates "1617?-
1692", and BM, 146:85). A modest vindication of Oliver Cromwell, London,
1698, is a reply to Ludlow's Memoirs and it was reprinted in Somers tracts,
1811, 6:416-42 (cf. BM, 146:85-6 for this and further related works).

To the Reader (says no one in history or scripture better deserved to die than Charles I, for his persecutions, cruelties, and bloodshed; here is

the original case against him, says Cook, with some examples added): p. [2]

at front.

Answered by: Samuel Butler (1612-1680), 1. The plagiary exposed ...
Being a reply to a book intitled King Charles's case, formerly written by
John Cook ... and since copied out under the title of Collonel Ludlow's
[pseud.] Letter. London, 1691. 2. Also issued as: A vindication of the
royal martyr King Charles I. London, 1705. 3. Also issued as: The secret
history of the Calves-Head Club. London, 1706, 1707, & 1709. 4. Also issued as: The Whigs unmasked: being The secret history ... London, 1713.
5. Also issued as: The hellish mysteries of the old republicans, set forth
in vinciation of King Charles ... London, 1714. 6. Also issued as: King
Charles's case truly stated: in answer to Mr. Cook's pretended case of that
blessed martyr. In Somers tracts, 1748, vol. 4, & 1811, 5:237-46, where
Butler's authorship is questioned, with Birkenhead suggested as one whose
style this more closely resembles. (Cf. BM, 30:1230, for all 6 titles.)

That strong feelings still survived about the rights of monarchs is clear

from the omission of the printer's name and concealment of that of the pub-

lisher/bookseller (evidently a Whig) from the imprint, as well as from the

defensive phrase following; but the year was 'glorious' because the succ-

ession of George I had occurred without disturbance. The republication of

this work in 1714, the year of the first Hanoverian king, would have served

as a reminder of the fate in store for arbitrary monarchs in England. Cook

however, was one of some 50 named exclusions from the 1660 Act of Indemnity

and Oblivion, and he was executed Oct. 1660, one of 13 regicides to die

(cf. DNB, 'Cook').

King Charles refusing to plead to the charge of high treason, Cook, app-

ointed Solicitor-General by the High Court of Justice for the people of

England against the King, could not deliver his case. It is here present-

ed (in 1649) more in evidence than in self-justification apparently. Add-

ressed to the President of the High Court, Cook expatiates upon the blood-

shed caused by the King (5-6000 slain at Edghill) and his indifference to

these evils; he describes the limited powers entrusted to English kings:

they may not impose nor subtract without common consent, may not commit

anyone to prison for any cause, and to these and other limitations they are

bound by the coronation oath; yet King Charles subverted laws every day.

Cook evinces history (though the note to this work in Somers says Cook

failed to offer grounds in law so drew upon insinuations incapable of

proof, or when proved, fell short of meriting the penalty demanded). The

King was destructive of people, Parliament, and property, says Cook; a

manipulator of English, Scottish, and Irish affairs, sold preferments and

monopolies (p. 20), committed barbarities in Ireland (p. 28-31), and be-

trayed the Protestants at La Rochelle (p. 31-5). For all this, Cook summ-

arized, far more crimes than those of all kings before, the blood of the

tyrant must pay; the blood of his innocent victims cries out for it. Cook

himself has no fear he says, and he calls on the Justices to do their duty.

   NUC(Pre-1956)121:227 (& 1649 & Dutch transl., 1751, 1882, & Somers tracts

reprints); BM(to 1955)43:534-5 (& 1649 & Dutch transl., 1751, 1771, &

Somers tracts reprints). Cf. Thomason,1:722, Feb. 9 (1649); WingSTC:C6025

(1649 ed., under: Cooke); London Library (Suppl. 1920):173(1649).

[DEFOE, Daniel], 1661?-1731.

   The secret history of the White-Staff, being an account of affairs under

the conduct of some late Ministers, and of what might probably have happ-

ened if Her Majesty had not died. The fourth edition. London: printed for

J. Baker at the Black-Boy in Pater-Noster-Row. 1714. Price one shilling.

1 p.l., 71 p. 8°(in 4s) 20 cm.

Authorship: Moore's attribution is without question, but Rothschild says it is controversial, giving grounds; Defoe himself disclaimed authorship (in his The secret history of The secret history ... London, 1715). Some information the work contains was exclusive to Robert Harley, Earl of Oxford, and John Dunton seems to have considered Harley as being involved (cf. his Queen Robin title, noted below); Defoe and Swift were both his writers, but Swift was clearly in the dark (cf. his letter to Arbuthnot, 19 Oct. 1714, quoted in Rothschild). Halkett & Laing, 5:211 assign this to Defoe, and Stonehill, NUC and BM concur. Wright (Defoe), p. 202, suggests the author was Defoe's collaborator, the 'Friday' of Robinson Crusoe. Contemporaries clearly thought it was Defoe though: cf. my notes to A detection of the sophistry, part 2, 1714, and parts 1 and 2 of The history of the Mitre and Purse, 1714, both below.

Transl. into Dutch as: De sekreete historie van de Witte staf ... Amsterdam, 1715.

The first 4 editions all appeared before 2d Oct. 1714 (cf. Moore).

In 3 parts: The secret history of the White Staff ... Part II. London, 1714, and The secret history of the White Staff ... Part III. London, 1715, both printed for Baker; subsequently, the 3 Parts were issued as one pamphlet.

A pirated false continuation was offered before 27th Oct. 1714 (cf. Moore).

Answered by: 1. [Bolingbroke, Henry St.-John, 1st Viscount], Considerations upon The secret history of the White Staff ... London [1714], q.v., above. 2. A detection of the sophistry and falsities of ... The secret history ... Containing an inquiry ... London, 1714. 3. A detection ... Containing a further inquiry ... Part II. London, 1714, q.v. below. 4. A detection ... Part III. London, 1715; extracts from A detection pt. 1 (& 2?) and

The secret history were presented in alternate paragraphs as 5. The Secret history of the White-Staff ... With a detection of the sophistry ...
of the said pamphlet. London, 1714. 6. John Dunton, Queen Robin ... the
true secret history of the White Staff, in answer to that false one lately
publish'd by the Earl of O[x]ford. London [1714]. 7. [Daniel Defoe], The
secret history of The secret history of the White Staff, Purse and Mitre.
London, 1715 (a disclaimer of his authorship of The secret history), itself
answered by: [William Pittis], Queen Anne vindicated from the base aspersions of some late pamphlets publish'd to screen the mismanagers of the
four last years ... London, 1714/5 (cf. BM,5:727). 8. The history of the
Mitre and Purse, in which the first and second Parts of The secret history
... are fully considered ... London, 1714, q.v. below (attributed to Bp.
Francis Atterbury and to William Pittis). 9. The history of the Mitre and
Purse continued ... Part II. London, 1714 (q.v., below), itself answered
by: Considerations on The history of the Mitre and Purse. Shewing, that
the design of the three late managers, the Staff [Harley, Lord Oxford],
Mitre [Bp. Atterbury] and Purse [Lord Harcourt, Chancellor], in setting their
historians to work, was only to raise a little dust that they might escape
in the cloud. ... London, 1714 (attributed to Defoe, but not in Moore,
and also to William Pittis). Most of these appeared in more than one issue
or edition, and doubtless there are other Whig responses in the acrimonious
controversy, as well as references within yet other works, such as the critique in: Charles Povey, An inquiry into the miscarriages of the four last
years reign. London, 1714 (p. 28-30), q.v., below.

Further to this is: Daniel Defoe, An appeal to honour and justice ...
by Daniel De Foe. Being a true account of his conduct in publick affairs.
London, 1715. (Moore, 307; pub. in Feb., Defoe tries to clear his name and
arouse public sympathy, with brilliant casuistry and literary skill.)

Said to have been written at Harley's instigation (though Harley made a
prudential disavowal of any complicity), and Defoe had indeed been in Harley's service; but his patron was now a prisoner in the Tower (mostly for
the unpopular terms of his peace with France), and this is a loyal defence
of Harley's policies. The importance of the work may be readily judged
from the lively 'battle of the pamphlets' which ensued. Defoe opens cau-
tiously by observing that while Ministers gain credit for the merit of
others, they also bear guilt for others' crimes. He adduces historical
examples, and reviews recent events up to Dr. Sacheverell's impeachment,
the supersedeas (writ of stay) to the White-Staff (symbol of the Treasurer's office), and the fall of the Whig Ministry; here the "Secret History"
begins (p. 8). The problems of the new Tory Ministry are discussed, and
their relation to events and decisions, the resentments between Whig and
Tory, and the attempts of Harley (called "the Prime Minister") at accom-
modation - all given by Defoe in a spirit of justification of Ministry policies and actions. Examples are given concerning Catalans in Spain, pensions in Scotland, the problems of Jacobite infiltration, and of the absolutist demands of the October Club (p. 23). The White Staff (Harley) was
constantly met with Whig and High-Church opposition to moderation. The
Ministry's relations with Hanover and the Pretender were distorted by Whigs,
and the "Staff" (Harley) felt such duty to the Queen that he neglected "that
which Politicians call Self-Preservation", and so was gradually supplanted
in the Queen's favour by the malicious insinuations of the Whigs (p. 50-
51). At length he was obliged to resign (his gallant speech to the Queen
is reproduced: p. 54-6), whereupon he explained to the other faction the
problems they faced, and how moderation would have saved them. The White-
Staff retired, and soon after the Queen died; though sound in constitution,
her death was from "something which affected her Heart": the others must

consider "how far they contributed to that fatal Blow" (p. 61-2). Some
say had she lived longer the schemes for bringing in the Pretender would
have succeeded; but in fact had she lived, she and the Staff would have
"overthrown all the wicked Schemes those Men had Laid" (p. 64). But the
Queen's eyes were opened, and 2 days after Harley's dispossession she was
convinced that the others couldn't be trusted; the other faction stumbled,
but the Queen died, and their fate had she lived is plain. Neither Queen
nor Ministry had the power to capitulate to France, bring in the Pretender,
and suppress liberty, and the Queen more than likely saw the treachery of
these men who said otherwise, for she chose to reign without them. They
were "Planet-struck", and their leader raged against the Staff for ruining
them: it is "impossible to supplant him with the Queen", said he, so our
only recourse is for "France and the Lawful Heir". But that secret history
must be for another volume (p. 63-71).

NUC(Pre-1956)136:644 (2d-4th, combined, & other eds.); BM(to 1955)50:129
(1st-4th eds., etc.); Morgan,BBH:Q180 (many eds.); Moore(2d ed.):280 (1st-
4th eds. noted); Rothschild:766; London Library,1:637 (4th); Wright(Defoe),
no. 160; BPL(Defoe):153 (numerous eds.); Kress:2902 (pt. 1 & 2, 1714, &
3d ed.).

A DETECTION of the sophistry and falsities of the pamphlet, entitul'd,
The secret history of the White Staff. Containing a further enquiry into
the Staff's conduct during the late management, particularly with respect
to the Pretender, and the correspondence the faction held with the court of
Bar-le-Duc. Part II. London: printed for J[ames]. Roberts, near the
Oxford-Arms in Warwick-Lane, 1714. (Price 6d) 1 p.l., 35 [i.e. 33] p.
8°(in 4s) 20 cm.

Page 33 misnumbered 35.

A reply to: Daniel Defoe, <u>The secret history of the White-Staff</u> ...
London, 1714, <u>q.v.</u>, above.

Further to: <u>A detection of the sophistry and falsities of ... The secret
history of the White Staff. Containing an inquiry ...</u> London, 1714.

Further to this is: <u>A detection of the sophistry ... Containing a further inquiry ... Part III.</u> London, 1715. Extracts from Part I (and II?),
and from <u>The secret history</u> were presented in alternate paragraphs as <u>The
secret history of the White-Staff ... With a detection of the sophistry
... of the said pamphlet.</u> London, 1714.

The author deals with both part 1 and (after p. 22) part 2 of Defoe's
<u>Secret history</u>. The first part of this enquiry into Defoe's work was "par-
ticularly with respect to the Protestant succession"; it being well received, says the author, he will continue his honest attempt to save people
from the falsities of the Staff (Robert Harley, leader of the late Tory
Ministry), and from thinking him a friend when he was "betraying to France".
Our fears were ridiculed "by even the very Author of the <u>Staff's</u> Secret
History, in his <u>Reviews</u>, <u>Mercators</u>" and other papers (p. 2; that Defoe was
the author was thus openly accepted). Defoe admits Jacobites were in the
administration, and tries to "mitigate the Guilt" of the Ministry in allowing this; but did the "late managers" take one step against Jacobites or
for the Hanover succession? No; yet it would have been easy for the Staff,
the "Master of Affairs", to have remedied this by declaring himself. The
author then sets out to demonstrate that the apparent contradicions in the
Staff's actions, which Defoe is at pains to defend, were in fact consistent
in favouring the Jacobites, the "Chevalier de St. George" (the Pretender,
resident at Bar-le-Duc in Lorraine, France), and the French (in the peace
treaty). Many details ignored by Defoe, or presented as innocent, are here
given a nefarious construction. A weak Ministry required the protection of

France, and needed peace to protect its friend from imminent defeat itself (p. 9-14). "I know the Staff's Historian so well" (again pointing to Defoe's authorship), he can't deny to me his ignorance in history (p. 12). The remainder of the pamphlet deals with the events towards and terms of the ruinous peace, all favouring France and against the Allies and the Hanover succession, and including extracts from part 2 of Defoe's Secret history dealing critically under concealed names with Lord Harcourt, Bishop Atterbury, and Lady Masham (p. 24-6). The author disagrees with the Staff's assessment, and his conclusion is a defence of Lady Masham against the slanders of the Staff.

  BM(to 1955)104:492; Morgan,BBH:Q190 (36 p.). Cf. NUC(Pre-1956)140:697 (Pt. 2, Dublin, 1714); Hazen(Walpole):2677 (part no. not identified); Kress:2905 (3 pts.; 1714-15, & pt. 1, 6th ed.), S1388 (8th ed.).

  THE FEARS of the nation quieted; in a letter to a Whig-gentleman. London: printed for J[ames]. Roberts, at the Oxford-Arms, in Warwick-Lane, 1714. 1 p.l., 3-54 p. 8°(in 4s) 20 cm.

  First (and only?) edition.

  Your last letter is apprehensive about the peace, says the writer in a mock defence of Tory policies and of the power of France and Spain together imposing the Pretender upon us. He then discusses the balance of power, Britain and Holland in a trade and religious alliance against France, past and present: the Commons zeal for this, the Court party's opposition, and the royal prerogative and parliamentary advice under Charles II (p. 3-10). Court intimacy between France and England is, you say, the past and present cause of our insecure peace treaties. The greatest obstacle to "universal Monarchy" is the free people of England; without them, the Allies are too weak to oppose France (p. 11-14). This freedom was nearly lost, to your mind, by our doctrines of hereditary right, passive obedience, and non-resistance, bolstered by Jacobites, and assisted by Louis XIV and our Popish enemies, who condemn the revolution principles and may resort to arms. Our separate peace, deserting our Allies, will not encourage them to come to our aid, you feel, for we showed greater aversion to them than to the French (p. 15-20). You allow we must have a large standing army, to balance that of the French; but then, you say, we might as well have continued the war: we were winning, France made weak; we could have kept faith with our Allies, had the Spanish dominions in the Emperor's hands, saved our trade from France, and restored the balance of power - all being war objectives (p. 23-30). The author then replies to other matters from the "Whig-Gentleman's" letter: the intricacies of the Spanish succession, Louis XIV's "Designs to set a Pretender over us", Whig cries of danger and Tory claims of security and the evils of this strife (but you complain, the writer says, of the Tory untruths in Abel Roper's journal Post-boy and Swift's Examiner; p. 40-3), and a review of the main foreign and domestic points of party contention, with Whig solutions - Tory remedies, you con-clude, being only "Prayers and Tears" (p. 31-50). The author ends this deliberate recounting of his "Whig-Gentleman" correspondent's "horrible Apprehensions" on a satirical note of reassurance: after all England has done for France (in the peace treaty), no matter how powerful she becomes "she can never possibly forget the Services we have done her ... so that you may banish all your Fears"; but let's not change our Tory Ministry, or France may forget these obligations to us. If this doesn't quiet your fears, then I know of no other arguments (p. 50-4) - thus damning rather than defending the Tory position.

NUC(Pre-1956)168:231 (this ed. only); Morgan,BBH:Q231 ("6d." - sixpence - follows date on t.-p., else same).

THE HISTORY of the Mitre and Purse, in which the first and second parts
of The secret history of the White Staff are fully considered, and the
hypocrisy and villanies of the Staff himself are laid open and detected.
... London: printed for J[ohn]. Morphew near Stationers-Hall. 1714.
(price I shilling) 1 p.l., [3]-72 p. 8°(in 4s) 19 cm.

Authorship: attributed to Francis Atterbury and to William Pittis (cf.
NUC, etc.).

First edition (cf. BM).

A reply to: Daniel Defoe, The secret history of the White-Staff ... 1st
and 2 d parts, both London, 1714; see above, part 1, for other notes.

Answered by: Considerations on The history of the Mitre and Purse. London,
1714 (attributed to Defoe, but not in Moore, and also to William Pittis).

Bound with, and further to this is: The history of the Mitre and Purse
continued ... Part II. London, 1714 (not as issued, from the condition of
the t.-p. of Part II), q.v., following entry.

Defoe's Secret history, 1714, had been a loyal defence of his patron,
Robert Harley. The author here, writing after Defoe's first two parts had
appeared and Queen Anne had died (1st Aug.), refers to Defoe not by name
but knowingly as a hired mercenary writer, and sets out to put his "Filthy
Work" in a "true Light"; that is, to present a High-Church Tory counter-
viewpoint. In demolishing Defoe's arguments one by one, the present author
uses the term 'Mitre' for Bishop Francis Atterbury, called a Papist by
Defoe but here represented as an ardent Protestant and impeccable defender
of the Anglican Church (he was later banished for Jacobitism); the Purse
is used for Simon Harcourt (Lord Harcourt), the Chancellor who, if ever he
erred it was in his attachment to the Staff (p. 9). The latter name is
used for Robert Harley (Earl of Oxford), who is vilified at every turn
through the rest of the book, starting with King William's opinion of his

"Dissimulation" at the Treaty of Ryswick (1697; p. 12), Harley's ingrat-
iating himself with Queen Anne (p. 21), his getting posts for his friends
(p. 27-8), driving Dr. James Drake (author of the Tory Memorial of the
Church of England, London, 1705, q.v.) to an early grave (p. 30), yet
rising to the highest posts a sycophant can gain (p. 31-47), when his Ministry gained power, to his contact "with the Enemy for a separate Peace,
in Breach of the Public Faith" (p. 54), made easy by the wartime (Spanish
Succession) losses of landed gentlemen (i.e. Tories) and the credulity of
the Queen under Staff's influence (p. 57); next, a treacherous peace which
favoured France, lost our trade, led to Dunkirk being rebuilt at Mardyke;
and then the dissimulation of the Schism Act (1714, against dissenters)
for political expediency, blaming the Pretender; till at last the Queen did
"spurn him from her Presence" before she died (p. 63-72). The Mitre and
Purse are still in good esteem, while the Staff is hated - but this will
fill another volume (The history of the Mitre and Purse continued, 1714,
q.v., next entry).

NUC(Pre-1956)248:178 (1st-3d & Dublin eds., 1714); BM(to 1955)104:492
(1st-3d eds.); Morgan,BBH:Q48 (under Atterbury); Kress:S1392 (2 pts.).

THE HISTORY of the Mitre and Purse continued, wherein the villanies of
the Staff are further detected, and the conduct of the late Ministers, that
would not join with him in betraying their Queen and country, is more amply
set forth in the discovery of several private transactions not yet made
publick. Part II. ... London: printed for J[ohn]. Morphew near Stationers-Hall. 1714. (Price one shilling.) ['one shilling' lined out in ink
and '6' added.] 1 p.l., 3-24 [i.e. 40] p. 8°(in 4s) 19 cm.

Authorship: attributed to Francis Atterbury and to William Pittis (cf.
NUC, etc.).

First edition (cf. BM).

Pages 33 to 40 misnumbered 17 to 24.

A reply to: Daniel Defoe, The secret history of the White-Staff ... 1st
and 2d parts, both London, 1714; see above, part 1, for other notes.

Answered by: Considerations on The history of the Mitre and Purse. London, 1714 (attributed to Defoe, but not in Moore, and also to William Pittis).

Further to: The history of the Mitre and Purse - see next note.

Bound with: The history of the Mitre and Purse, in which the first and
second parts of The secret history ... are fully considered ... London,
1714 (not as issued, from appearance of t.-p.), q.v., preceding entry.

The demands for publication of the first part of this work, caused important omissions regarding great men censured for mismanagement while under
the Staff (Robert Harley), making publication of this second part essential. The author admits that the writer of The secret history (unnamed,
but it is apparently with him whom he has since conversed in person, p. 4)
is not a Papist or Jacobite but rather in favour of dissenters (!), and
he appears to allow that the Staff is as guiltless of Popery as is his advocate (Defoe the "Hireling"). However, in Scotland, the Staff ignored
encroachments between Presbyterians and Anglicans, and other problems; he
allowed the printer of a libel of his own to go undefended; and even his
friends the Mitre (Bp. Francis Atterbury) and the Purse (Lord Simon Harcourt) had to discover his treachery and dissimulation to the Queen, at
whose feet the Staff then threw himself (p. 5-13). The Queen resumed her
favours to him, which however he continued to abuse, till she "was precip-
itately lost to all our Hopes", her life sacrificed to the ambition of Staff,
whose arrogance might have brought us another war had not the French observed the treaty and acknowledged the succession of Hanover (p. 14-19).

The Purse proclaimed the King (George I), then examined our defences against the Pretender, and found only "the scandalous Neglect of the Staff"
(p. 21), and difficulties in raising funds, which he cleverly overcame to
"balance his Accounts" in readiness for His Majesty's arrival. And the
Mitre, who with "truly Heroic Sorrow" performed the Queen's funeral rites
(while the Staff "seem'd rather to Rejoice than Lament"), yet chose to
serve her successor and offered him his submission, notwithstanding the
malicious insinuation that he held the interest of the Pretender (p. 21,
i.e. 37; Atterbury was in fact later banished for his Jacobitism); and
both Purse and Mitre gave the King a loyal and hearty reception. The Staff
had thought his imposition upon the Queen might be continued with the
King; but His Majesty saw his designs and the Staff was despised at Court,
his counterfeit joy finding only contempt. The author's envoy is a mordant quatrain from Juvenal, showing ambition crushed under the weight of
greed (p. 24, i.e. 40).

   NUC(Pre-1956)248:178 (this ed. only); BM(to 1955)104:492 (1st & 2d eds.,
1714); Morgan,BBH:Q49 (under Atterbury; & 2d ed., 1714; & Q48 has 3d.,
1714); Kress:S1392 (2 pts.).

   THE PEACE-MAKER, or The art of cultivating peace; in a letter to a friend.
London: printed for John Baker, at the Black-Boy in Pater-Noster-Row. 1714.
Pr. 3d. 1 p.l., 23 p. 8°(in 4s) 20 cm.

   Morgan has a variant title, but perhaps in error: Peace-makers, in a
letter to a friend, or the art of cultivating peace ..., otherwise the same.

   The author, devout and evidently a dissenter, adopts the epistolary form
though his substance is more akin to a sermon. He reflects on the blessings of peace, and the sins of the nation which disturb it and cause "all
our other Evils", so obstructive to the Queen (he thus writes before 1st

Aug. when Anne died). With many Old Testament references, the author all-
udes darkly to the "present Posture of Affairs", to "imminent Danger", and
to a "Kingdom divided against itself" (p. 1-8). 'Divide and rule', say.
our enemies. Britain is poor, weak, our Church lacking in confidence, and
the Schism Act (1714, Tory and Anglican in spirit) is offensive to thousands - but God's will be done, so do not discompose yourself (the author
writes to his friend; p. 9-14). Then he confides the secret of "Cultivating Peace", most "taken from God's Word": prayer, love, charity, and for-
giveness are necessary, as is the casting out of envy and malice; we must
have wholesome civil laws, good doctrine, and reconciliation, and God's
mercy - lest He should teach us "profitable Lessons by the Rod of his Ang-
er". Grant the Queen divine wisdom to rule by, and her people the Protestant succession of Hanover (p. 15-21).

   NUC(Pre-1956)446:370; Morgan,BBH:Q486 (Peace-makers, in a letter ...).

[POVEY, Charles], 1652-1743.

An inquiry into the miscarriages of the four last years reign. Wherein
it appears by sixty five articles, that a scheme was laid to raise the
grandeur of France and Spain, break the Confederacy, make a separate peace,
destroy the Establish'd Church, sink the trade of the nation, betray the
Queen, and bring in the Pretender. As also a design to reform the army,
by putting in Irish officers to command it, and for making private leagues
in order to hasten and support the intended restauration. With other particulars relating to the forwardness of a rebellion in Scotland, the great
encrease of Popery in Ireland, the occasion of the Queen's death, and the
discovery of an immense sum of money taken out of the Treasury, and not
accounted for. Presented to the freeholders of Great Britain, against the
next election of a new Parliament. The sixth edition. London: printed for

the author, and are to be sold at Mr. Robinson's, a looking-glass shop,
over against Serjeants-Inn, Fleetstreet. 1714. (Price three pence, on
royal paper 6d.) 1 p.l., 3-32 p. 8°(in 4s) 19 cm.

Authorship: DNB, 'Povey', and Halkett & Laing,3:157; also attributed to
Swift (cf. Morgan), but Swift is the supposed author of a reply to this
(see below).

Title: 5th ed. in NUC has note "Published in 1714 also with title: An
enquiry ..." but no such spelling found in NUC or BM titles.

Appeared in at least eight editions in the same year, 1714 (cf. NUC,
Morgan, and DNB, 'Povey'), though one was "A false Edition" without the
coat of arms (p. 32) which distinguishes "the true Copies" from the "Count-
erfeits"; the latter should be torn wherever found, "according to Act of
Parliament" ("Note", p. 32).

"Advertisement", 1., p. 3: "every true Britain" (sic; i.e. Whig) is urged
to distribute copies of this book "before new Members of Parliament are
chosen", so the Tories will not be re-elected. Quantity rates available.
Free copies in Ireland. 2., p. 31-2: a compendious volume, in Latin, English, and French, to be compiled of articles, speeches, etc., of the Tories during the "Four last Years Reign", with notes, for European distribution, that all may know the "fatal Consequences" of a "Self-interested"
Ministry, and also the happiness brought by the new (Whig) Ministry. Gifts
invited for the book's completion, to "the Seven Gentlemen", via Mr. Robinson, and curious events of the Tory Ministry also accepted.

Answered by: Francis Atterbury, English advice, to the freeholders of
England. [London?], 1714, q.v., above, and: Jonathan Swift, supposed author,
The management of the four last years vindicated: in which her late Majesty,
and her Ministry, are fully cleared from the false aspersions ... in ...
An enquiry into the miscarriages ... Recommended ... against the next

election of a new Parliament ... [London], 1714, (2d ed., 1715), q.v.,
below.

Further to this is: Charles Povey, A memorial of the proceedings of the
late ministery ... Writ by the author of An inquiry ... London, 1715.

The burden of the text is carried in the title. Povey begins by asserting that the prizes of a balance of power and secure peace would have been
won by Marlborough with another battle, instead of the premature Tory peace;
the French were beaten. The early years of Queen Anne were happy at home,
victorious abroad, the Church of England safe, the bishops wise, not "false
brethren" (as Dr. Sacheverell had claimed, cf. his The perils, 1709, above),
while the last four Tory years have seen England "under the blackest Cloud"
while France and Spain have enjoyed "The Sun of Prosperity" beamed to them
from England (p. 4-5). "The Election of a new Parliament is now coming on"
and we must maintain the deliverance King George I has brought to us, not
lose it to the Tories, who would have excluded him from the throne (p. 6-8).
Povey then sketches "Seven dark Planets", short parodies of the Tory Ministers (including Harley), "those who would have sold us, carry'd off in
Fetters" (p. 9-10). Then follow the 65 articles relating to the conduct
of all those Tories (called 'Romans') "oblig'd to surrender their Offices"
under George I, starting with the false alarm by Dr. Sacheverell that the
Church was in danger (p. 10-11). These articles form a partisan history,
domestic and foreign, of the Tory Ministry as seen by a keen advocate of
the revolution principles, ending with (article 65, p. 28-30) a critique
of Defoe's The secret history of the White Staff (London, 1714, q.v.,
above), a canting work written "to vindicate his own Actions, and expose
the Guilt of others" (the White Staff was the symbol of the Treasurer's
office). Povey quotes freely from Defoe's work. He concludes by inviting
the Examiner (Swift's journal) to "contradict with Truth this short History",

to prove Povey has given a false account of the Tory Ministry (p. 30).

Elsewhere, Povey says his life was in danger because of this pamphlet (DNB,

'Povey').

NUC(Pre-1956)468:280 (2d to 8th eds., 1714); BM(to 1955)194:125 (1st to

3d, 6th eds.); Morgan,BBH:Q512 (1st to 3d., 6th, 8th eds., all 1714);

London library,2:607; Kress:2918 (unnumbered & 5th eds., 1714).

RYMER, Thomas, 1641-1713.

Of the antiquity, power & decay of parliaments. Being a general view of

government, and civil policy, in Europe: with other historical and poli-

tical observations, relating therunto. By Tho. Rymer, Esquire, late Hist-

oriographer-Royal. ... London: sold by J[ames]. Roberts, near the Oxford-

Arms in Warwick lane. 1714. 2 p.l., 73, [3] p. 8°(in 4s) 17 cm.

Half-title: Mr. Rymer Of the antiquity, power & decay of parliaments,

&c.; running title (black letter): The antiquity, power and decay of parl-

iaments.

First pub. London (?), 1684 (2d ed. 1704; cf. DNB, 'Rymer', and Morgan

Q557; unfound in NUC, BM), the present ed. being posthumous.

Books printed for D. Browne, W. Mears, and J. Browne (on various subjects):

3 p. at end.

Further to this is (apparently) Rymer's Of the power of Parliaments with

political observations relating thereunto: being a general view of govern-

ment, and civil policy in Europe. Reprinted on occasion of Capt. Steele

[later Sir Richard Steele] being expelled the House of Commons [Mar. 1714,

for seditious libel]. London, 1714 (cf. Morgan,Q557, who says "This seems

to be a part of his Of the antiquity, power & decay ..."; NUC has 3d ed.,

1715, of Of the power.)

Though written (in epistolary form) "in this my retirement" (p. 1), Rymer

was still Historiographer Royal (the post applied for by Swift, April 1714 -
cf. DNB, 'Swift' - after Rymer's death), and fully occupied with his re-
search as editor of the official published transcript of conventions between
Britain and other powers, 1101 to 1654, entitled Foedera - no doubt the
source of much of his information on governments here. After caveats
against bias by nation, era, etc., and comments on the love of liberty in
Europe, Rymer expounds upon the development of government from ancient
to Christian times, and from the common council of Germany, France, and
England to modern assemblies. The story is one of struggle: absolutism
and the sword against the power of the people and peace. Rymer ends with
a discourse on the growth of the 3 estates, in various lands, from the monarch, aristocrats, and people in Polybius' Greece, and 'Rex', 'Principes',
and 'Omnes' in the Rome of Tacitus, to Germany, France, and other European
powers, but always "The Emperor is clearly one of the States" (p. 65-9) -
and so is the English King a part of the Parliament. He concludes with a
note on political frauds in history (p. 71-3).

NUC(Pre-1956)512:487; BM(to 1955)210:329 (both have 1714 only).

A SPEECH to the people against the Pretender, at the publication of Her
Majesty's proclamation, and upon the vote of the Honourable House of Commons. ... London: printed, by Ferd[inand]. Burleigh, 1714. Price two-
pence. 1 p.l., [3]-15 p. 8°(in 4s) 16 p.

Authorship: Morgan gives this to "Stuart, Prince James Edward Francis",
drawing no doubt from BM, where it is placed under "James Francis Edward"
(the Prince of Wales, or Old Pretender) as subject.

Second ed.? (cf. Morgan).

A space-filler at the end (p. 15) advertises: "The grand mystery laid
open, &c. printed by Ferd. Burleigh in Amen-corner".

Addressed to "Gentlemen, Countrymen, and Britons", this opens with a reference to measures taken against the Pretender by Her Majesty (this was therefore written before Queen Anne's death in Aug. 1714) and the Commons, and continues with a warning of the danger to religion, liberty, and happiness, if he comes to the English throne. Shall we have the Hanover succession, or the Pretender, a boy bred under tyranny who, embittered by his father's misfortune, would destroy Parliament? Don't be deluded by empty assurances, or this "Bulwark of the Reformation" (England) will fall under a Popish King who will alter our laws (p. 3-11). It is just for men to risk their lives to keep their land from slavery, and Protestant Europe will assist us against France, whom we conquered in battle but who now wants a "Universal Monarchy". I speak, fellow citizens, not from doubt of your courage, but because I see "how nearly we are threatned", and to say that if the Pretender ascends the throne we shall be scorned by contemporaries and posterity (p. 12-15).

BM(to 1955)114:592 (1st & 2d eds., 1714). Cf. NUC(Pre-1956)561:131 (has 22 p., printer's address, price 3d, 1714); Morgan,BBH:Q656 (but 22 p., price 3d, & "2d ed., 1714", no imprint given - same as above, price 2d?).

[SWIFT, Jonathan], 1667-1745, supposed author.

The management of the four last years vindicated: in which her late Majesty and her Ministry, are fully cleared from the false aspersions cast on them in a late pamphlet, entituled; An enquiry into the miscarriages of the four last years reign, &c. and the malice of the faction in that, and in other late libels, is expos'd. Recommended to all true Englishmen, against the next election of a new Parliament. ... [s.l.; London,] Sold by J[ohn]. Morphew near Stationers Hall, 1714. (Price six-pence.) 1 p.l., [3]-48 p. 8°(in 4s) 19 cm.(unbd.)

Jonathan Swift
Engraved by Andrew Miller from the portrait by Francis
Bindon. (From Ralph Straus, <u>The Unspeakable Curll</u>,
London, Chapman and Hall, 1927, opposite p. 192, and
 here reproduced with the publishers' permission.)

Authorship: Halkett & Laing and Stonehill assign to Swift without query, as does Morgan; but Swift is conjectural in Rothschild, and not listed even as doubtful in Teerink-Scouten. The work is signed (p. 48): "C.B.". Lacking firm evidence, I have used the NUC form of entry.

First edition; 2d ed., 1715; also Dublin, [1714?].

A reply to: Charles Povey, An inquiry into the miscarriages of the four last years reign. London, 1714, q.v., above.

Printed marginal notes of sources.

Provenance: Geo. Rouyou (? t.-p. autogr.).

Here is another in the flurry of factional pamphlets issued to influence "the Honest Freeholders and Voters of Great Britain", to whom it is addressed (p. [3]), in the usual epistolary form. The "next Election" (t.-p.) was held in Feb. 1715, when the Whigs were returned overwhelmingly. This is a Tory contender in the lists, for "the Whigs have had a fair Field" to present their case; it is difficult even "to break in upon them". One tract is singled out to "be the Test for all", the contender for the "blackest Libel" of all: Povey's Inquiry; he had set forth in 65 articles his charges against the Tories, the peace favouring defeated France and Spain, and the Pretender, being foremost. After several pages of general denunciation, the author lights on the Tory victory in the new Parliament, 25 Nov. 1710, the ensuing jubilation everywhere, and evidence that the Ministry had no intention to "raise the Grandeur of France and Spain, or bring in the Pretender" (p. 11), but to continue the war: yet, an unequal burden of expense had been laid on us by the Allies, and we tried to curb the Whig embezzlements, for the millions spent to shorten the war were now the cause of its continuation, for profit; so Parliament agreed with the Queen in ending this impoverishing war. Is this raising the grandeur of France? Peace had been attempted before, when it was a sweet word; and then, as

later, in concert with the Dutch, who were asked to bear a more even share
of costs if war continued; but they pleaded inability (p. 20). So, the
Queen is vindicated from the imputation of deserting her Allies. Many
official documents and letters are cited or transcribed, and private in-
cidents of state related (to all of which Swift was privy through his high
contacts) in evidence against Povey's charges - especially letters to and
from the Queen (on the Dutch desire for peace, p. 23; amnesty for the Catalans, p. 30; and removal of the Pretender from Lorraine, p. 38). The
Queen and Ministry offered a reward for the Pretender, so the charge of
Jacobitism is groundless, as is the charge of designing to destroy the
Church of England, against which are cited 5 official articles supporting
the Church (p. 41). The final pages refute the rest of Povey's accusa-
tions, drawing upon an intimate knowledge of Church and state events.

NUC(Pre-1956)579:218 (& 2d ed., 1715); Morgan,BBH:Q663; Rothschild:2211;
London Library,2:193 (under title; & Dublin, 1714?); Kress:2935.

A TENDER and hearty address to all the freeholders, and other electors
of Members for the ensuing Parliament of Great Britain, & Ireland. In
which the conspiracies of the faction, for four years last past, are plac'd
in a true light. London: printed for J. Baker in Pater-Noster Row. 1714.
Price 3d. 2 p.l., 3-18 p. 8°(in 4s) 19 cm.

Attributed to Charles Povey (1652?-1743) - cf. Morgan.

Half-title: An address to the freeholders.

First (and only?) edition.

"Any Gentlemen that are willing to take a Number [of these pamphlets] to
give away, shall have a considerable Allowance [in price]" (a propaganda
device still in use): verso of half-title.

One of many pamphlets addressed to freeholders (electors, as absolute

owners of land) after the death of Queen Anne, pressing various issues
prior to the "Approaching Choice" (p. 3), the general election of a new
Parliament, February, 1715 (this was pub. Dec. 1714, cf. Madan). Here the
concern is with the "Calamitous State" resulting from the "Two Last Parliaments" under the "Corrupt Ministry" of the Tories. There follows a
catalogue of miseries abroad and at home, all leading England to the brink
of ruin, including the destruction of the Dutch 'barrier' against France,
Popish and Jacobite activities in Scotland, the growth in number and arming of Papists in Ireland, the "False Cry of the Church's Danger" by Dr.
Sacheverell, favouring of the Pretender, and a private peace with France
(Spanish Succession War; p. 4-9). Some other woes lamented are: poor relations with the Dutch Allies, domestic debt and corruption, delay in the
destruction of Dunkirk, decline in trade, and high duty on commodities for
the poor. Yet, the moment King George came, stocks rose prodigiously,
showing the general faith in "a True English Protestant House-of-Commons"
as against those who gave us the "Bill of Commerce with France" (1713) and
the "Bill of Schism" (against dissenters, 1714). An entreaty to avoid all
representatives of the last Ministry, and a summary of charges against them
(most of which are dealt with in separate Whig pamphlets), concludes the
work.

   NUC(Pre-1956)586:292 (this ed. only); Morgan,BBH:Q673 (this only);
Madan(Speck):1111 (this only).

[TOLAND, John], 1670-1722.

The art of restoring. Or, The piety and probity of General Monk in
bringing about the last restoration, evidenc'd from his own authentic letters: with a just account of Sir Roger, who runs the parallel as far as he
can. In a letter to a Minister of State, at the Court of Vienna. ...

The fourth edition. London: sold by J. Roberts, near the Oxford-Arms, in

Warwick-Lane, 1714. Price 6d. viii, 48 p. 8°(in 4s) 19 cm.

Errata: p. [ii].

Morgan indicates 10 editions pub. in 3 months, 1713 (1st) & 1714.

The Preface ("To Count George ... My Dear Kinsman"), a supposed letter

dated at "Vienna, Jan. 2. 1714", concerns Harley, and plots and bribery at

home and abroad (especially French) against the Hanover succession; the text

in reply (to "My Lord") is dated at "London, August 20, 1713", but contin-

ues till October (see end of annotation, below).

The author compares and contrasts the position of "Sir Roger" (Robert

Harley, Earl of Oxford) and his alleged Jacobite commitment to restoring

the Pretender, with the manipulations of "General Monk" (George Monck, Duke

of Albemarle), who facilitated the Restoration of Charles II, 1660. The

Jacobites, says Toland, in their libels (as in The conduct of the Allies,

1712, by Swift) plainly want to change the Hanoverian succession, saying it

is absurd to have a Popish Emperor (in the Treaty of The Hague) and Papist

French King (in the Treaty of Utrecht) guarantee a Protestant succession -

though the Jacobites also quarrelled with the Dutch for their guarantees.

It is not so much our souls as our liberty at risk, however, and this con-

cern, and ties of blood and closeness to the House of Hanover, we share

with the Emperor, against France (p. 1-4). The balance of power favours

France, as it did at the time of Cromwell, and Harley designs to place the

French viceroy (the Pretender) on the British throne. There follows a

diatribe against the pride, vanity and low cunning of Harley, and the char-

acter of Monck "between whom and Sir Roger several comparisons may be ...

made", though without bad reflection on the blessed Restoration of Charles

II, of course (p. 5-13). The remainder of the pamphlet deals with Monck's

part in the Restoration, based on his own copiously-quoted letters. Monck,

like Harley, had "been of all parties, till at last he came to enjoy great
Power" (p. 15), when his "Perjury and Dissimulation" brought back the King
(p. 32). Similarities with Harley are pointed up throughout, and even
their epitaphs should be alike; of Harley: "That he never said a plain
thing, nor ever did an honest thing" (p. 36), and of Monck (but will "do
every whit as well for Sir Roger"): "... he verifies, That whoever will
rise, Must be content to have Knave Writ on his grave" (p. 39). There is
much more to say but, Toland finishes, "This is a long-winded letter ...
begun in August, and hardly ended in October". Morgan comments that "this
pamphlet created a sensation" when published.

   NUC(Pre-1956)596:321 (NIC; 1713, & 1st-7th eds.); BM(to 1955)162:640-41
(1st, 3d-5th eds., under: Geo. Monk); Carabelli: 180-2 (1st; 1713; 2d-4th,
1714); Morgan,BBH:P607 (1st, 1713; 4th-10th, 1714); Hazen(Walpole):2677:3;
Rothschild:2437; London Library (Suppl. 1920):731.

[_____].

   The grand mystery laid open; namely, by dividing of the Protestants to
weaken the Hanover succession, and by defeating the succession, to extir-
pate the Protestant religion. To which is added, the sacredness of parliamentary securities: against those, who wou'd indirectly ... attack the
publick funds. ... London: printed by Ferd[inand]. Burleigh. 1714.
(Price Four Pence). 1 p.l., 3-31 p. 8°(in 4s) 16 cm.

   Authorship: Morgan notes an attribution to Defoe, but unconfirmed in
Moore; Carabelli cites numerous authorities for Toland's authorship;
Halkett & Laing and Stonehill agree.

   Also published with imprint: London, printed for J. Roberts, 1714, price
6d., 48 p., & that has likely priority of issue, for the 2 errata of J.
Roberts edition, p. 48, not present here, have been corrected in the text

(p. 7 and 10).

The author, a deist active in establishing the Protestant succession, writes before August, when Queen Anne still lived. Fearing the Pretender (James Edward) may land in England, Toland reports that both Queen and Commons have offered rewards for his capture, while others try to keep out the Elector (of Hanover). The Papists in Ireland are openly arming, though this is denied by the Examiner and Post-boy (Tory journals); while in England, anyone above a farmer praises the peace with France and declaims against the Dutch, as do their confederates the nonjurors. In England, Ireland, and Scotland, men are enlisting for the Pretender; invasion is being planned, and the Protestant succession menaced. "Of our disbanded Soldiers vast numbers are gone to France", to march back with the Pretender; but it would still be a French victory (p. 3-8). High-Churchmen threaten the Church of England (Toland opposed Dr. Sacheverell) by crying danger, from dissenters and Low-Churchmen, thus dividing "The Bulwark of the Reformation", England, against herself, and assisting Rome, France, and the Pretender, by widening the breaches (p. 9-11). Toland then exposes some Tory and foreign leaders for abetting this disunion among Protestants, to alienate Hanover; but if we can hold together, we can defy France and the Pope. So, let us pray for the Queen, our dear country, and the Protestant succession (p. 12-18).

In a concluding section headed "The sacredness of Parliamentary securities, &c." (p. 19), Toland says the public debt arises from corruption; the exhausted treasury requires "little Tricks" to cover it, by Ministers who are rewarded for their success. Anyone without tricks is counted a "sad Politician". Religion and liberty mean nothing to such men, in the dangerous task of ruining their enemies; and turncoats harbour the most implacable malice (p. 19-21). If the Pretender promised to make good all funds, some would accept, preferring private interest to public good. If our

Parliament fails us, where is security? Cicero is quoted for guidance, and

the Pretender and Jacobites are seen as threats to public funds while Han-

overians are for Parliament and guarding the funds. An extract from the

5th July _Examiner_ on the need for British independence, ends the work.

BM(to 1955)195:826 (? no printer or collation given). Cf. Morgan,BBH:

Q683 (1st ed., J. Roberts, 48 p.); Carabelli:185 (printed for J. Roberts,

48 p.); NUC(Pre-1956)596:324 (printed for J. Roberts, rest of imprint, &

collation, omitted).

[WAGSTAFFE, William], 1685-1725.

The state and condition of our taxes, considered; or, A proposal for a

tax upon funds: shewing, the justice, usefulness, and necessity, of such

a tax, in respect to our trading and landed interest, and especially if we

engage in a new war. With some directions to the freeholders of Great

Britain, concerning the choice of the next Parliament. By a Freeholder.

... London: printed for John Morphew, near Stationers-Hall, 1714. Price

6d. 2 p.l., 5-46 p. 8°(in 4s) 18 cm.

Half-title (1st p.l.): "The state ... considered, &c."

First edition; 2d and 3d eds., 1714, 24 p.

A freeholder was the absolute owner of an estate and, as such, enfran-

chised to vote for a Member of Parliament. On the eve of the national

election, after the "coming over of the King", George I, we must, says the

author, be cautious who we choose to represent us. Wagstaffe, a physician,

complains that though the expensive war made high taxes necessary, they are

not "laid equally on all People in Proportion to their Wealth"; the "Coun-

try Gentlemen" are especially burdened, even though they are as loyal and

freedom-loving as others (p. 6-11). Landed and moneyed interests should be taxed equally, then we'll see who wants to continue the war and to humble France - not the poor, taxed on coals, candles, soap, and leather. Is the moneyed interest willing to pay one fifth of its wealth (as have land-holders) for the security of our constitution, when they have paid nothing at present? (p. 12-16). A general excise would stimulate trade, pay the costs in the event of another war, be more equitable, and make our island strong again by financing a protective fleet, not an army - as Clarendon's History observes (p. 17-26). Dr. Wagstaffe praises Ormonde and Bolingbroke (p. 26-9) and reckons it wise to re-elect the present honest, public-spirited, loyal and altogether felicitous (and Tory) Parliament, giving many reasons, suggestions for it to consider, and some regarding its mem-bership. Don't be deluded (Wagstaffe closes) by the cant of a false peace (by the Whigs), when havoc and high taxes make peace essential. Let Whig and Tory distinctions cease; let's differentiate only between those who want peace, and those for war and heavy taxes (p. 31-46).

NUC(Pre-1956)644:668 (1st-3d eds.); BM(to 1955)79:28 (1st-3d); Morgan, BBH:Q710 (1st-3d); Kress:2937 (1st & 2d eds.).

Completed 31 August 1982

Laus Deo

APPENDICES

APPENDIX A

The "Faults" Controversy, 1710

The controversy began with Benjamin Hoadly's The Thoughts of an
Honest Tory (London, 1710), but most of the pamphlets which sprang from
this one contain the word 'faults' in their titles. For this group,
therefore, the appellation 'Faults' controversy is appropriate and convenient. Strangely enough, although the qualifications for belonging to the
group are recognizable in most of the titles, there does not seem to have
been any attempt to bring all these titles together - as, for example,
Madan has done for the Sacheverell controversy.

The 'faults' group of pamphlets is really a continuation of the furor
raised by Henry Sacheverell's two sermons of 1709, The Communication of Sin
and The Perils of False Brethren. In the latter it was their ringing cry
against "Resistance upon any Pretence whatsoever" to the monarch which
raised the wrath of Parliament, and culminated in bringing impeachment
(albeit in mild form) upon Sacheverell's head early in 1710. There had been
a small dress rehearsal of this controversy a few months before the Sacheverell frenzy, when this same Hoadly had responded sharply to Bishop Offspring Blackall's The Divine Institution of Magistracy, London, 1709 (q.v.
in the Catalogue), setting the fur flying between High and Low-Church

adherents, Tories and Whigs, in a group of lively pamphlets. Hoadly's opening shot in this new 'faults' cannonade (item 1, below) was heavily critical of the activities and propaganda of the Tories, ever since the impeachment. That Hoadly was raising new issues, distinct from those of the Sacheverell affair, was understood by Madan, for he excludes almost all of the 'faults' titles from his bibliography. Nevertheless, Hoadly strongly argued for the 'revolution principles', against the Tory, High-Church doctrines of the hereditary right of kings, passive obedience, and non-resistance to royal commands, so that the 'faults' controversy comes within the wider contentious arguments voiced by Sacheverell.

Hoadly posed satirically as a Tory, deploring the infamy of 'his' party's principles and practices. This set the tone for many of the subsequent works, such as The Thoughts of an Honest Whig, in which the Tory author parodies Hoadly in pretending he speaks for the Whigs. Simon Clement's Faults on Both Sides is the first use of the key word, and forms a strong presentation of Robert Harley's policy of moderation towards both sides in the dispute. This work, in which Harley undoubtedly had a direct hand (cf. J.A. Downie, Robert Harley and the Press, Cambridge University Press, 1979, p. 119-22), was reprinted many times, in English, French and Dutch. The subsequent titles in the series appear in the bibliography below.

Seven titles in this group are owned by Queen's University, and thus appear in the main Catalogue. These are denoted by an asterisk preceding the item number. The remainder of the titles listed have not yet been acquired for the Collection, and it should be noted that I have not examined these works. The information given has been gathered from the sources cited in each entry; and while this method of compilation is undoubtedly subject to hazard, it seemed useful to bring these related titles together in this preliminary form, as an appendix to the foregoing Catalogue of the Collection as it presently exists.

The bibliographies cited are identified in the list of sources which precedes the Catalogue, and the principles of description and transcription follow those set forth for the Catalogue in the Introduction.

A Preliminary

Bibliography of the "Faults" Controversy

*1. [Hoadly, Benjamin], bp. of Winchester, 1676-1761.

The thoughts of an honest Tory, upon the present proceedings of that party. In a letter to a friend in town. London, sold by A[nn] Baldwin, in Warwick-Lane. 1710. Price 2d.

[2], 14 p. 8°

Reprinted in Somers tracts, 1814, 12:672, and in Hoadly's Works (1773), 1:630. For other notes, see entry in the Catalogue.

NUC(Pre-1956)248:478; BM(to 1955)104:611 & 240:347; Morgan,BBH:M318; Madan(Speck):483; Rothschild:1141.

2. [_____].

Another edition. London, 1710.

[2], 14 p. 8°

No comma after "Tory" and "London" on title-page. For other notes see entry in the Catalogue for item 1.

BM(to 1955)104:611; Madan(Speck):484.

Also (without specifying t.-p. variation) Morgan,BBH:M318.

----

*Items in the Catalogue or the Appendix of additions.

3. [_____].

Another edition. London, 1710.

16 p. 8°

Title-page as in item 1, but with a colon after "London". For other notes see entry in the Catalogue for item 1.

Madan(Speck):485.

*4. [Clement, Simon], fl. 1695-1714.

Faults on both sides: or, An essay upon the original cause, progress, and mischievous consequences of the factions in this nation. Showing that the heads and leaders on both sides have always impos'd upon the credulity of their respective parties, in order to compass their own selfish designs at the expence of the peace and tranquility of the nation. Sincerely intended for the allaying the heats and animosities of the people, and persuading all honest, well-meaning men to compose their party-quarrels, and unite their hearts and affections for the promoting the publick good, and safety of their Queen and country. By way of answer to the thoughts of an honest Tory. _____ En quo discordia cives Perduxit miseros _____ _____ Virg. London: printed and sold by the booksellers of London and Westminster, 1710.

56 p. 8°

A reply to item 1, and answered by item 12, and partly by item 28; "Part the second" (item 14) is actually another reply. Reprinted in Somers tracts, 1814, 12:678. For other notes, see entry in the Catalogue, and the Somers reprint.

NUC(Pre-1956)231:275 (under Richard Harley); BM(to 1955)71:303; Morgan,BBH:M284; London Library, 1:1081. Cf. Rothschild:85 (2d ed., but extensive notes).

*5. [_____].

   "The second edition." London: printed and sold by the booksellers

of London and Westminster, 1710.

   56 p. 8°

   A reprint from the type used for the 1st edition, but on different

paper. For other notes, see entry in the Catalogue.

   NUC(Pre-1956)231:275 (under Richard Harley); BM(to 1955)71:303;

Morgan,BBH:M284; London Library, 1:1081; Rothschild:85; Hazen(Walpole):

89:2:4.

6. [_____].

   Another edition. London, 1715.

   24 p. [8°?]

   Morgan,BBH:M284n. refers also to a 1730 edition. For other notes,

see entry in Catalogue for item 4.

   NUC(Pre-1956)231:275 (under Richard Harley).

7. [_____].

   Misslagen aan weerkanten, of schetse Van de eerste Oorzaak, den Voor-

gang en de verderflyke gevolgen van de verdeeltheden der Engelsche

Landaard: Toonende Dat de Hoofden en Leydslieden van wederzyden, altoos

de ligtgeloovigheyd hunner byzondere partyen misleyd habben enz. ...

Dienende tot antwoord van't Boekje, geheeten De gedachten van eenen

eerlyken Tory ... Uyt het Engels vertaald, Door W. Sewel. Amsterdam,

J. Swart, 1710.

   110 p. 8°

   A Dutch translation of item 4.

   Knuttel:15870.

8. [_____].

   Fautes des deux côtez, par rapport à ce qui s'est passè depuis peu en

Angleterre, traduit de l'Anglois. Rotterdam, Fritsch et Böhm, 1711.

[collation unavailable]

French translation of item 4.

NUC(Pre-1956)231:275; Morgan,BBH:M284n.

9. [_____].

Fautes des cotez, par un rapport à ce qui s'est passé depuis peu en Angleterre, traduit de l'Anglois. Cologne, P. Marteau, 1711.

lxxx, 142 p. 8°

Another French translation of item 4.

Knuttel:15942.

*10. The thoughts of an honest Whig, upon the present proceedings of that party. In a letter to a friend in town. London: printed in the year 1710.

16 p. 8°

Stonehill:2427 has the author as Benjamin Hoadly, but in fact this is a response to Hoadly's The thoughts of an honest Tory (no. 1, above), in which the author parodies Hoadly's satirical approach: he pretends he is a Whig dissenter, but in fact is a Tory criticizing the Whigs. For other notes, see entry in the Catalogue.

NUC(Pre-1956)593:59; BM(to 1955)256:397; Morgan,BBH:M699; Madan(Speck): 486.

11. _____.

Another edition. London, 1720.

16 p. 8°

For notes, see item 10, and the entry in the Catalogue for item 10.

NUC(Pre-1956)593:59.

12. Faults in the fault-finder: or, A specimen of errors in the pamphlet, entitul'd Faults on both sides. London, A[nn]. Baldwin, 1710.

47 p. 8°

A reply to item 4, above, and answered by item 18; it was supplemented

by item 23. For other notes, see entry in the Catalogue for item 13.

NUC(Pre-1956)167:545; BM(to 1955)71:304; Morgan,BBH:M283.

*13. _____.

"The second edition." London: printed, and to be sold by A[nn].

Baldwin, near the Oxford-Arms in Warwick-Lane, 1710. (Price 3d.)

24 p. 8°(in 4s)

For notes, see entry in the Catalogue.

NUC(Pre-1956)167:545; BM(to 1955)71:304; Morgan,BBH:M283; London Lib-

rary, 1:810; Rothschild:85n, 88.

* 14.   Faults on both sides: part the second. Or, an essay upon the origin-

al cause, progress, and mischievous consequences of the factions in the

church. Shewing, that the clergy, of whatsoever denomination, have

always been the ring-leaders and beginners of the disturbances in every

state; imposing upon the credulity of the laity, for no other end than

the accomplishing their own selfish designs, at the expence of the

peace and tranquillity of the nation. Faithfully produced from the most

eminent authorities. Sincerely intended for allaying the heats and

animosities of the people, and persuading all honest, well-meaning men

to compose their party quarrels, and unite their hearts and affections

for promoting the public good, and safety of their Queen and Country.

By way of a letter to a new Member of Parliament ... [Two-line quotat-

ion from Lucan.] London: printed and sold by the booksellers of London

and Westminster, 1710.

38 p. 8°(in 4s)

This is not a continuation of Clement's work, item 4 above, but a re-

ply to it in defence of Hoadly, presenting a Whig viewpoint. Reprinted

in Somers tracts, 1814, 12:708, and (cf. BM, 'Faults') 1751, v.3.

NUC(Pre-1956)167:545; BM(to 1955)71:303; Rothschild:85n,86; Morgan, BBH:M284n.

15. [Trapp, Joseph], 1679-1747.

Most faults on one side: or, The shallow politicks, foolish arguing, and villanous designs of the author of a late pamphlet, entitul'd Faults on both sides consider'd and expos'd. In answer to that pamphlet: shewing, that the many truths in modern history related by the author of it, do not make amends for his many falsehoods in fact, and fallacies in reasoning ... London: printed for John Morphew, near Stationers-Hall, 1710.

63 p. 8°

Authorship: Stonehill:1449. A High-Church Tory pamphleteer who assisted Dr. Sacheverell at his trial, Dr. Trapp here angrily criticizes Clement's moderate Tory work, item 4, but recognizes its general historical accuracy. This was answered by Clement's A vindication of the Faults on both sides, item 18 below.

NUC(Pre-1956)600:44; BM(to 1955)71:304; Rothschild:85n,2447; Morgan, BBH:M713; BPL(Defoe):169.

*16. [_____].

Most faults on one side: or, The shallow politics, foolish arguing and villanous designs of the author of a late pamphlet, entitul'd Faults on both sides, consider'd and expos'd ... London, John Morphew, 1711.

70 p. 8°

Evidently the 2d edition. For other notes see item 15.

NUC(Pre-1956)600:44; BM(to 1955)71:304; Morgan,BBH:M713 (? has "1711" only); BPL(Defoe):169.

17. [_____].

"The third edition, corrected." London, John Morphew, 1711.

63 p. 8°

For notes, see item 15. BM also has another edition, same imprint

but 70 p.

NUC(Pre-1956)600:44; BM(to 1955)71:304; BPL(Defoe):170.

18. [Clement, Simon], fl. 1695-1714.

A vindication of the Faults on both sides, from the reflections of

the Medley, the Specimen-maker, and a pamphlet, entituled, Most faults

on one side. With a dissertation on the nature and use of money and

paper-credit in trade ... By the author of the Faults on both sides ...

London, printed and sold by the booksellers of London and Westminster,

1710.

43, [1] p. 8°

Clement's defence of Robert Harley's mediation policy between Whigs

and Tories, as expressed in his own work, item 4; a reply to item 12,

and to the Tory Dr. Trapp's Most faults, item 15. It was supported by

item 20, and answered by item 23. The medley was a Whig journal, London,

1710-12 (cf. Union list of serials, 3d ed., and Morgan,BBH:N262), in

which Faults on both sides had been attacked. Specimen-maker has not

been identified. Reprinted in Somers tracts, 1815, 13:3 (q.v. for use-

ful notes), and 1752, v. 3 - cf. BM, 'Faults'.

NUC(Pre-1956)638:411; BM(to 1955)71:304; Morgan,BBH:M286; Kress:2680.

19. [_____].

Second edition. London, 1710.

[collation unavailable].

Morgan,BBH:M286.

20. [Defoe, Daniel], 1661?-1731.

A supplement to the Faults on both sides: containing the compleat
history of the proceedings of a party ever since the Revolution: in a
familiar dialogue between Steddy and Turn-round, two displac'd officers
of state. Which may serve to explaine Sir Thomas Double; and to show
how far the late Parliament were right in proceeding against Dr. Sacheverell, by way of impeachment. London: printed for J. Baker, at the
Black-Boy in Pater-noster-row, 1710. (Price 1s.)

   2 p.l., 3-76 p. 8°

Authorship: Moore, and Stonehill:2395. Page 49-76 misnumbered 41-68
(cf. BM). This is another presentation of Robert Harley's moderate views
in support of items 4 and 18; it advocates a coalition ministry under
Harley, who employed both Clement and Defoe in his plan to reconcile
Whigs and Tories. This work is advertised in p.[2] of the booklist
at the end of The re-representation: or, A modest search, London, 1711
(q.v. in the Catalogue). Sir Thomas Double at court was an anonymous
work by Charles Davenant.

   NUC(Pre-1956)577:23; BM(to 1955)50:136; Morgan,BBH:M191; Moore(2d
ed.):194; London Library, 1:1081; BPL(Defoe):169.

21. [_____].

   Variant. London, 1710.

   2 p.l., 3-76 p. 8°

   In this, pagination, catchwords, etc., have been corrected.

   BM(to 1955)50:136.

22. [_____].

   Other editions. London, 1710.

   Moore reports "five known editions", and some variants; BM has two
1710 editions, and a variant.

23. A supplement to Faults in the fault-finder in answer to the Vindication of "Faults on both sides". London, printed and sold by A[nn]. Baldwin near Oxford-Arms in Warwick Lane, 1711. ([Price] 3d.)

   47 p. [8°?]

   This (if it is not a ghost) is further to item 12, and a reply to
item 18.

   Morgan,BBH:N567.

24. [Defoe, Daniel], 1661?-1731.

   Faults on both sides; the second part: containing the compleat history of proceedings ever-since the Revolution; in a familiar dialogue
between Steddy and Turn-round, two displac'd officers of state. Which
may serve to explain Sir Thomas Double; London: printed for J. Baker;
at the Black-Boy in Pater-noster-row, 1710. (Price 1s.)

   32 p. 4°

   Pages 21-24 misnumbered 20-23 (cf. NUC). Authorship: Moore, and Rothschild. This appears to be a hasty reprint (cf. Moore) of item 15, and
it is not the same work as item 14, which has the subtitle "part the
second". It is a continuation of Robert Harley's argument for reconciliation: cf. item 20. The semicolon after 'Double' is from NUC & Moore.

   NUC(Pre-1956)167:545; Moore(2d ed.):194n.; Rothschild:86n.; Morgan,
BBH:M284n.(?); BPL(Defoe):43.

25. A letter from a High Church-man to a Whig. [London? 1710?]
   [collation unavailable]

   No copy known to be extant, but its existence is implied by item 26.
   Madan(Speck):524.

26. [_____].

   Colophon: Edinburgh, reprinted by John Reid junior, 1710.

   4 p. [8°?]

Caption title. This attacks the political record of the Whigs, and
defends the High-Church doctrine of passive obedience and non-resistance. It is in part a reply to item 1, and partly to another work by
Benjamin Hoadly: The French king's thanks to the Torries of Great
Britain (London, A[nn]. Baldwin, 1710).

NUC(Pre-1956)328:665; Madan(Speck):525.

27.   A true history of the honest Whigs. A poem. London: printed in the
year 1710.

16 p. 8°

A reply to item 1 and an echo of the title to item 10, this work is
attributed to a disillusioned Whig (cf. Madan). It is hostile to the
Whigs, especially to the alliance of low-churchmen and dissenters, and
it supports Dr. Sacheverell's High-Church arguments.

NUC(Pre-1956)602:611; Madan(Speck):487.

28.   An answer to that part of the pamphlet entitul'd, Faults on both sides,
which relates to the deficiency of the English army in Spain, at the
time of the Battle of Almanza. Being the substance of Her Majesty's
message to the House of Commons concerning it. London: printed, and
to be sold by A[nn]. Baldwin, near the Oxford-Arms in Warwick-Lane, 1710.
(Price Two Pence.)

16 p. 8°

A reply to part of item 4. In the Battle of Almanza, 25 April, 1707,
the British army under a French Huguenot was defeated by the French
army, under an English son of James II.

NUC(Pre-1956)17:587; BM(to 1955)71:304; Morgan,BBH:M34; Rothschild:
85n,87; Kress:2644.

29.   [Steele, Sir Richard], 1672-1729, and [Addison, Joseph], 1672-1719.

The Tatler's ecclesaistical thermometer or weather glass exemplifying

Faults on both sides, but in reverse to a late book ... Most faults

on one side. [London?], 1710.

fol. broadside.

Exemplifies item 4, and opposes the High-Church Tory work, item 15.

The Tatler, London, 1709-11, conducted by Steele and Addison was a

Whig journal.

Morgan,BBH:M672.

30.   A vindication of ye Church of England, or An essay upon an essay

called Faults on both sides (1710). [London? 1710]

[collation unavailable]

A reply to item 4, and not to be confused with item 18. Evidently

a Tory work.

Morgan,BBH:M733a.

31.   Faults on no side: or, Everyone in the right. In answer to Faults on

both sides. [London, 1710]

4 p. [8°?]

Evidently a response to Clement's work, item 4.

NUC(Pre-1956)167:545.

32. [Defoe, Daniel], 1661?-1731.

R——'s [i.e. Rogue's] on both sides. In which are the characters of

some r——'s not yet describ'd; with a true discription of an Old Whig,

and a Modern Whig; an old Tory and a modern Tory; a highflyer, or mot-

ly; as also of a minister of state. By the same author. London, printed

for John Baker, at the Black-Boy in Pater-Noster-Row, 1711. Price 6d.

2 p.l., 36 p. 8°

First edition. Signatures: [A]^2, B-E^4, F^2 (D2 incorrectly signed D3 -

cf. NUC). Unseen but assumed to be relevent, as Defoe's contribution to

the altercation. Defoe was writing for Robert Harley at this time, as was Clement (item 4), who had also responded to Hoadly's original pamphlet (item 1). The meaning of the possessive apostrophe in 'rogue's, if any, is not clear.

NUC(Pre-1956)136:641; BM(to 1955)50:127; Moore(2d ed.):198; Morgan,BBH: N155; BPL(Defoe):147.

33. [_____].

The second edition. London, 1711.

2 p.l., 36 p. 8°(?)

Signatures: [A]^2, B-E^4, F^2 (cf. NUC).

NUC(Pre-1956)136:641; BPL(Defoe):147.

The following later titles do not appear to be part of the same controversy, though they bear similar titles:

34. [Honeyman, James], 1675(ca.)-1750.

Faults on all sides. The case of religion consider'd: shewing the substance of true godliness ... Newport, Rhode-Island, printed for the author ... 1728.

11 p.l., 150 p. [8°?]

NUC(Pre-1956)253:419; BM(to 1955)71:303.

35. Faults on both sides, or whether the church or dissenters are in fauts [sic]: being an enquiry into the cause, proceedings, and dangerous consequences of the factious parties in the kingdom. ... London, printed by D. Brown in Fleetstreet [1714].

16 p. 4°

Morgan notes that another edition of this, also [1714], is entitled Fauts on both sides.

Morgan,BBH:Q320a.

*   *   *

APPENDIX B

Year Count of Tracts in Morgan

Dr. William Thomas Morgan's Bibliography of British History (1700-1715)
is the most comprehensive source of titles I have consulted, for the period
of this Catalogue. A brief glance at the bibliographical citations for the
entries will verify that 'Morgan' is hardly ever absent. As a mirror of
the pamphlets published during these early years of the eighteenth century,
Morgan's book seems best qualified to reflect the most accurate image.
Reproduced here is a table of the numbers of publications listed in Morgan
for the period it covers, year by year. As mentioned elsewhere in this
Catalogue, the year 1710 saw the greatest amount of press activity. It was
the five years to the end of Queen Anne's reign (1714) which produced the
highest numbers, and the year 1715 (the year of the Fifteen Rebellion) still
maintained a productivity of over six hundred items. With 1716, and the
passage of the Septennial Act, the number of publications dropped back to
the four-hundreds again. The supernova had burned itself out.

1700 - 498	1704 - 521	1708 - 462	1712 - 758
1701 - 514	1705 - 481	1709 - 456	1713 - 681
1702 - 560	1706 - 437	1710 - 770	1714 - 755
1703 - 443	1707 - 499	1711 - 670	1715 - 651

1716 - 495

APPENDIX C

Who Was 'Eugenius Philalethes'?

Although I have not made a quantitative analysis of word and phrase occurrence and patterns in the text, such as has been applied to the works of Swift[1], there is internal evidence to suggest that Some modest animadversions ... by Eugenius Philalethes, pseud. (London, 1710, q.v. in the Catalogue), could very well have been written by Charles Leslie, 1650-1722.

Leslie was one of the most outspoken of the nonjurors, and irrepressibly prolific. Although a deeply-convinced believer in the divine right and hereditary succession of monarchs and the subordinate doctrines, his arguments are conveyed in a literary style of wit and kindly satire, and presented in an orderly, intelligent manner which persuades by its steady conviction and moderate fairness. Dr. Johnson went so far as to observe[2] that Leslie was the only reasoning nonjuror, and one "who was not to be reasoned against".

General

Charles Leslie's favourite topic is resistance and non-resistance.

---

1. Louis T. Milic, A quantitative approach to the style of Jonathan Swift (Paris, 1967). Professor Milic coins the useful phrase "word-class frequency distribution".
2. DNB, 'Leslie'.

He is one of the most zealous High-Church writers of the time. Queen Anne's reign is the most active period of his writing. Leslie, a lawyer, uses close argument: point-by-point refutation, with specific page references to the text he is criticizing.

Leslie uses the pseudonym 'Philalethes', in his journal The rehearsal, 1704-9. None of these points is in itself (or even taken together) conclusive - the pseudonym 'Philalethes' is a fairly common one, for example.

Style

Many of Leslie's arguments are similar to those in Some modest animadversions: stress on resistance, frequent references to the lesson of Charles I, numerous citations of the Old Testament.

'The Good Old Cause' is a favourite expression, two of Leslie's titles beginning with these words, and they are used in Some modest animadversions, e.g.: p. 13.

His references to resistance and non-resistance are always forceful and agitated. This is a typical High-Church topic, but it is not typical to discuss it with such strength of emotion.

Leslie has a habit of referring to his opponent directly, as 'Sir', or 'Mr', or 'Doctor'; e.g., Leslie's Good old cause: p. 6, 9, 20, 21, 25, and his Best answer ever: passim; and so also in Some modest animadversions: p. 9, 11, 12, 15, 44, 46, 51.

Leslie also has a particular habit of making deferential references adjacent to a reprimand; e.g., in his Good old cause further discuss'd: p. 6, 9, 20, 21, 25; and so too, in Some modest animadversions: p. 10, 11, 12, 15, 44, 45, 47, etc.

In conclusion, I note that in Herbert Davis' edition of Swift's Drapier's letters (p. xiii), evidence similar to that above is accepted for Swift's authorship of a comment in the Dublin Weekly news-letter: the comment "states in his unmistakable language a few of the points which he was afterwards to elaborate in the Second letter; and gives a contemptuous description of William Wood ..." - just as Leslie is contemptuous of resistance.

APPENDIX D

The Order of the Bibliographical Notes

A. Notes concerning the whole edition or issue.

First priority: - Errata, caption title (when there is no title-page), other notes for special attention (but matters affecting text of whole edition).

Second: - 1. authorship; 2. translator, author of an abridgement, etc, editor (matters affecting the whole text of the edition in hand); 3. signed parts (with place and date when given); 4. translator, editor, etc. of parts; 5. other author attributions.

Third: - Title (variants, title(s) of earlier or later editions), sub-title variations, translated from and into, caption title and half-title (give these titles when they differ from title-page title; when there is no title-page, see 1st priority, above), etc. Title in red and black; or, within a black mourning border; running title; added title-page, engraved.

Fourth: - Imprint notes, including: edition(s), issue(s), variant(s), and prior and subsequent editions when significant; publisher(s); place of publication.

Fifth: - Collation: 1. explanation of pagination irregularities seen as common to the whole edition; 2. same for gatherings; 3. size (_e.g._ large paper edition), etc.

Sixth: - Contents, 1. multivolume works with different titles; 2. Bound with _as issued_ (see also B, 2nd), a. with separate title-pages, b. with only caption or half-titles; 3. list of books, advertisements, etc.; bibliographies, bibliographical footnotes, dedications; 4. irregularities of typography, paper, plates, common to whole edition.

Seventh: - Links with related titles: Answered by, A reply to, Further to, etc.

B. <u>Notes concerning the specific copy</u>

First priority: - Condition, 1. imperfections affecting text or plates; 2. other imperfections, of paper, ink, binding, etc.; 3. special paper, typography, binding, etc.

Second: - Bound withs (_not_ as issued; see also A, 6th, above), binder's title.

Third: - Provenance: ex libris, ms. inscriptions, etc.

These bibliographical notes are followed by the annotation, then the bibliographical citation, for each entry.

APPENDIX E

The following titles were

acquired by Queen's University Library after the

compilation of this Catalogue was completed.   They will be

found in the Index with their page numbers preceded by an *.

AN ACCOUNT of a dream at Harwich.   In a letter to a Member of Parliament about the Camisars.   London, printed for B. Bragg.   1708.   15p.   NUC(Pre-1956) 2:548.   Signed (p. 15): A.M.   Caption title: An account of a strange dream of A____ M____m.

ADDISON, Joseph, 1672-1719.

The campaign: a poem, to His Grace the Duke of Marlborough.   By Mr. Addison.   London, printed and sold by H. Hills, 1710.   16 p.   NUC(Pre-1956) 4:29.   Two copies.

AN ADDRESS to the Oxfordshire addressors and all others of the same strain ...   London, printed for A. Baldwin, 1710.   15p.   NUC(Pre-1956) 4:104.

ANIMADVERSIONS upon a seditious libel, intituled, The exorbitant grants of William III. examin'd and question'd,

&c. Wherein the author's assertions, that the kings of England have their title by conquest, are hereditary and indeposable, and that there was no such thing as an original contract betwixt them and their subjects are examin'd; ... London, printed for A. Baldwin, 1703. 28 p. NUC(Pre-1956)17:175. Reply to: The exorbitant grants of William III (London, 1703).

ARGUMENTS relating to a restraint upon the press, fully and fairly handled in a letter to a bencher, from a young gentleman of the Temple. With proposals humbly offer'd to the consideration of both Houses of Parliament. London: printed for R. and J. Bonwicke, 1712. 51 [1] p. NUC(Pre-1956)20:409.

ASGILL, John, 1659-1738.

An argument proving, that according to the covenant of eternal life revealed in the Scriptures, man may be translated from hence into that eternal life, without passing through death ... London: printed in the year 1715. 87 [1] p. NUC(Pre-1956)23:316. Signed (p.87): J. Asgill. (Bound as no. [1] with his :

A collection of tracts. London, 1715.) First pub.: 1700.

[ASGILL, John] 1659-1738.

The assertion is, that the title of the House of Hannover to the succession of the British monarchy (on failure of issue of her present Majesty) is a title hereditary, and of divine institution. The 3d ed. London, printed by J. Darby. 1715. 38 p. NUC(Pre-1956)23:316. (Bound as no. [2] with his: A collection of tracts. London, 1715.) Second ed., corr.: 1710; 1st ed., 1710. Half-title: Mr. Asgill Dejuredivino.

ASGILL, John 1659-1738.

A collection of tracts written by John Asgill Esq; from the year 1700 to the year 1715. Some relating to divinity; and others to the history of the monarchy, the succession of the Crown, and consititution of the government of Great Britain. London, printed by J. Darby. 1715. 1 vol., various pagings. NUC(Pre-1956)23:316. The contents, each with individual t.-p. and paging, are listed separately in this Appendix, even those pub. after 1714 since all are bound together.

[ASGILL, John] 1659-1738.

An essay for the press. London, printed for A. Baldwin. 1712. 8 p. NUC(Pre-1956)23:316. (Bound as no. [3] with his: A collection of tracts. London, 1715.)

ASGILL, John, 1659-1738.

Mr. Asgill's defence upon his expulsion from the House of Commons of Great Britain in 1707. ... London, printed, and sold by A. Baldwin. 1712. 87 [1] p. NUC(Pre-1956)23:317. (Bound as no. [4] with his: A collection of tracts. London, 1715.) Further to this is his: Mr. Asgill's extract ... London, 1714, q.v. in this Appendix.

ASGILL, John, 1659-1738.

Mr. Asgill's extract of the several acts of Parliament for settling the succession of the Crown in the House of Hannover, for declaring the rights and liberties of the subject, and for attaining and abjuring the Pretender, &c. Being his apology for an omission

in his late Defence, publish'd September 1712. London, printed for J. Roberts. 1714. 24 p. NUC(Pre-1956) 23:317. Further to his: Mr. Asgill's defence ... London, 1712, q.v. in this Appendix. (Bound as no. [5] with his: A collection of tracts. London, 1715.)

ASGILL, John, 1659-1738.

The Pretender's declaration abstracted from two anonymous pamphlets: the one entitled Jus sacrum; and the other, Memoirs of the Chevalier St. George. With some memoirs of two other chevaliers St. George in the reign of King Henry VII. The 2d ed. London, printed by J. Darby. 1715. 46 p. Cf. NUC(Pre-1956)23:317. First ed.: London, 1713. (Bound as no. [6] with his: A collection of tracts. London, 1715.) First pub.: 1713.

ASGILL, John, 1659-1738.

The Pretender's declaration English'd by Mr. Asgill. With a postscript before it, in relation to Dr. Lesley's letter sent after it. London, printed for J. Roberts. 1715. 24 p. NUC(Pre-

1956)23:318. (Bound as no. [8] with his: A collection of tracts. London, 1715.) Refers to a letter of Dr. Charles Leslie, 1650-1722.

ASGILL, John, 1659-1738.

The succession of the House of Hannover vindicated, against the Pretender's second declaration in folio, intitled, The hereditary right of the Crown of England asserted, &c. The 2d ed. London, printed for J. Roberts. 1714. 75 [1] p. NUC(Pre-1956)23:318. (Bound as no. [7] with his: A collection of tracts. London, 1715.) First pub. same year.

[ASTELL, Mary] 1666-1731.

Moderation truly stated: or, A review of a late pamphlet, entitul'd, moderation a vertue. With a prefatory discourse to Dr. D'Aveanant [sic], concerning his late essays on peace and war. London: printed by J.L. for Rich. Wilkin. 1704. 1 p.l., lxvi, 2 ℓ., 120 p. NUC(Pre-1956)24:448. Prefatory discourse (p.i-lxvi) signed: Tom. Single. [pseud.]. Errata: p. lxvi and verso of

following leaf. Added title page precedes p. 1.

[ATTERBURY, Francis, Bp. of Rochester] 1662-1732.

English advice, to the freeholders of England. [London?] Printed in the year 1714. 30 p. NUC(Pre-1956) 25:213. Imprint trimmed.

ATTERBURY, Francis, Bp. of Rochester, 1662-1732.

A sermon preach'd in the cathedral church of St. Paul; at the funeral of Mr. Tho. Bennet, Aug. 30 MDCCVI. London: printed by H. Hills, 1706. 16 p. Cf. NUC(Pre-1956)25:215 (1707 ed.) Thomas Bennet was a London bookseller (cf. Plomer).

ATTERBURY, Francis, Bp. of Rochester, 1662-1732.

A sermon preach'd in the Gild-Hall Chappel, London, September 28, 1706. Being the day of the election of the Right Honourable the Lord Mayor. London: printed and sold by Hen. Hills. [1706?] 16 p. NUC(Pre-1956)25:215.

THE BALLANCE of power: or, A comparison of the strength of the Emperor and the French King. In a letter to a friend. London; printed for A. Baldwin, M.DCC.IX [i.e. 1711]. 15 p. NUC(Pre-1956)32:400.

[BARRINGTON, John Shute, 1st viscount] 1678-1734.

A dissuasive from Jacobitism; shewing in general what the nation is to expect from a popish king; and in particular from the Pretender. ... London: printed for John Baker. 1713. 47 p. Cf. NUC(Pre-1956)37:9.

[BARRINGTON, John Shute, 1st viscount] 1678-1734.

The revolution and anti-revolution principles stated and compar'd, the constitution explain'd and vindicated, and the justice and necessity of excluding the Pretender, maintain'd against the book entituled, Hereditary right of the Crown of England asserted. By the author of the two disswasives against Jacobitism. London: printed and sold by Edward Young. 1714. 92 p.

NUC(Pre-1956)37:10. Errata: p. 92. Reply to George Harbin, The hereditary right of the crown of England asserted (London, 1713.)

BISSET, William, d. 1747.

The modern fanatick. With a large and true account of the life, actions, endowments, &c. of the famous Dr. S____l. London: printed: and sold by A. Baldwin. 1710. 1 p.l., [4], 63 p. Part [I]. Bound with his: The modern fanatick. Part III. (London, 1714), q.v. in this Appendix. Pt. II pub. 1710 [i.e. 1711 N.S.] NUC(Pre-1956) 59:108. Concerns Dr. Henry Sacheverell.

BISSET, William, d. 1747.

The modern fanatick. Part II. Containing what is necessary to clear all the matters of fact in the first part; and to confute what has been printed in the pretended vindication of Dr. Sacheverell, relating to myself. Being the first book that ever was answer'd before it was made. ... London: printed, and sold by A. Baldwin, 1710. 39 p. NUC(Pre-1956)59:108.

Parts I & III also appear in this Appendix.

BISSET, William, d. 1747.

The modern fanatick. Part III. Being a further account of the famous doctor, ... London. Printed for James Roberts. 1714. 1 p.l., [6], 34, [6] p. Concerns Dr. Henry Sacheverell. Bound with his: The modern fanatick. [Part I] (London, 1710), q.v., in this Appendix. NUC(Pre-1956)59:109.

[BOLINGBROKE, Henry Saint-John, 1st viscount] 1678-1751.

A letter to the Examiner. [London] printed in the year 1710. 16 p. NUC (Pre-1956)64:513.

[BRAMHALL, John, Abp. of Armagh] 1594-1663.

A warning for the Church of England. ... London printed, and sold by the booksellers of London and Westminster, 1706. 52 p. NUC(Pre-1956)72:255. First pub. as: A fair warning to take heed of the Scotish discipline (London, 1649).

BRETT, Thomas, 1667-1743.

True moderation. A sermon on Phil. IV. 5. London: printed for John Wyat. 1714. 24 p. Cf. BLC(to 1975)42:151.

BURNET, Gilbert, Bp. of Salisbury, 1643-1715.

A sermon preach'd before the Queen, and the two Houses of Parliament, at St. Paul's on the 31st of December, 1706. The day of thanksgiving for the wonderful successes of this year. ... Printed by Her Majesty's special command. London: printed by W.B. for A. and J. Churchill. 1707. 32 p. Half-title: The Bishop of Sarum's thanksgiving sermon, December 31. 1706. Cf. NUC(Pre-1956)85:642.

[BURNET, Gilbert, Bp. of Salisbury] 1643-1715.

A vindication of the Bishop of Salisbury and passive obedience, with some remarks upon a speech which goes under his Lordship's name. [London] Printed in the year 1710. 16 p. NUC (Pre-1956)85:648. Unopened.

[BURNET, Sir Thomas] 1694-1753.

Essays divine, moral, and political
Viz. I. Of religon [sic] in general.
II. Of Christianity. III of priests.
... By the author of the Tale of a
tub ... With effigies of the author.
London: printed in the year, 1714.
NUC(Pre-1956)85:665. A satire on
Jonathan Swift, Tale of a tub (London,
1704).

A COLLECTION of all the addresses
that have been presented to Her
Majesty, since March the 25th, 1710.
[London? J. Morphew? 1710?] 47 [1] p.
NUC(Pre-1956)115-287. Caption title.
Twelve numbers in 1 vol. Index at end.

A COLLECTION of the addresses which
have been presented to the Queen since
the impeachment of the Reverend Dr.
Henry Sacheverell. In two parts. Part
II. London, printed: and sold by John
Morphew, 1711. 1 p.l., 45 p. fol. Cf.
NUC(Pre-1956)115:357. Eleven numbers
in 1 vol.

COMPTON, Henry, Bp. of London, 1632-
  1713.

Seasonable advice to the ministers

of the church of Great Britain, (especially those in and about the City of
London) not to meddle, as some have
done, with matters of state, or controversial preaching. Taken verbatim out
of the present bishop of London's
seventh letter of the conference with
his clergy, held in the year 1686.
... London: printed, and sold by R.
Halsey. 1710. 7 [1] p. NUC(Pre-1956)
118:280.

CONCORDIA discors: or, An argument to
prove, that the possession of Dunkirk,
Port Mahon, Gibraltar, and other places
by the English, may be of worse conse-
quence to these nations, than if they
had still continued in the hands of
the French, or Spaniards. To which is
added the history of standing armies;
... London: printed for S. Popping,
1712. 1 p.l., 40 p. NUC(Pre-1956)118:
461.

[DAVENANT, Charles] 1656-1714.

An essay upon the national credit of
England; introductory to a proposal
prepar'd for establishing the public
credit; ... Humbly submitted to the

Honourable House of Commons. London: printed by A.R. ... and are to be sold by B. Bragg [1710] 4 p.l., 40 p. NUC(Pre-1956)134:73.

[DEFOE, Daniel] 1661-1731.

A new test of the Church of England's loyalty: or, Whiggish loyalty and church loyalty compar'd. [Edinburgh] Re-printed in the year, 1703. 23 p. NUC(Pre-1956)136:574.

[DEFOE, Daniel] 1661-1731.

Plunder and bribery further discover'd in a memorial humbly offer'd to the British Parliament. London, printed in the year, 1712. 48 p. NUC(Pre-1956) 136:578.

[DEFOE, Daniel]1661-1731.

The secret history of the White Staff, being an account of affairs under the conduct of some late ministers, and of what might probably have happen'd if Her Majesty had not died. Part II. The 2d ed. London: printed for J. Baker. 1714. 71 [1] p. NUC(Pre-1956) 136:644. Part I pub. same year, Part III in 1715. Defence of Robert Harley,

Earl of Oxford.

THE DESCRIPTION of a Presbyterian; Humbly address'd to those gentlemen, that by the imputation of High Church are lately added to that famous party, ... [London?] Printed, in the year 1710. 16 p. NUC(Pre-1956)140:321.

DOCTOR Sacheverell's defence, in a letter to a Member of Parliament. Or, Remarks upon two famous pamphlets, the one entituled, A true answer to Doctor Sacheverell's sermon, preach'd before the Lord Mayor, November 5. 1709. The other (a sham-pamphlet) entituled, Doctor Sacheverell's recantation. By R.G. London: printed for John Reade. 1710 [i.e. 1709]. 16 p. NUC(Pre-1956) 145:385. A true answer is by White Kennet, and Dr. Sacheverell's recantation may be by Defoe (cf. NUC).

[DUMONT, Jean, Baron de Carlscroon] d. 1726.

Les soupirs de l'Europe &c. or, The groans of Europe at the prospect of the present posture of affairs. In a letter from a gentleman at the Hague to a Member of Parliament. Made into English from the original French. [London] Printed in the year 1713. 128 p. 2 fold. geneal. tables. NUC(Pre-1956)151:474.

THE EXORBITANT grants of William the III. Examin'd and question'd. Shewing the nature of grants in successive and elective monarchies; and proving by law and history, that Crown-lands are inalienable ... And that kings set up by Parliament can dispose of no lands but with the consent of Parliament ... London printed, and sold by B. Bragg, 1703. 30 p. NUC(Pre-1956)164:545. Signed (p. 30): B.B. (B. Bragg?).

THE FALSE steps of the Ministry after the revolution: shewing that the lenity and moderation of that government was the occasion of all the factions which have since endanger'd the constitution. With some reflections on the license of the pulpit and press. In a letter to my Lord - - - -. The 2d ed. London: printed for J. Roberts. 1714. 1 p.l., 34 p. Cf. NUC(Pre-1956)166:326. First ed. pub. same year.

FAULTS ON both sides: part the second. Or, An essay upon the original cause, progress, and mischievous consequences of the factions in the church ... By way of letter to a new Member of Parliament. London: printed and sold by the booksellers of London and Westminster, 1710. 38 [2] p. NUC(Pre-1956)167:545. A defense of Hoadly; see Appendix A.

[FLEETWOOD, William, Bp. of Ely] 1656-1723.

The thirteenth chapter to the Romans, vindicated from the abusive senses put upon it. Written by a curate of Salop; and directed to the clergy of that county, and the neighbouring ones of North-Wales; ... London: printed for A. Baldwin. 1710. 1 p.l., 22 p. NUC (Pre-1956)174:685.

GREAT BRITAIN. Commissioners Nominated to Treat of a Union between the Kingdoms of England and Scotland.
Articles of the Treaty of Union agreed on by the commissioners of both kingdoms, on the 22d of July 1706. Edinburgh, printed by the heirs and successors of Andrew Anderson, reprint-

ed at London for Andrew Bell [1706]
16 p. NUC(Pre-1956)

GREAT BRITAIN. Parliament, 1701.

House of Commons.

A state of the proceedings in the
House of Commons, with relation to the
impeached lords: and what happened
thereupon between the two Houses.
London, printed for Edward Jones, and
Timothy Goodwin. 1701. 2 p.l., 5-61
p., 1 *l.* NUC(Pre-1956)214:552. The
impeached lords were Lord Somers, Earl
of Oxford, Earl of Halifax and Earl
of Portland.

[HALIFAX, George Savile, 1st marquis
of] 1633-1695.

Cautions to those who are to chuse
members to serve in Parliament. To
which is added a list of those that
voted for and against the Bill of
Commerce, as publish'd in a late
pamphlet intituled, A letter from a
Member of the House of Commons to his
friend in the country, &c. London,
printed for J. Baker, 1713. 32 p.
NUC(Pre-1956)227:99. First ed.: 1695.

THE HISTORY OF the first and second
session of the last Parliament. ...
By G.F. Gent. London, printed and
sold by J. Baker, [1714] 104 p.
NUC(Pre-1956)248:161.

THE HISTORY OF the Mitre and Purse,
in which the first and second parts of
The secret history of the White Staff
are fully considered, and the hypocrisy and villanies of the Staff himself
are laid open and detected. The 2d ed.
London: printed for J. Morphew. 1714.
(price 1 shilling) 72 p. NUC(Pre-1956)
248:178. The Mitre and the Purse relate
to, respectively, Bishop Francis Atterbury
and Lord Harcourt the Lord Chancellor.
The secret history of the White Staff, by
Daniel Defoe, is a defence of Robert
Harley, the Earl of Oxford.

[HOADLY, Benjamin] Bp. of Winchester,
1676-1761.

The election-dialogue, between a
gentleman, and his neighbour in the country, concerning the choice of good members for the next Parliament. London,
printed, and sold by A. Baldwin.

1710. 16 p. NUC(Pre-1956)248:471.

[HOADLY, Benjamin, Bp. of Winchester]
1676-1761.

The fears and sentiments of all true
Britains; with respect to national
credit, interest and religion. London:
printed and sold by A. Baldwin, 1716.
16 p. NUC(Pre-1956)248:472.

[HOADLY, Benjamin] Bp. of Winchester,
1676-1761.

A letter to the Reverend Dr. Francis
Atterbury: occasion'd by the doctrine
lately deliver'd by him in a funeral-
sermon on I Cor. 15. 19. August 30.
1706. London: printed and sold by H.
Hills, 1706. 16 p. NUC(Pre-1956)248:
473.

[HOADLY, Benjamin] Bp. of Winchester,
1676-1761.

Some short remarks upon the late address of the Bishop of London and his
clergy to the Queen. In a letter to
Dr. S.M.-l-g E. London: printed for
A. Baldwin, 1711. 24 p. NUC(Pre-1956)
248:478. Henry Compton was the Bishop
of London.

[HODGES, James] fl. 1697-1706.

A letter from Mr. Hodges at London.
To a Member of the Parliament of Scotland. Edinburgh, printed by the heirs
and successors of Andrew Anderson,
1703. 8 p. NUC(Pre-1956)249:158.
Signed (p. 8): J. Hodges.

HUMFREY, John, 1621-1719.

Free thoughts upon these heads. Of
predestination, redemption, the salva-
bility of the heathen, the Judicial covenant, justification, ... Subjection
to our present Queen. London; printed
for T. Parkhurst ... and Jonathan
Robinson ... and sold by J. Morphew.
1710. 1 p.l., [2], 64 p. NUC(Pre-
1956)260:209. Errata: p. [2], 1st
count.

[JANSSEN, Sir Theodore, bart.] 1658?-
1748.

General maxims in trade, particularly
applied to the commerce between Great
Britain and France. London, printed
for Sam. Buckley, 1713. 1 p.l., 5-23
p. NUC(Pre-1956)277:436.

JUS SACRUM; or, a discourse wherein it is fully prov'd and demonstrated, that no prince ought to to [sic] be depriv'd of his natural right on account of religion, etc. London, J. Baker, 1712. 44 p. NUC(Pre-1956)287:92.

[KING, William] 1663-1712.

Rufinus: or An historical essay on the favourite-ministry under Theodosius the Great and his son Arcadius. To which is added, a version of part of Claudian's Rufinus. London, printed, and sold by John Morphew. 1712. 1 p.l., 61 p. Satire against the Duke of Wellington. Also attributed to Robert Shippen. NUC(Pre-1956)296:516.

[LESLIE, Charles] 1650-1722.

The Bishop of Salisbury's proper defence, from a speech cry'd about the streets in his name, and said to have been spoken by him in the House of lords, upon the bill against occasional conformity. London and Westminster, 1704. 58 p. NUC(Pre-1956)328:210.

L'ESTRANGE, Sir Roger, 1616-1704.

Two cases submitted to consideration. I. Of the necessity and exercise of a dispensing power. II. The nullity of any act of state that clashes with the law of God. ... Now published to prove the divine institution of government, and to vindicate the Lord Bishop of Exeter's arguments against the weakness and trifling of Mr. Hoadly's assertations. London: printed for W. Hawes, 1709. 16 p. NUC(Pre-1956)328:504. First ed.: London, 1687; this is 2d ed. A defence of the Bishop of Exeter against Bishop Benjamin Hoadly.

A LETTER, directed to the Honourable Robert Harley, Esq; Speaker to the Honourable House of Commons, relating to the great abuses of the Nation. [London, 1701] 4 p. NUC(Pre-1956)328:650.

A LETTER from a Dissenter in the city to his country-friend. Wherein moderation and Occasional Conformity are vindicated, ... London: printed, and are to be sold by the booksellers of

London. 1705. 14 p. NUC(Pre-1956) 328:654.

A LETTER to a friend, giving some account of the proceedings in Her Majesties Court of Queens-bench, in the case of the Ailesbury electors: with the arguments of the learned judges pro and con. London: printed for Benj. Bragge. 1705. 11 p. fol. NUC(Pre-1956)329:21.

A LETTER to a new Member of the ensuing Parliament. [London? 1702?] 8 p. Cf. NUC(Pre-1956)329:37. Caption title; at head of title: Dec. 23. 1701.

A LETTER to the good people of Great Britain. London, printed for A. Baldwin, 1710. 8 p. NUC(Pre-1956)329:84. Signed at end: A.B., but NUC gives Joseph Rawson as supposed author.

MACKWORTH, Sir Humphrey, 1657-1727.

Peace at home; or, A vindication of the proceedings of the Honourable the House of Commons, on the bill for preventing danger from occasional conformity. Shewing the reasonableness and even necessity of such a bill for the better security of established government, for preserving the publick peace ... London: printed by Freeman Collins, and are to be sold by J. Nutt, 1703. 1 p.1., [6], 12 p. NUC(Pre-1956)352:478. Folio.

MILBOURNE, Luke, 1649-1720.

The people not the original civil power, proved from God's word, the doctrine and liturgy of the Established Church, and from the laws of England. In a sermon preach'd at the parish-church of St. Ethelburga, on Thursday, Jan. 30. 1706/7. Being a day of solemn fasting ... for the ... murder of K. Charles the first ... The 5th ed. London, printed for George Sawbridge. 1709/10 [i.e. 1710]. 23, [1] p. Title within mourning border. NUC (Pre-1956)383 :405. First ed.: 1707 (cf. NUC).

[MILBOURNE, Luke] 1649-1720.

Tom of Bedlam's answer to his brother Ben Hoadly, St. Peter's-poor parson, near the Exchange of principles. London: printed and sold by H. Hill. 1709. 1 p.l., 3-16 p. NUC (Pre-1956)383:406. Attack on Bp. Benjamin Hoadly, Rector of St. Peter-le-Poor Church, Broad St., London (1704-21), by a supporter of Dr. Sacheverell.

MR. WALPOLE'S case, in a letter from a Tory Member of Parliament, to his friend in the country. 2nd ed. corr. [London?] printed in the year, 1712. 44 p. Cf. NUC(Pre-1956)387:589. Morgan, BBH, suggests Walpole or Wagstaffe as the author.

[OLDMIXON, John] 1673-1742.

A defence of Mr. Maccartney. By a friend. The second edition. London: printed for A. Baldwin, 1712. 3 p.l., 31 p. NUC(Pre-1956)429:310.

A PLAIN, honest, easy, and brief determination of the late controversy concerning that non-resistance of the higher powers, which is required by the Apostle in his Epistle to the Romans ... [London? 1710] 8 p. Caption title. Taken from a book called:

Free thoughts upon these heads ... (cf. p. 7), unfound, NUC, BLC. NUC (Pre-1956)460:467. Ms. note on authorship in this copy: by John Humfrey.

PUNCHANELLO, Seignioro, pseud.

Punch turn'd critick, in a letter to the honourable and (some time ago) worshipful rector of Covent-Garden. With some wooden remarks on his sermon, preach'd the 30th of January, 1711. [London] Printed in the year 1712. 16 p. Signed (p. 16): Seignioro Punchanello. NUC(Pre-1956)475:333. Ms. note on authorship in this copy: Robert Lumley Lloyd.

[RAWSON, Joseph] 1664-1719, supposed author.

A letter to the Reverend Dr. Henry Sacheverell. On the occasion of his sermon, and late sentence pass'd on him by the Honourable House of Lords. By a Cambridge-gentleman. London: printed for John Morphew, 1710. 1 p.l., 14 p. NUC(Pre-1956)482:613. Signed (p. 14): A.B. A reply to (probably): The perils of false brethren (London, 1709).

THE REASONS of those lords that enter'd their protests. In Dr. Sacheverell's case, &c. London: printed in the year 1710. 20 p. Cf. NUC(Pre-1956)483:524.

THE REPRESENTATIVE of London and Westminster in Parliament, examined and consider'd. Wherein appears the antiquity of most of the burroughs in England; ... By a gentleman. London, printed for S. Crouch, 1702. 1 p.l., 40 p., incl. tables. NUC(Pre-1956) 489:184.

REVOLUTION-PRINCIPLES: being a full defence of the Bishop of Asaph's preface to his Four sermons: in answer to the objections which have been made against it; proving them to be all groundless, by scripture, law, and reason. London: printed for A. Baldwin. 1713. 1 p.l., [6], 36 p. NUC(Pre-1956)490:449. Reply to William Fleetwood, Bp. of Ely, Four sermons.

THE REVOLUTION no rebellion: or, Serious reflections offered to the Reverend Mr. Benjamin Hoadly, occasion'd by his considerations on the Bishop of Exeter's sermon preach'd before Her Majesty, March, the 8th, 1708. By a citizen of London: a lover of the present establishment both in church and state. London: printed and sold by the booksellers of London and Westminster. 1709. 16 p. Cf. NUC(Pre-1956)490:449.

[RIDPATH, George] d. 1726.

The peril of being zealously affected, but not well: or, Reflections on Dr. Sacheverel's sermon, preach'd before the Right Honourable the Lord Mayor, aldermen, and citizens of London, at the Cathedral Church of St. Paul, on the fifth of November, 1709. London, printed for J. Baker. 1709. 24 p. NUC(Pre-1956)494:371.

THE RIGHT of the sovereign in the choice of his servants. Shewing the necessity of the present change of the Ministry, and the folly and design of the last. With a list of the ministers and officers displac'd soon after Sacheverel's tryal, ... London: printed for J. Roberts, 1714. 1 p.l., 34 p. NUC(Pre-1956)495:149.

SACHEVERELL, Henry, 1674?-1724,

defendant.

An impartial account of what pass'd most remarkable in the last session of Parliament, relating to the case of Dr. Henry Sacheverell. [London] printed for Jacob Tonson, 1710. 47 p. NUC(Pre-1956)513:282.

SACHEVERELL, Henry 1674?-1724.

The nature, guilt and danger of presumptous sins set forth, in a sermon preach'd before the University of Oxford, at St. Mary's, Septemb. 14th, 1707. Oxford: printed by Leon. Lechfield, for John Stephens, bookseller: London. 1708. 2 p.l., 24 p. NUC (Pre-1956)513:283.

SECRET MEMOIRS, relating to the present war between the Confederates and the Fr. King, in the Empire, Flanders, Spain and Italy; as also that of the kings of Swedeland, Poland and Czar of Muscovy: with some thoughts on the insurrection in Hungary, ... Written by a person of quality in a letter to his friend. London: printed, and sold by John Morphew. 1707. 52 p.

NUC(Pre-1956)536:75.

THE SENSE of the nation, concerning the Duke of Marlborough, as it is express'd in several acts of Parliament in the votes and joint-addresses of both Houses, and in Her Majesty's ... answers. London, printed for S. Popping, 1702 [i.e. 1710?] 28 p. NUC (Pre-1956)538:434. Contents dated Oct. 1702 to Feb. 1709 (O.S., 1710 N.S.).

[SHIPPEN, William] 1673-1743.

Faction display'd. A poem. From a corrected copy. London: printed and sold by H. Hills. 1709. 16 p., NUC (Pre-1956)544:132.

SNAPE, Andrew, 1675-1742.

A sermon preach'd before the Right Honourable the Lord-Mayor, the aldermen and citizens of London, at the cathedral church of St. Paul, on Monday the 30th of Jan. 1709/10. Being the anniversary fast for the martyrdom of King Charles the first. London, printed for Jonah Bowyer, 1710. 30 p. NUC(Pre-1956)552:660.

SOME PLAIN observations, recommended to the consideration of every honest Englishman; especially to the electors of Parliament-Members [London? 1705] 4 p. fol. NUC(Pre-1956)555:693. Source of pub. date given in NUC.

[SOUVERAIN, Matthieu] d. ca. 1699.

Platonism unveil'd or, An essay concerning the notions and opinions of Plato, and some antient and modern divines his followers; in relation to the Logos, or Word in particular, and the doctrine of the Trinity in general. In two parts. [London?] Anno Dom. 1700. 1 p.l., [2], 139 p. NUC(Pre-1956)558:667. Transl. from his: Le platonisme devoilé. (Cologne, 1700) Two parts in 1 vol., paged continuously; caption title, pt. 2: p. 102.

STEELE, Sir Richard, 1672-1729.

A letter to a Member of Parliament concerning the bill for preventing the growth in schism. By Richard Steele, Esq; the second edition. London: printed, and sold by Ferd. Burleigh. 1714. 23 p. NUC(Pre-1956)566:157. First ed. pub. the same year.

[STEPHENS, Edward] d. 1706.

A petition and demand of right and justice by one of the Commons of England, on behalf of himself and the rest. In a letter to his representative in the present House of Commons. To M.C. Esq; [London, 1702] 4 p. NUC(Pre-1956)567:561. Caption title. Signed (p. 4): E.S.

A SUPPLEMENT to the Faults on both sides: containing the compleat history of the proceedings of a party ever since the revolution: in a familiar dialogue between Steddy and Turn-round, two displac'd officers of state. London: printed for J. Baker. 1710. 76 p. NUC(Pre-1956)577:23. "Pub. in the same year with title: Faults on both sides; the second part" (NUC)

[SYKES, Arthur Ashley] 1684?-1756.

The innocency of error, asserted and vindicated. In a letter to --------. By Eugenius Philalethes [pseud.] The 2d ed., corr. With a preface in answer to the Remarks, &c. lately made upon it. London: printed for John Wyat.

1715. 1 p.l., 31 p. NUC(Pre-1956)
579:677.

[TRAPP, Joseph] 1679-1747.

The true genuine Tory-address, and the
true genuine Whig-address, set one
against another. To which is added,
a further explanation of some hard
terms now in use, for the information
of all such as read, or subscribe
addresses. Being an answer to a late
scandalous paper, falsly call'd, The
true genuine Tory-address, etc. London,
1710. 12 p. NUC(Pre-1956)600:48.
Reply to Bp. Benjamin Hoadly, The
true, genuine, Tory-address (London,
1710).

TRIMNELL, Charles, Bp. of Norwich,
    1663-1723.

A sermon preach'd before the Lords
Spiritual and Temporal, in Parliament
assembled, in the Abbey Church at Westminster, on the 30th of January 1711/12;
being the day of the martyrdom of King
Charles I. By Charles Lord Bishop of
Norwich. London: printed for D.
Midwinter, 1712. 24 p. NUC(Pre-1956)
601:463.

THE TRUE, genuine modern Whigg-address.
To which is added, An explanation of
some hard terms now in use, for the
information of all such as read or
subscribe addresses. [n.p. 1710] 4
p. NUC(Pre-1956)602:609. A parody of
Bp. Benjamin Hoadly, The true, genuine,
Tory-address (London, 1710).

A VIEW of the management of the late
Scotch Ministry, with respect to the
Protestant succession, union, &c.
London: printed in the year 1709. 31
p. NUC(Pre-1956)637:109. Caption
title: A brief view of the late Scots
Ministry. Dated (p. 31): November
15. 1708.

WAKE, William, Abp. of Canterbury,
    1657-1737.

The Bishop of Lincoln's and Bishop
of Norwich's speeches in the House of
Lords, March the 17th. at the opening
of the second article of the impeachment against Dr. Sacheverell. London:
printed for John Morphew, 1710. 31 p.
NUC(Pre-1956)645:162. This bishop was
Charles Trimnell; his "Bishop of
Norwich's speech" has a special t.-p.;

continuous paging.

[WALPOLE, Robert, 1st earl of Orford]
1676-1745.

Four letters to a friend in North
Britain, upon the publishing the tryal
of Dr. Sacheverell. London, printed
in the year 1710. 2 p.l., 27 p. NUC
(Pre-1956)647:18.

[WILDMAN, Sir John] 1621?-1693.

The Pretender an imposter: being that
part of the Memorial from the English
Protestants to Their Highnesses the
Prince and Princess of Orange, concerning their grievances, and the birth of
the pretended Prince of Wales. Which
is more than a sufficient answer to the
old depositions about that matter lately published. London 1711. 40 p.
NUC(Pre-1956)663:477.

[WILLES, Sir John] 1685-1761.

The speech that was intended to have
been spoken by the terrae-filius, in
the theatre at O_____d [Oxford], July
13, 1713. Had not his mouth been
stopp'd by the V. Ch------r [Vice Chan-
cellor]. London printed: and sold by

E. Smith, 1713. 2 p.l., [3], 30 p.
NUC(Pre-1956)664:366.

WHO PLOT Best; the Whigs or the
Tories.

Being a brief account of all the
plots that have happen'd within these
thirty years ... In a letter to Mr.
Ferguson. London, printed by A.
Baldwin, 1712. 21 p. NUC(Pre-1956)
661:381.

A WORD to the present Ministry; with
two or three in vindication of our
High Church House of Commons: and six
or seven to the electors of Members
for the next ensuing Parliament.
London: printed for John Morphew, 1713.
12 p.

I N D E X

to the Catalogue and Appendix E

This index is only to the pamphlets cited in the Catalogue: in both the main Catalogue, and in the supplementary Appendix E of later acquisitions. Listed are the titles, and authors when known, of every work given as a main (i.e. separate) entry. In addition, every other eighteenth-century pamphlet identified in the notes to the entries is included, but with a lower-case 'n'('note') following the page number. (Modern works of reference cited are given in the list of sources at the front of the book.) A parenthetic numeral after a page number denotes the number of instances that author or title are mentioned on that page. An asterisk preceding a page number indicates a supplementary entry, unannotated, all of which appear in Appendix E. Journals are represented in italics (underlined).

The arrangement is A-Z, authors and titles in a single alphabet, ignoring initial articles. For authors, designations of nobility or of status in religion are disregarded (though barons are usually entered under their titled rather than family names), unless the title is required to distinguish between similar names. Author attributions are not indexed unless accepted as authors in the entries. Titles bearing frequently-used first words, such as 'Letter' and 'Sermon', are each combined in a single entry beginning with that first word followed by a colon, the titles thereafter in A-Z order each beginning with a dash, and separated by semi-colons.

259

N

O

P